Understanding
Judaism

Understanding Judaism

The Basics of
Deed and Creed

Rabbi Benjamin Blech

JASON ARONSON INC.
Northvale, New Jersey
London

Jason Aronson Inc. softcover edition—1992

This book was set in 11/13 Times Roman
by Simcha Graphic Associates of Brooklyn, New York.

Library of Congress Cataloging-in-Publication Data

Blech, Benjamin.
    Understanding Judaism : the basics of deed and creed / Benjamin Blech.
      p. cm.
    Includes bibliographical references and index.
    ISBN 0-87668-650-1 (hardcover)
    ISBN 0-87668-291-3 (softcover)
    1. Commandments (Judaism). 2. Judaism—Doctrines.
  3. Judaism—Essence, genius, nature.   I. Title.
  BM520.7.B58 1991
  296—dc20

                              90-24947

Manufactured in the United States of America. Jason Aronson Inc. offers books and cas-
settes. For information and catalog write to Jason Aronson Inc., 230 Livingston Street,
Northvale, New Jersey 07647.

The wine belongs to the owner
and thanks are given to the butler — Baba Kamma 92b

To dedicate is to acknowledge debt.
Who made this book possible?

Those who came before . . .
I am a tenth-generation Rabbi.
My father, Rabbi Benzion Blech, of blessed memory,
showed me the beauty of a life of saintliness and scholarship.
My mother, Gertrude, continues to inspire me in her maternal role
as the proverbial "woman of valor."

Those who now share the days of my life . . .
My wife, Elaine, has given me more than her love;
her greatest gift has been the sustaining confidence and support
that allowed me to believe in myself
and to bring this work to fruition.
My children — Tamar and Steven, Yael and Stephen, Jordana and
Aryeh, and Ari — gave me the encouragement to write
and, more significantly, the contentment of a father who knows
he is blessed with the finest children on earth, as well as the
greatest grandchildren — Avital, Eitan, Talia, and Yair.

Those who today are the seeds of our future . . .
It is my students who helped form the thoughts,
style, and content of these pages.
To them go the thanks of a grateful teacher who has learned most
from his disciples.

And a final note of appreciation
to those very special individuals — Daniel Federbush,
Yitz Grossman, Herb Mehl, and Joel Rebibo —
who, each in his own way, helped turn the ideas for this book
into reality.

Contents

THE WAY OF CREED

Preface

lie Wiesel, universally recognized as the scribe of the Holocaust, summarized our contemporary uniqueness in these words: "We are the most cursed of all generations and we are the most blessed of all generations. We are the generation of Job, but we are also the generation of Jerusalem."

Historians may well take note of the attempted genocide of our people and the subsequent return to our biblically promised homeland as the two major events of religious significance in the twentieth century. Yet there is another reality of Jewish life, asserting itself in the aftermath of the Holocaust and the birth of Israel, which could prove to have even greater meaning. The unspeakable murder of six million innocents who perished just because they were Jews led the survivors to seek a better understanding of their tradition and heritage, which had almost become obliterated. The ultimate irony of the post-Nazi era is that the "Final Solution" has in fact been followed by a religious revival, a movement of *ba'alei teshuvah*—religious returnees to our faith—never before witnessed in all of Jewish history, both with regard to intensity as well as numbers.

God did not die in Auschwitz. What was made clear to Moses
by way of metaphor at his first encounter with the Almighty became miraculously manifest as we contemplated the failure of
Hitler, the modern-day Haman, who sought total destruction of
our people. Why did God initially appear to the man selected for
leadership in "a bush burning with fire, and the bush was not
consumed"? Clearly, it was not meant to demonstrate that God
could perform a miracle. Any one of an infinite number of amazing conjurer's feats could have been chosen. But the *seneh*—the
Hebrew word for "bush," and the site later designated as Sinai,
where the Torah was given—was a plant whose indestructibility
would serve as paradigm for the unique power of the Jewish
people throughout history. Against all laws of nature, running
counter to the principles of history as codified by Toynbee as well
as the example of every other nation before or since, Jews were
offered to the fires of crematoria and the torches of timeless
enemies and yet "were not consumed." Our people and our faith
defied all logic to illustrate the miracle of survival; Israel and the
message of Sinai share with the *seneh* the remarkable gift of indestructibility.

Contemporary survivors might have been forgiven if their
theological response to the loss of close to two-thirds of our
people was rejection of the God of their fathers. Indeed, some
chose the road of religious denial. Yet, many others viewed irra-
tional events as a spiritual challenge. Perhaps it was not so much
God in the heavens who failed His children, but human beings
below who proved how barbaric their behavior was when guided
solely by secular standards and values. Even as men, women, and
children were turned into bars of soap, and a self-proclaimed
master race embodied a demonic cruelty, a hunger arose in the
hearts of those who learned of these deeds to comprehend the life
purpose of the human species, created "in the image of God."

The Germans left us with questions—six million at the minimum. It became the supreme task of the post-Holocaust generation to seek and to probe, to ask and reflect, to try to comprehend
a faith that had stood the test of time, but seemed to fail the confrontation with reason and a continued belief in a God both
omnipotent and beneficent.

Thousands of years ago in the first Holocaust in Jewish history, which took place in Egypt, the battle cry was "Let my people go." In our own time, the aftermath of a period of incomprehensibility, Rabbi Adin Steinsaltz gave birth to a new slogan: "Let my people know."

Knowledge is more than power. As Solomon wrote in the *Book of Proverbs:* "If you lack knowledge, what do you have? If you have knowledge, what do you lack?" Survivors had to understand the purpose of their survival. And the answer would have to be more than trite reference to "tradition" or a "fiddler on the roof." "Let my people know"—and tens of thousands of Jews searched for answers in synagogues, adult education courses, Jewish studies programs, *chavurah* study groups, and in the hundreds of new schools that sprung up to provide sustenance for the spiritual seekers of our generation.

Where did all these ba'alei teshuvah come from? Mystics suggested a fascinating response. Six million of our people had perished. Among them were approximately two million children—infants, youngsters, and teenagers—prevented from fulfilling their life potential. Was it possible that God allowed these souls a "second chance," that in fact the magnitude of the ba'al teshuvah movement reflects the multitude of these reincarnated souls scattered throughout the world? Perhaps an outrageous suggestion, but no more farfetched than any other to explain the preponderance as well as the passion of these "returnees" whose existence and religious conviction cannot be accounted for in any rational manner.

It is within the context of this contemporary phenomenon that this book was born. Yeshiva University was one of the first institutions of higher Jewish learning to see the need and feel the responsibility for dealing with the ba'alei teshuvah. A special division, the Jewish Studies Program, was established. The curriculum, it was agreed, would have to include the basic core of Jewish studies that had always been typical of the classical Yeshiva program. There would be readings from original texts in Torah, Talmud, and Codes of Jewish Law as well as the most famous commentaries. Yet one nagging question remained. An overview of the philosophy and theology of our faith is a natural result of intensive study for decades. Those growing up "within the system" would eventually understand the basic conceptual principles behind Halakhah—the deed, and Agadah—the creed. But how could one speed up the process? What was one to do for all those who wanted, as in the time of Hillel the Elder, to learn "all of Judaism on one foot?" To the heathen who asked to learn all the Torah on one foot, Hillel had responded: "What is hateful to you, do not do unto your neighbor," and then added, "and the remainder go and study." But the time needed to master the subject matter is far too long to allow us the luxury of withholding a minimal response for the present. Jews today stand "on one foot" and ask for sufficient information to allow them to function in the interim, as well as to be inspired to continue their intellectual search in the future.

What we need, I was told when approached to teach a course of this nature, was a class for which no book had yet been written—a book on the essence of Judaism, summarizing basic principles of deed and of creed. Many years of trial and error followed. What is it that people most needed and wanted to know about Judaism? Contact with congregants in my congregation at the Young Israel of Oceanside, with students in classes at Yeshiva University, as well as with inquisitive and intellectually challenging individuals of all ages, backgrounds, and professions whom I addressed in lecture tours in Australia, the Orient, Israel, and the United States, afforded me profound insight. Slowly the outlines and full development of a basic course in Judaism came into being.

What happened as this material was taught and refined over the years exceeded my fondest expectations. Many told me that these lectures proved to be the most important source for their religious commitment and spiritual growth. Rabbinical students audited the classes and found the subject matter relevant and personally helpful even at their advanced stage of Jewish learning.

The incident that I most cherish, however, concerns an obviously much-older-than-college-age gentleman who had been given permission by the university to sit together with freshmen for this course. As was my custom when I noticed someone clearly not taking the class for credit, I asked this visitor to meet with me afterward so that I might learn more about his identity and desire for further Jewish education.

What he told me remains with me to this day. "I am a doctor"—and as soon as he gave me his name I recognized him as a world-famous surgeon with an exceedingly large medical practice on Park Avenue. "Permit me to tell you why I am here," he added. "I have come to a stage in my life where I realize that I know a great deal about the human body, but I know very little about the soul. The older I get and the more I understand about human beings, I recognize that the latter is far more important than the former. It is time for me to rearrange my priorities. I intend to set aside time from my schedule to discover more about myself, my roots, my people, and my God. Hopefully that will make me not only a better human being, but a better doctor as well."

For one full year this prominent professional attended classes without missing a session. I often thought of how difficult it must have been for him to rearrange his commitments. Yet he did so unfailingly. I felt we had created a special bond, both of friendship and student—teacher. Imagine how stunned I was to hear from his lips, after our last session together, what sounded like words of rebuke.

"There is only one thing for which I cannot forgive you, Rabbi," he told me. "I have learned so much from you. How dare you deprive those who cannot physically attend this class of your lectures? I will not forgive you until this course, which has changed my life, becomes a book available to everybody."

I can only pray that this work makes the necessary amends. May those who study this book be as enlightened, inspired, and enriched as were the countless students whose comments and questions helped to create it.

Introduction

re you religious?

      Ask that question to a Christian and it means one thing. Ask it to a Jew and it means quite another.

    This is not simply because Judaism and Christianity disagree about the identity of God or even whether the Trinity is compatible with a monotheistic faith. It goes far deeper than that: it concerns the very meaning of the word "religious." When a Christian refers to religion he is speaking of *creed*. When a Jew relates to God he is far more concerned with *deed*.

    For a Christian, "Are you religious?" means one thing: Do you believe in the divinity of Jesus? Faith is everything. What you *believe* is far more important than what you *do*. And the reason for this is crucial to understanding the role of the founder of Christianity. The Christian doctrine of salvation rests on the belief that Jesus died on the Cross to atone for the sins of mankind. Jesus's death was necessary because man could not achieve perfection himself through good works. His spirit was stained by original sin. His soul was sullied so that no matter what he did he would be unable to *earn* the keys to the kingdom of God. Vicarious atonement, forgiveness granted via the death of Jesus, is the Christian's

xvii

only hope. The Crucifixion refutes the possibility of man's *self-perfection.*

As Paul stated in the New Testament: "If uprightedness could be secured through the law, then Christ died for nothing" (Galatians 2:21). In other words, if deeds could achieve the desired effect, asks Paul, why would God have found it necessary to send a personal envoy of sacrifice?

Christianity therefore rejected the law and gave a new interpretation to the Covenant at Sinai. This is the crucial distinction between the Old Testament and the New. The Torah was assuredly given to the Jewish people at Mount Sinai, but its laws were no longer binding, according to Christianity. How could God have given directives that He Himself later saw fit to change? Christianity responds that the Old Testament was only given in order to prove that it could not be kept. "For no human being can be made upright in the sight of God by observing the law. All that the law can do is to make man conscious of sin" (Romans 3:20). The Five Books of Moses were, in this light, superseded, so that with the coming of Jesus, Jews would finally recognize that grace is the only legitimate option. Believe in the Lord Jesus Christ and you shall be saved is the message of John 3:16 and 6:47.

Jews do not usually understand what this doctrine, of cardinal importance to Christianity, really means. The exclusive emphasis on faith produces two conclusions incompatible with Judaism: someone may be extremely wicked, but if that person believes that Jesus was the son of God and died for the sins of all people, then that person is destined for heaven. On the other hand, someone who never acknowledged Jesus as savior, but who may have spent a lifetime doing good, is doomed to an eternity of hell, since creed is more significant than deed.

Of course this is an extreme point of view, and one that, in practice, would find little support among the majority of Christians, secular and clergy alike. The emphasis on belief, however, is a fundamental tenet of Christian dogma and, if carried to its logical extreme, becomes somewhat of a reductio ad absurdum: for a just God to allow a Hitler or an Eichmann into Paradise on the basis of a mere profession of faith seems unthinkable.

For a Jew, the question "Are you religious?" asks whether or not you live up to that commitment made at Mount Sinai when

God informed us that we would be His people provided that we act according to the dictates of His Torah.

George Foot Moore, a prominent non-Jewish scholar writing on Judaism, was most impressed by the moment of revelation—not for what it said, but for what it didn't say. For the Jew, revelation was not a means for man to see what God looked like. Revelation had nothing to do with Divine appearance. Rather, revelation was God's way of letting the Jews know what was important to Him. He revealed His purpose rather than His person, His values rather than His vision. Revelation was not for man to see God; it was for God to endow man with a view of his potential for goodness and Godliness.

Every year on the High Holy Days the Jew is judged. His life is reviewed, as it will be at the end of his days. And what is the standard for this evaluation? As the Midrash puts it, every good deed performed creates a "good angel"; every bad deed brings forth an "angel of evil." And in the month of Tishrei, when the astrological sign is Libra, God takes out the universal scales. He places the good angels on one side, the bad on the other, and the ultimate outcome is determined not by what a person may have *believed* throughout the year, but by the effect of his *deeds*.

Judaism is a religion of 613 commandments. And as Moore put it, "Judaism, unlike Christianity, is not a religion of 'this thou shalt believe' and 'this thou shalt not believe,' but of 613 laws divided into 'this thou shalt do' and 'this thou shalt not do.'"

Perhaps the most striking way to illustrate the distinction between Judaism and Christianity is to imagine someone seeking to become a convert to either religion. The potential convert to Christianity will first be taught a catechism and told: Affirm your belief in its doctrines and you will have found spiritual fulfillment. The potential convert to Judaism is initially rebuffed and told the words spoken long ago by Naomi to Ruth: Return to your people and your god.

The full text of their dialogue is deduced by the Sages from Ruth's famous statement of acceptance. "For wherever you go, I will go; where you lodge, I will lodge; your people are my people and your God is my God" (Ruth 1:16).

When Naomi understood that Ruth wanted to convert, she warned her daughter-in-law that Jewish women do not visit places of idolatry and immodesty. Ruth replied, "Wherever you go"—and only where you are permitted to go—"will I go."

Naomi continued that it is forbidden to dwell in a house that does not have a mezuzah, a reminder of divine protection, on the doorpost. If so, vowed Ruth, only in those domiciles "where you lodge, will I lodge."

Our people are different, Naomi added. We are restricted in all of our actions. We observe 613 commandments. Ruth responded that she will obey the laws of God in their entirety. 'Your people are my people.' Finally, Naomi cautioned Ruth that God is a God of justice. Failure to heed His law, once accepted, will bring dire consequences. Ruth responded: "Your God is my God."

In Judaism, if someone believes in God but rebels against Him, he is compared to Nimrod, who is described in the Bible (Genesis 10:9) as "a mighty hunter before the Lord." The rabbis of the Talmud deduce from this description that Nimrod acknowledged God but chose to act against His will. His acceptance of the Almighty's existence *compounded* the crime; to know, to believe, and yet to transgress, is the ultimate aberration.

Conversely, a person who is unaware of the name of God as revealed at Sinai and who nevertheless lives a life of holiness balances the scale in favor of divine approval. *Hasidei umot ha-olam, yesh lahem heleq be-olam haba* (Maimonides, *Hilkhot Teshuvah* 3:5, quoting earlier sages). The Talmud teaches that the righteous of all nations have a share in the World to Come. This is in marked contrast to the precepts of the Church, which damns all who deny Jesus as Savior.

Judaism's emphasis on deed is highlighted in a verse in Jeremiah, in which the prophet, speaking for God, castigates the people: "Me they have forsaken and My Torah they have not kept" (16:11). In a remarkable analysis of this text, the Jerusalem Talmud detects an important idea in the sequence of the words. "Me they have forsaken"—it is as if God is saying I could almost forgive the personal slight. After all, what does it matter to Me whether they call Me by My Name or not? Far worse than that is the conclusion: "My Torah they have not kept." They *act* in ways abhorrent to Me, and this I cannot forgive.

Though the following words do not actually appear in the text of Jeremiah, they are so clearly implied that the Talmud does not hesitate to offer them as the words of the Almighty: *Halevai oti azvu ve-et Torati shameiru*—"*Would that they had forsaken Me and kept My Torah.*" God would be delighted if the ways of humanity were righteous, even if the price were divine denial.

People often speak of Judaism and Christianity as two different *faiths* and sometimes refer to a Judaeo-Christian tradition. But language has betrayed us. Semantically we have fallen victim to a kind of assimilation that almost goes unnoticed. In fact, Judaism and Christianity are not two different *faiths*; likewise the word "religion" should not be incorrectly defined as "a personal system of belief."

Christianity is a creed that asks for a commitment of faith, but Judaism demands more. Today we find Jews who say: "I may not keep kosher, I may not observe the Sabbath, perhaps I don't keep any of the laws of the Torah. But I am a very 'religious' person. I am a Jew at heart." What is the meaning of this remark? It is that Jews today, living in a Christian world—where religion is defined by standards other than deed—are identifying themselves as "pious" Jews by Christian standards.

Are you a good Jew, in Jewish terms, means: Do you observe the Torah and the mitzvot? Do you keep the Covenant made long ago at Sinai—at which, according to our Sages, every Jewish soul of every generation was present? Do you join in affirming those words that persuaded God to make us His people—*na'aseh ve-nishma*—"we will *do* and we will hear" (Exodus 24:6)?

Being a "Jew at heart" is not enough. The words of David in the Book of Psalms ring out clearly: "All my bones, all my limbs proclaim the greatness of God" (Psalm 35:10). The stress is on actions, not thoughts; on body, not simply minds.

Does this mean that belief plays no role in Judaism? Of course, that cannot be. The very first commandment is "I am the Lord, your God, who took you out of the land of Egypt, the house of bondage" (Exodus 20:2). A Jew must believe. As Ibn Ezra, a prime commentator on the Torah, explained: If there is no Commander, there can be no command. However, the purpose of belief in one

Deity is to ensure that the mitzvot are kept. Belief in God is not the message but rather the medium. The goal is not God but a life of holiness, for which belief is simply a prerequisite. The first of the Ten Commandments is but the means to an end; it is followed by nine obligations related to proper behavior.

A diagram illustrating the differences between Judaism and Christianity would look like this: Christianity would have one circle beneath the word religion and in it would be the phrase: "Believe in the Lord Jesus Christ and thou shalt be saved." Judaism would have two circles. A small circle on top would contain the words "I am the Lord, your God." These words are there because, as Ibn Ezra wrote, the number 10 without 1 leaves zero. It is not possible to have genuine goodness without a belief in God. The first commandment in the small circle is the conduit to the 612 other commandments. The 612 mitzvot constitute the large circle of deeds, which encompasses the true goals of our faith. Judaism requires belief so that you *do* what is demanded of you. Christianity mandates belief alone as necessary for entering the Kingdom of Heaven.

Let us see what Judaism has to teach us about both of these categories. What must a Jew do? What must a Jew believe? Let us proceed first with deed—because we have established that for the Jew that is the first priority.

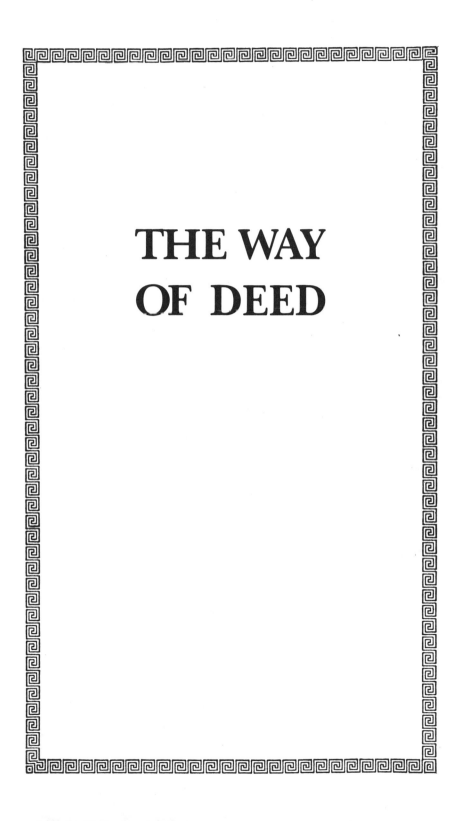

THE WAY
OF DEED

Part I

Which Is the Most Important Mitzvah?

1

If You Had
to Choose
Only One Mitzvah

magine the following scenario from the Middle Ages. A Jew is imprisoned, but for some reason the feudal baron decides to show him some mercy. "You will remain my prisoner forever," declares the baron, "but, as an act of kindness, I will allow you one day of freedom a year. On that day you may return to your family and your community and you may freely practice your religion. Furthermore, I do not care which day you choose. But remember, you only have one day a year. On but one day can you have your freedom. And on but one day can you practice your religion. You have a day to be a Jew. Decide for yourself which one it shall be."

What a difficult choice that would be! If the prisoner picks Passover, he will be able to observe the Seder, eat matzot, and drink the four cups of wine. If he selects Rosh Hashanah, he will have the chance to hear the shofar (ram's horn trumpet) and pray in the synagogue. If he chooses Sukkot (the Festival of Booths), he will be able to dwell in a sukkah. Purim? He'll be able to hear the scroll of Esther. Or should the prisoner choose Shabbat? Or Shavuot (the day the Torah was given at Sinai)?

The story actually happened back in the sixteenth century. The details were exactly as given. The prisoner could not make up his mind and turned to one of the rabbinic giants of his generation, the Radbaz (the Hebrew acronym for **R**abbi **D**avid **b**en **A**bi **Z**imra). The answer is found in his Responsa (Queries and Responses).

Which day would you choose is another way of asking a far more fundamental question: Which mitzvah is most important in the Jewish religion? If given a choice of performing but one mitzvah, which would it be? Of course a Jew is normally obligated to affirm, "I will do them all." But when the situation makes clear that *all* is impossible and a choice must be made, which will it be? How does one select from among 613 alternatives?

A good case might be made for any number of calendrical possibilities. Every one of the holidays and holy days has much to commend it. But, startling as it may seem, neither Shabbat nor Yom Kippur, neither Rosh Hashanah nor Sukkot, were the suggested options. The Radbaz answered: "The day you must choose is the *very first day available,* be it a Shabbat, a weekday, or any holiday" (1:87).

Choose the very first day. Why? Precisely so that you will not be forced to choose between mitzvot. The Radbaz bases his ruling on the Mishnah in *Ethics of the Fathers,* which states: "Rebbe (Rabbi Yehudah HaNasi) said: 'Be as scrupulous in performing a "minor" mitzvah as you are with a "major" one, for you do not know the rewards given for mitzvot'" (2:1).

At first glance, there seems to be a contradiction within the Mishnah itself. Rebbe speaks of a minor mitzvah and a major one. Yet the very point of the Mishnah is that "all mitzvot are created equal"; that one, in fact, may not distinguish between them. So how can Rebbe use adjectives like minor and major? The answer, of course, is that he is merely applying those terms that we might casually use, based on our own erroneous perceptions. It is we who might label some mitzvot as more and some as less important. That is because we might assume mitzvot that are more difficult, more costly, or more demanding are somehow more significant. But that is precisely the warning of the Mishnah's author. Be as careful with one as with the other—because you do not know the measure of reward granted by God for any individual mitzvah. It is not for us to understand the relative merit of mitzvot. God and

God alone knows what weight to give every action in the cosmic scheme of reality. For us, every mitzvah must be equal simply because each one shares its source in the divine imperative. Each is to be observed because God said so. That is true for the simplest act, and it is true for the most demanding one as well.

It is here that a profound point begins to emerge. If we were to give preference to one mitzvah over another for whatever reason, it is then we who become final arbiters of the purpose of commandments. To rank one law above another might not seem a crime, but whenever we call one thing more important than the next, we also diminish the one not chosen for highest priority.

Treat all mitzvot equally, because to do otherwise is to say I think that this particular law is not so important. If I like the ethical parts of the Torah, but do not feel constrained by the rituals, then of course I will say the former is what God really cares about. Do I find rituals rich in symbolism, pageantry, and beauty, but laws restricting me in my business practices too confining? Then obviously God only meant to be taken seriously when He told me to pray to Him, but He was not serious when He insisted I not prey upon my fellow man.

Selectivity is the sin that allows us to pick and choose from the law and hence to redefine it. "More important" and "less important" are terms that eventually turn Torah into a manual of personal preference. What I like is what God demanded. What I find unpleasant is what God never intended. The humorous sign in the antique store aptly sums up the dangers of this approach: "We buy your old junk. We sell antiques." When it suits us, the most precious objects of the past simply become old junk. And when we want to, we can express reverence for the antique and hallowed heritage of our ancestors.

Rabbi Yehudah HaNasi was simply clarifying the most fundamental requirement for proper acceptance of Torah. If the law comes from God, then its jurisdiction is absolute. To introduce personal evaluations is to diminish and ultimately to destroy. We do because God said "do," and this divine mandate applies equally to every law, no matter what our opinion of it. That is what creates the constitutional foundation of the Torah. One may well paraphrase the point of the Mishnah as follows: All mitzvot are created equal—with liberty and justice implicit in identical measures for all, as commanded by the Almighty.

That is the point of the Mishnah that the Radbaz used as the basis for his response to the Jew forced to "select" a day of religious observance. Choose the first day so that you don't in fact choose, but rather God chooses for you. Choose the first day, because if you are granted the freedom to practice your religion on any one day, you dare not defer it to another and thereby declare that you are "looking for something better."

But the matter doesn't end with the words of the Mishnah. True, the Radbaz found his source there, but from where did the author of the Mishnah derive his dramatic conclusion? We have an obligation to understand the biblical basis of this concept. It is in the final words—"for you do not know the reward given for the respective mitzvot"—that we have an allusion to the reasoning behind the Mishnah's ruling.

Does the Torah in fact teach us the concept of reward? If by this question we mean, does the Torah make clear that Heavenly favor is bestowed upon those who lead a life dedicated to fulfilling God's will, the answer is yes. The second paragraph of the *Shema* (Hear O Israel) is the most definitive expression of this principle. "And it will be, if you listen to my commandments, which I command you this day to love Hashem,* your God, and to serve Him, with all your heart and with all your soul—then I will provide rain for your land in its proper time, the early and late rains, that you may gather in your grain, your wine, and your oil. I will provide grass in your field for your cattle and you will eat and be satisfied. Beware lest your heart be seduced and you turn astray and serve gods of others and bow to them. Then the wrath of Hashem will blaze against you. He will restrain the heavens, so there will be no rain and the ground will not yield its produce. And you will swiftly be banished from the goodly land which Hashem gives you. Place these words of Mine upon your heart and upon your soul; bind them for a sign upon your arm and let them be Tefillin between

---

* The Tetragrammaton (YHVH), which Jews do not pronounce and for which they substitute the name *Adonai* during prayer and chanting of the Torah; at all other times, the appellation *Hashem,* which literally means *The Name,* is used.

your eyes. Teach them to your children, to discuss them while you sit in your home, while you walk on the way, when you retire and when you arise. And write them on the doorposts of your house and upon your gates, in order to prolong your days and the days of your children upon the ground that Hashem has sworn to your ancestors to give them, like the days of the heavens on the earth" (Deuteronomy 11:13–21).

But let us ask the question in a more specific form. Does the Torah indicate exactly what reward is given for each mitzvah? We are told in the Mishnah in *Ethics of the Fathers,* "you do not know," i.e., the reward of mitzvot is unspecified.

Why not? Would it not have made many difficult laws far more appealing? Had we been told that doing such and such gives us God's promise of a specific reward, would that not have served to motivate us? Why weren't divine gifts spelled out as heavenly inducements? The answer is implicit in another Mishnah in *Ethics of the Fathers:* "Antigonos, the man of Socho, said: 'Be not like servants who serve their master for the sake of receiving a reward; instead, be like servants who serve their master not for the sake of receiving a reward'" (1:3). Is this a talmudic discussion on labor–management problems? The Sages are clear that the words address themselves to all human beings in their relationship as servants to the Master on High. What it teaches us is a basic concept concerning proper ethical performance. To do a good deed for the sake of reward diminishes it. If a child only listens to a parent on the promise of payment, then the very act has been demeaned. It is no longer an expression of parental honor, but rather pragmatic gain. "I will give you a dollar if . . ." turns the deed into a monetary transaction.

Antigonos taught that in our relationship to God we must not make observance conditional upon divine recompense.

There is a fascinating custom Jews observe to this very day, based on Antigonos' principle. When we recite the third paragraph of *Shema,* the phrase *lema'an tizkeru* ("so that you will remember [the mitzvot]") must be pronounced in an unusual manner. The "z" sound in *tizkeru* has to be prolonged so that the word is not mistaken for *tiskeru* meaning "in order that you receive reward." This, of course, would be repugnant, the very antithesis of proper motivation. Hence, every effort must be made to avoid even the most remote reference to this allusion. We do not do mitzvot for the sake of reward; we observe because we want to please Him, not ourselves.

This is why the Torah did not state a reward alongside each mitzvah. To do so would have created exactly the wrong relationship between deed and purpose. If the reward were stated, then the *peras* (prize) would have become primary. It would have become our first priority.

But God, so to speak, has a problem. It is the same problem that surfaced in the aftermath of the Mishnah in which Antigonos taught that we must serve God without intent to receive reward.

Zadok and Boethus were two students who heard the words of Antigonos and misunderstood his intent. They listened to the teaching that reward was to be expunged from their theological vocabulary and understood that there is no reward for individual mitzvot. Worship the master without intent to receive reward— because the reward of a good deed is the deed itself, they reasoned. Do not expect more since there is no more. From there it was a short step to the heresy that there is no hereafter or final accounting. These students became founders of the Sadducees and the Boethusians—movements far removed from traditional observance—because of their failure to grasp the proper role of reward in our religious system.

Antigonos was subsequently castigated for not being clear enough in his remarks. There are those who believe that a later Mishnah in *Ethics of the Fathers* was written to prevent just such a problem. *Ḥakhamim hizaharu bedivreikhem*—"Wise men be careful with your words" (1:11). To allow oneself to be misunderstood in the religious realm may have disastrous consequences.

Let us now analyze the new biblical problem. We have explained that God could not state a reward alongside every mitzvah, for that would encourage mere pragmatic performance, doing for the sake of reward. But, never to indicate heavenly payment might lead to the heresy of Zadok and Boethus.

What is the ideal solution? How can God suggest that recompense exists, but prevent it from becoming the prime motivation?

The Torah found a remarkable compromise. To prove that reward is part of God's plan, a principle of testimony as applicable in the courts was employed. We know that testimony in the Jewish legal system is only admissible when it comes from two witnesses. Thus, it is not at all strange that there are, in fact, two cases in which a mitzvah is linked to a specific reward. The first appears in conjunction with the Fifth Commandment: "Honor your father and mother so *that your days may be long upon the land which the Lord your God gives you*" (Exodus 20:12).

The second is in Deuteronomy: "If a bird's nest chance to be before you on the way in any tree or on the ground, with young ones or eggs and the mother sitting upon the young, or on the eggs, you shall not take the mother with the young; you shall let the mother free, but the young you may take for yourself so *that it may be well with you and you may prolong your life*" (Deuteronomy 22:6–7).

Honoring parents and sending away the mother bird before removing the eggs upon which she is sitting—these are the two laws that share a unique biblical characteristic. For both of them, we are told, there is a reward. And if two cases jointly testify to this characteristic of the Almighty, then we may rightly assume it is so for all other commandments as well.

Elsewhere a reward is not stated so that we do not act out of wrong motives. Two times, of necessity, it is mentioned, thereby establishing the existence of the principle.

One question still lingers. God could not reveal the reward alongside every mitzvah because of the Antigonos principle. He had to nonetheless validate the reward concept by the use of two mitzvah "witnesses." But of all 613 possibilities, why did He choose precisely these? What is so unique about honoring one's parents and separating the mother bird that they serve as paradigms for a powerful truth?

The Talmud noted a distinctive feature about each of these laws, which makes their selection comprehensible. If one were to rank all the mitzvot of Judaism according to a standard of difficulty, then exhibiting the honor due to parents would be at the extreme end of the scale.

The Babylonian Talmud in *Kidushin* gives countless illustrations of rabbis who performed what we might call incredible feats of self-control in honoring their parents.

Dama, son of Nethinah, was once wearing a gold-embroidered

silken cloak and sitting among Roman nobles when his mother came, tore off his cloak, struck him on the head, and spat in his face—yet he did not shame her.

Whenever the mother of Rabbi Tarfon wished to climb into bed, he would bend down—allowing his mother to step on his back—to let her ascend. He went and boasted thereof in the school. His colleagues said to him: "You have not yet reached half the honor due her" (*Kidushin* 31a,b).

Accepting the mistreatment of senile parents, and self-abasement in the service of aged parents, are not only expected but deemed insufficient and paltry in terms of proper filial responsibility.

Understandably, honoring one's parents is considered the most difficult mitzvah in Judaism.

And what is the easiest mitzvah to fulfill? A man walks on the road and sees a mother bird sitting on her young. To take the egg he must first, according to law, shoo the mother bird away. It is nothing more than a wave of the hand, requiring minimal energy, no preparation, and no expenditure of funds. It is, as the Talmud in *Hulin* tells us, the simplest mitzvah to observe. Remarkable indeed that the principle of divine reward is elucidated by the two laws that circumscribe all of the 613 mitzvot—the very mitzvot that range from easiest to hardest. Now we understand why precisely these two laws were chosen. There is a reward given for the easiest and hardest mitzvot and for everything in between.

But we have not yet put our finger on the most important conclusion. What is the reward promised for honoring your father and mother? And what is the reward promised for sending away the mother before taking the eggs? Longevity. Not only is there a reward for both the easiest and the hardest, but the reward is *identical* in both cases.

It behooves us to clarify that the reward of longevity is not what it may seem to be. History records another heretic who strayed owing to a lack of proper biblical comprehension. Rabbi Elisha Ben Avuyah once witnessed a scene that seemed to refute everything he had studied. A father turned to his son and, pointing out an egg in the branches, asked him bring it down. The young lad, immediately obeying his father, rushed to that spot, saw that the mother bird was sitting on the egg, and shooed her away. Having fulfilled precisely those two mitzvot for which the Torah promises long life, he then descended the tree, slipped, and fell to his death. Rabbi Elisha Ben Avuyah felt that he had seen reality disprove the Torah, and renounced his faith. When the matter came to the attention of Rabbi Akiva, he clarified it to his students. If God, Who is eternal and infinitely good, promises "length of days" and "a good life" as rewards, then truly He cannot refer to this world, which is limited in duration and goodness. The rewards are not given on earth but in the afterlife, which is both infinitely good and infinitely long.

That is the gift promised equally for honoring parents and separating the mother bird. Why precisely these two mitzvot? Because being at opposite ends of the scale of difficulty, they clearly include all others. And having the identical reward, a reward clarified by our Sages as encompassing the benefits of eternity, the most difficult law and the simplest therefore teach the equality of all mitzvot from God's perspective.

We may now, with Maimonides, add a few words to the text of the Mishnah which appear self-evident: Be as careful with minor mitzvot as with major ones, because as a rule you do not know the reward given for mitzvot. Note, however, that in the two cases where you do, the reward for the hard and the easy are indistinguishable. Use that standard as a paradigm. Accept all with the same degree of love and enthusiasm. As far as you are concerned, they all came from the same source. And for all you know, the reward given for performance of each and every one is identical, because "all mitzvot are created equal."

2

If You Are in the
Middle of a Mitzvah

he man who could be free for just one day a year had to choose the first opportunity to perform a mitzvah. His choice was in fact to make no choice. Radbaz used as his source the words of Rebbe in the Mishnah: "Be as scrupulous in performing a minor mitzvah as you are with a major one, for you do not know the rewards given for mitzvot."

This statement, we discovered, was predicated on a biblical insight. The reward indicated for the easiest as well as the most difficult laws were identical, teaching us to regard all commandments equally.

Halakhah has codified this concept in a way that reflects both theology and legal stricture. The idea that all mitzvot are equal is the basis of a remarkable law. What serves as our source for a halakhic ruling will therefore be for us yet another biblical confirmation of our premise and the principle of the Radbaz.

The Talmud teaches us that a person engaged in the performance of one mitzvah is exempt from fulfilling another (i.e., until the first mitzvah is completed). One might assume that this means that one is not required to leave one holy act for another. The Rashba (R. Shlomo ben Adres, Sephardi, Barcelona, 1235–1310) and later halakhic authorities agree that the legal ramifications go much further. The dictum does not imply that one *need* not forsake one mitzvah for another, but that one is not *permitted* to abandon one religious act to fulfill another.

The Mishnah expresses this in the principle "messengers of mitzvah are exempt from fulfilling the mitzvah of Sukkah" (*Sukkah* 25a). Rashi (Rabbi Shelomo Yiẓḥaqi, 1040–1105), the famed commentator of Troyes, illustrates this with the case of a messenger who was sent long distances to secure the release of captives held for ransom. He found himself traveling at the time of the Sukkot holiday and faced the following dilemma: Should he interrupt his journey for the duration of the holiday in order to find a sukkah in a town or city, and continue on his holy mission afterward, or should he ignore the demands of the holiday, since he is already busily engaged in fulfilling a different commandment of God? Speed up the release of the prisoner or sit in a hut as required to commemorate the Exodus from Egypt?

It is to this situation that the Mishnah addresses itself. And it is in this situation that the commentators rule not only that the messenger may continue on his journey if he so desires, but that he *must* do so, and not leave one mitzvah for another.

The rationale is obvious. To do otherwise would meant that, in this case, the messenger has concluded that the mitzvah he is presently fulfilling is less important than the one to which he wants to turn. Leaving one for the sake of the other entails a choice between mitzvot, and that is something a Jew dare not do. This explains why one who is engaged in the performance of a mitzvah is exempt from any other for the duration, because no other law can have a claim upon our time or effort if we are already engaged in fulfilling the will of God.

The law is applied in many other cases as well. The Talmud in *Berakhot* teaches us: "Someone who is confronted with the death of a relative whom he is responsible to bury, is exempt from the recitation of *Shema,* the putting on of Tefillin, and the recitation of prayer as well as all other mitzvot of the Torah" (17b). Here, too, the meaning is not only that an *onan* (a living relative who finds himself in the time period from death until burial) need not pray, but that he is not allowed to pray or to fulfill other mitzvot, since his first obligation is to bury the deceased. To leave the deceased, even to pray or recite the *Shema,* creates a hierarchy of importance. The resulting devaluation of the "interrupted" commandment prohibits the forsaking of any one mitzvah.

But even the Talmud must have a source for such a dramatic conclusion. Let us follow the discussion in the Babylonian Talmud in *Sukkah* (25a).

Mishnah:
Those who are engaged on a religious errand are free from [the obligation of] Sukkah.

מה"מ דת"ר בשבתך בביתך פרט לעוסק במצוה ובלכתך בדרך פרט לחתן . . .
מאי משמע אמר רב הונא כדרך מה דרך רשות אף כל רשות לאפוקי האי דבמצוה עסוק.
מי לא עסקינן דקאזיל לדבר מצוה וקא אמר רחמנא ליקרי
אם כן לימא קרא בשבת ובלכת מאי בשבתך ובלכתך
בלכת דידך הוא דמיחייבת הא בלכת דמצוה פטירת

Gemara:
From where do we know this? From what our Rabbis taught: "When you sit in your house" excludes the man who is occupied with a religious duty. "And when you walk on the way" excludes a bridegroom. . . . How is this inferred?—Rav Huna said, "It is compared to 'the way'; just as 'the way' refers to a secular way, so must every act be secular (i.e., for your own purpose), thus excluding such a man who is occupied with the performance of a religious duty. But does it not refer to where one is going on a religious errand [also]? And does not the Divine Law nevertheless say that one should read?—If so, the verse should have said, 'When sitting and when walking'; why [then does it say,] 'When *you* sit and when *you* walk? [It must consequently mean:] When walking for your own purpose you are bound by the obligation, but when walking on a religious errand you are free."

Let us clarify the passage. The directions for reciting the *Shema* contain two types of phrases. The first is clearly related to time: "when you lie down and when you arise." The implications of this phrase are treated elsewhere in the Talmud. Next come two additional statements clearly relating to place: "When you sit in your house and when you walk on the road." Although these seem like extensions, talmudic genius clearly recognized them as *exclusions*. Had the text not defined the place where it would be incumbent to recite the *Shema,* the talmudic requirement would obviously have been universal. Why then state "when you sit in your house and when you walk in the road?" The answer must be to *exclude*: only when you sit and when you walk. That is, when you are obligated, but not in other circumstances.

It is on the basis of this reasoning that the Talmud excludes two kinds of people from reciting the *Shema:* a person in the midst of performing a mitzvah and a groom. A short aside is required to make sense of the latter. A groom on his wedding night cannot possibly have the required concentration for the proper reading of the *Shema.* He is naturally preoccupied with the nuptial activities that will follow. The sexual aspects of the wedding night are in fact a mitzvah, part of the very first law given to mankind: "Be fruitful and multiply." The groom's concern is a direct consequence of the law. He is in fact engaged in the performance of a mitzvah.

If the case of the groom belongs in the general category of one occupied with the performance of a mitzvah, why would the Talmud require two different phrases for the same idea? The answer is that the Sages drew a profound distinction between the groom and other situations of engagement in a mitzvah. The groom is in fact not actually in the midst of performing a mitzvah until he becomes physically involved in the sexual act. Yet we exempt him from the *Shema* the entire night. Why? Because if the Torah uses two phrases—"when you sit down *and* when you walk"—then it is extending the parameters of engagement in a mitzvah to include *physical* performance of an act as well *mental* involvement in its preparations. If the Torah expands the category, then we must find room not only for the one who is occupied with a mitzvah but even for one who is *preoccupied.* Whether one is physically engaged in the performance of a divine act or mentally engrossed in preparation for its performance, the biblical exemptions apply.

The Talmud asks the obvious question: How does the text itself indicate this? Even if we are to grant that these phrases are present in order to teach us that there is a person who need not recite *Shema,* how can we be sure that they refer to these cases?

The answer relates to a word that is used in a specific grammatical construction. The Torah states: "When you sit in *your* house, when you walk on *your* road." The Torah is referring specifically to the acts of sitting and going for one's own purposes, and that is when one must recite the *Shema*. But if one sits and goes because of an involvement that transcends one's private interest and fulfills the will of God, then the Torah has taught that you need not, and should not, recite the Shema.

Do what you were already in the midst of doing. Do not shift from one mitzvah to another. More precisely: Do not dare to "evaluate" God's commandments, forsaking one duty in order to perform another *you* think is more important.

Which is the most important mitzvah? Another biblical source confirms our constitutional principle that all mitzvot are created equal. We do not know the rewards given by God, and in the two cases where we do—the lightest and the most severe—the recompense is identical. Similarly, from the very paragraph that mandates the most important expression of monotheism, we are enjoined: Recite the *Shema except* if you are already engaged in another mitzvah—because if you are in the midst of fulfilling God's will, you can never say you believe another, more important duty is calling you in the service of the Almighty.

3

The Big and the Little

ne word summarizes all we have said. It appears in Deuteronomy as part of a covenant between God and the Jewish people, and although it is a peculiar word in context, it serves as the name of a Torah portion.

"And it shall come to pass as a consequence of your listening to these ordinances and carefully carrying them out that God will keep with you the Covenant and the mercy which He swore to your fathers, and He will love you and bless you and multiply you" (Deuteronomy 7:12–13).

The second Hebrew word in the verse, *eqev* ("as a consequence of"), whence the portion gets its name, is related to the name of the third Patriarch, Jacob (in Hebrew, Ya'aqov). Its root meaning is "heel." Why is such an unusual term used to describe the precondition for God's blessings? Rashi, the master commentator of the Torah, replies using a midrashic source: "If [even] the light mitzvot which a person tends to trample with his heels you will listen to . . . [then you will be entitled to God's blessings]."

There are indeed laws that people trample upon because they assume that they are not important. For this reason God says, "I will bless you if you keep the minor ones in the same way that you keep the ones you consider major."

19

Interestingly, the very word EQeV, referring to the simple laws often stepped upon by the heels of man, numerically adds up to 172 (Ayin = 70, Qof = 100, Veit = 2). This is important because the Ten Commandments comprise 172 words. What a remarkable correspondence between the words considered most important and those dismissed because of their seeming lack of importance!

"It shall come to pass as a consequence of your listening to these ordinances." Blessing for the Jew is predicated upon the recognition that all mitzvot are to be treated equally.

How Does One Convert to Judaism?

The *Shulḥan Arukh,* the Code of Jewish law, gives us the requirements for proper conversion. Let it be noted that Jews discourage converts. But that is only because we know that once one joins the Jewish fold, one is responsible for observance of all mitzvot. If we were to accept into Judaism someone who had no intention of keeping the commandments, we would be doing that person a grave injustice.

Only if we are certain that a prospective convert actually intends to abide by those commitments implicit in conversion are we to proceed. With this one proviso, we do in fact feel positively about adding to those who will acknowledge the oneness of God. That is, after all, our vision for the End of Days: "It will come to pass that God will be King over the entire world and on that day God will be One and His Name will be One" (Zechariah 14:9).

The Halakhah, the operative law, is clear. We must both discourage and encourage a prospective convert. We must speak of the reality of being a Jew, both the curse and the blessing. The *Shulḥan Arukh* reads as follows:

> When a Gentile comes to convert, you say to him: "What did you see that made you come to convert? Don't you realize that at this time the Jewish people is oppressed, despised, and banished, and that much suffering is being visited upon them?" If he responds, "I know, and I am not worthy to join you," then accept him immediately. Teach him the foundations of Judaism, which are the oneness of God and the prohibition of idol worship, and talk to him at

length about them. Teach him some of the commandments—some
that are easy and some that are difficult. . . . [*Yoreh De'ah* 268:2]

We must introduce the prospective convert to those mitzvot that
are regarded as serious and to those that are considered light. He
must affirm his commitment to both. What if he says, "I will do
everything with the exception of one small, minor matter. There is
not a single 'big thing' that I am not prepared to do, but surely it
cannot mean that much if there is only one small minor point, one
trivial matter that I must reject as insignificant." In such a case, we
must respond: "If you still do not grasp that one dare not make
distinctions, you are not ready to become a member of God's
people. To be a Jew means to respond with the same devotion to
every single demand of His will."

A Final Story

One of the most famous preachers in Jewish history was the
Magid of Dubno (Jacob Kranz, c. 1740–1804). His parables
became world famous. His "simple" tales conveyed the most profound teachings. One of his famous parables summarizes our
theme and clarifies its meaning.

In a little shtetl there lived a poor, pious Jew. He found himself
in indescribable poverty, unable to support his wife and children.
Although deeply religious, he felt he had no alternative but to
steal in order to feed his loved ones.

How does a pious Jew go about stealing? He did not know
where to turn. Force of habit led him to the synagogue. It was
there that he began to look around for something to take. But he
knew in his heart that he could never steal anything "really important."

He searched everywhere, but refused to even consider taking
the Torah scrolls themselves, the silver ornaments, the prayer
books, or the Bibles. They were too holy, too significant. If only
there were something that was not "so important."

It was a beautiful synagogue by the standards of the shtetl. It
had no fancy furniture, but a magnificent chandelier hung from
the ceiling, which lit up the room with what everyone felt were

spiritual rays emanating from God Himself. Light with which to read prayers to the Almighty. Light with which to study from God's holy books. Light with which to illuminate the entire world.

From that light he sought to find something, anything, of even the slightest value. He lowered his expectations. If there were something worth just a ruble. He found nothing on the main floor of the synagogue, so he climbed up to the attic to search there. In the dark, he began to probe. Fingers touching, feeling. At first there was nothing. And then, miracle of miracles, his fingers felt a small screw in the ground. It was made of metal. Surely he would be able to sell it for scrap. It would not be much, but it might allow him to buy a piece of bread. And most significant of all, he would not really be stealing anything of value. And so he began to loosen that small, insignificant screw and, no sooner did he manage to undo most of it, than he heard from below a thunderous crash. It took only a moment to realize that what had fallen was the chandelier, the most costly object in the synagogue. All because he had undone the screw that held it in place—the little thing that in retrospect carried with it so much more than he could have ever realized.

How powerful the message. There are small things attached to far greater objects, holding them in place and ensuring that they give light to the entire community. What is a little mitzvah? And who can tell how much effect its removal may have on the total picture?

Some years ago, the thirteenth space launch of the U.S. shuttle program met disaster. Scientists combed the debris and found that a faulty O-ring was responsible. That small item caused the death of the astronauts and millions of dollars in damage.

Who is to judge what is small and what is large, what is less and what is more important? So too is it with mitzvot. We dare not judge. What we deem insignificant may bear light to the whole world.

Part II

What about the Ten Commandments?

4

There Are No
Ten Commandments

e believe that at Mount Sinai, God taught Moses
613 Commandments. We also know that he singled
out ten of them for special treatment in two ways:
(a) these ten were written on two tablets, handed to Moses, and
kept in the holiest spot of the *mishkan* (the Tabernacle), and
(b) they were also spoken directly to the people, rather than
relayed via Moses, as were all the other laws of the Torah.

If God chose these ten for special treatment, then He Himself
made a choice. It would appear that they are the most important
laws of Judaism. Doesn't the existence of a Decalogue refute our
claim regarding the constitutional principle of equality of mitzvot? To the contrary. Once we understand the real meaning of the
Ten Commandments, we will see that they confirm our master
principle.

Let us begin by clarifying what really occurred at Sinai. Did the
Jewish people hear Ten Commandments from God Himself? The
answer, interestingly enough, is no. Although the text does not
introduce an interruption in the flow of the narrative, the commentators explain that Chapter 20, verse 16—"And they said to
Moses, you speak with us and we will hear, but do not let God

speak with us, lest we die"—occurred immediately after the second commandment. The people could not continue to listen to God directly. The voice was too strong, the implications for punishment in the future too grave if they were to accept the commandments from the Almighty Himself. "You speak with us and not God, lest we die," they pleaded with Moses. Thus, according to the Sages, only the first two were heard by the people from God directly. The following eight were communicated through Moses.

There are at least four confirmations of this account:

1.   The Babylonian Talmud, in tractate *Makot,* teaches us that there were a total of 613 commandments. Being sensitive to the teachings of *gematria* (numerology), the secrets of numbers hidden in letters of words, the Talmud notes the strange fact that the word TORaH adds up to only 611 (Tav = 400, Vav = 6, Resh = 200, Heh = 5). In our daily prayers, we recite: "Moses commanded the Torah to us." Why would the word "Torah" be defective in number, indicating that Moses only taught us 611 laws rather than 613? The answer is because two laws, the first two commandments, were not given to us by Moses, but came directly from God Himself.

2.   The medieval commentator Rabbi Avraham Ibn Ezra makes the cogent observation that the grammar of the Ten Commandments points us to the same conclusion. In the first and second commandments, God speaks in the first person: "*I* am the Lord, your God . . . You shall have no other gods before *Me*." Beginning with the third commandment, however, the text switches from second to third person. "You shall not take the name of *the Lord* your God in vain." "Remember the Sabbath day to keep it holy, because in six days *the Lord* made Heaven and the earth" (Exodus 20:8), etc.

3.   The Jerusalem Talmud finds an allusion to this in the declaration of faith every Jew makes twice daily. *Shema Yisrael Hashem Eloqeinu Hashem Eḥad.* "Hear, O Israel, the Lord is our God, the Lord is One" (Deuteronomy

6:4). In this phrase we proclaim not only *that* we believe, but *why* we believe. We know there is a God Who gave us the Torah, because we heard Him speaking to us. We were present at Sinai and God addressed us. *Shema Yisrael,* continue to hear, Israel, what you heard then. What did we hear? *Hashem Eloqeinu,* the Lord is our God, the summary of the first commandment ("I am the Lord, your God"), and *Hashem Eḥad,* the Lord is One, which is the second commandment ("You shall have no other gods before me"). Commandments one and two are in a class by themselves. They are the ones alluded to in the line of the *Shema* because they are the two laws that we in fact heard from Him without the need for Moses as an intermediary.

4. A final indication is contained in a brilliant insight offered by the Ḥatam Sofer (1762–1839). The first word of the Torah, BeREShiYT ("in the beginning"), alludes to the two most fundamental principles of our faith. The letter Shin, which appears on every mezuzah, stands for Shadai, the name of God. Surrounding the Shin are the letters Yod and Tav on one side, and Alef, Resh, and an enlarged Beit on the other.

Tav Yod Shin Alef Resh Beit

The total (Tav = 400, Resh = 200, Yod = 10, Alef = 1, Beit = 2) is 613. God and Torah meet in the very first word of the Torah. Interestingly, the word BeREShiYT is divided in a manner whereby the consonants Tav, Resh, Yod, and Alef, totaling 611, are supplemented by the enlarged Beit, which has a value of 2. Why was the Beit enlarged? Perhaps to intimate that the 613 Commandments may be divided into two categories: 611 that were taught by Moses, and two that came directly from the Almighty Himself.

At this point, if one were to repeat the question "Did God

recite all of the Ten Commandments to the Jewish people directly?" the answer would be no. We have established the distinction
between the first two and the remaining eight. But that is not the
end of the story.

The introductory verse to the Ten Commandments reads as
follows: "And God spoke all these words, saying" (Exodus 20:1).
Rashi, quoting the Midrash, finds a source for an additional
aspect of the story. The phrase "God spoke all these words" suggests that before He enumerated each of the Ten Commandments
to the Israelites, God uttered it all simultaneously, in one oral
expression. If one were to imagine it, it would be similar to a ca-
cophony of sound; as if 172 different people were each instructed
at one and the same moment to shout out a different word. God,
of course, had no problem producing so many words at precisely
the same instant.

But the Midrash does not explain why God would want to
make all the words be heard in one instant, when they could
obviously not have been understood by the people that way. If
God had to repeat them subsequently, for the sake of comprehension, what was the point of having them shouted out in one chilling
moment of incomprehensibility?

Neither Rashi nor the Midrash address themselves to this
problem. Understanding why God chose these Ten Commandments for special treatment will, however, allow us to resolve this
difficulty as well.

Are these really then the ten most important laws of Judaism?
Where is Yom Kippur? Where are the dietary laws of kashrut?
Where is family purity? Not one of our Sages suggests what the
contemporary mind so often assumes: "Well, I may not keep all of
the laws, but at least I keep what are obviously the most important, the Ten Commandments."

To suggest that these are the ten most important commandments is to ignore the simple truth that in Judaism there really are
no "Ten Commandments."

As shocking as that statement may seem, it becomes obvious
once we examine the Hebrew terminology. A commandment is a
mitzvah. In Hebrew, we refer to the *Taryag Mizvot,* i.e., 613

Commandments. There is, however, no equivalent phrase in all of Jewish tradition that refers to the "Ten Commandments" as *Aseret ha-Mizvot,* the Ten Mitzvot. Clearly one cannot speak of the "Ten Mitzvot," because that would imply the selection by God of ten commandments for special status, which is contrary to the concept of the equality of mitzvot. *Aseret ha-Dibrot* literally means "Ten Sayings." Rabbi Sa'adiah Gaon (882–942 C.E.) clarified what this means. In a remarkable little book called *Sefer Azharot,* he shows the link between each one of the 613 mitzvot and its prime category heading. Every one of the "Ten Sayings" is in fact a major category or principle. Under it may be subsumed countless other laws.

For example: Embarrassing someone in public is a sin. But where is it found in the Ten Principles? It is included in the laws forbidding murder, which in Hebrew is called *Shefikhat damim,* the shedding of blood. When one person kills another, the victim has not been allowed to continue living. When someone embarrasses another publicly, the humiliated party wishes he or she were dead and might even have preferred physical extinction to public shame. The Talmud teaches that when a person shames another publicly, God makes the blood rush from the latter's face. That, too, is a way of shedding blood, and it is viewed as a derivative of the sixth category or principle, "Thou shalt not murder." Maximurder and mini-murder are equally forbidden.

Where is Yom Kippur? Passover? Shavuot or Sukkot? Principle number four teaches us that God may be captured not only in space but also in time. Time is holy. The Sabbath day is to be used to reflect upon God both as creator and architect of history. Once we accept this concept on a weekly basis, we may readily grasp the need to develop and extend it in such a way that all significant dates associated with major incidents of the past are to be celebrated on an annual basis.

Not commandments, but principles. Not ten mitzvot, but ten categories. Write the number 613, the sum total of all mitzvot, and then add them individually: $6 + 1 + 3 = 10$. This is so because all 613 may be reduced to a more fundamental grouping. That grouping is in fact the *Aseret ha-Dibrot* uttered at Sinai. It would be wrong to say that God singled out ten laws, thereby suggesting that they were of greater importance. The ten, in fact, encompass the 613.

The Talmud long ago addressed the problem of those who thought that the Ten Commandments were selected as the ten most important laws of Judaism. Have you ever wondered why the ten singled out for such special status at Sinai are not recited on a daily basis? Our prayers include selections from the Torah—"Hear O Israel" and the song of deliverance at the Red Sea—as well as numerous chapters from the Psalms and elsewhere. Why not include something as important as the *Aseret ha-Dibrot*?

The Talmud relates that indeed this was once the case. Prayer today is an attempt to create a substitute for the sacrificial system practiced in the Holy Temple of Jerusalem. A sacrifice, a *qorban*, was meant to do what the root of that word (q.r.v.) implies: *qoreiv*, to bring us nearer to God in an audiovisual display of our relationship to the Creator. We humble ourselves and subdue our animalistic nature. We sacrifice the animal within us. In Freudian terms, the id is transformed by the superego in the service of God. The synagogue was a much later creation, necessitated by the destruction of the Temple and the abolition of animal sacrifice. Prayer was primarily an inferior alternative to the offering of *qorbanot*.

In spite of all this, the Talmud tells us that even in the days of the Temple, there were some prayers so basic to an understanding of our relationship with God that they were recited by the Priests (*Kohanim,* sing. *Kohen*) as part of the sacrificial service. One of these prayers, at a time when institutionalized liturgy as we know it was almost nonexistent, was the recitation of the *Aseret ha-Dibrot*.

What made such a basic part of prayer disappear from our liturgy? The answer revolves around a rabbinic response to an unfortunate misunderstanding. "The Rabbis negated the daily recitation of the Ten Commandments because of the libels of the heretics" (*Berakhot* 12a). Which heretics? In the current edition of the Talmud, Rashi's explanation of the word "heretics" is rendered as *Akum,* idolaters. Earlier, uncensored versions have Rashi in a more relevant version: *Talmidei Yeshu,* disciples of Jesus (the

Christians burned the Talmud numerous times and imposed censorship of "offensive passages," leading to a self-protective self-censorship—the correct edition of the Talmud). What we have here in fact is an early reference to Christianity and the early Judeo-Christians. It was they, with an eye on spreading their religion and making it far more appealing, who claimed that if God wrote these ten on the tablets, they and they alone must be the most important laws of Judaism. More is really not required. It would be an easy step from here to say, "I am religious because I observe these ten." For us, however, the ten are but a summary of the 613, and if one chose to select merely ten for observance out of more then 600 laws, one would in fact be committed to an extremely small fraction of God's total will.

The daily reading of the Ten Commandments was canceled so that people would not overemphasize their importance. The error we alluded to was directly addressed by the *Tanai'im,* the rabbis of Mishnaic times. Daily repetition of one small portion could be very misleading. Christianity chose to make the Decalogue its important commandments. Judaism, both by theology and by law, reaffirmed that the ten are not the whole; they are merely the summary of it.

When the Decalogue was mistakenly identified as the entire covenant, the rabbis preferred to exclude it from the daily service rather than allow it an exaggerated importance.

The error of our time—the assumption one can satisfy one's commitment to God by accepting no more than the ten laws on the tablets—was exactly what our Sages feared when they consciously legislated the exclusion of the Decalogue from synagogue service.

Why God Spoke "All the Words" Simultaneously

God chose to recite all ten laws in one instant, before He began to articulate each one in a comprehensible manner, because He wanted to ensure that we do not make the error of granting additional value to any one portion of the Divine law. We asked initially, what point would there be in having 172 words spoken together when no one could understand them? In so doing, God avoided a major difficulty. Had the ten categories been articulated one after the other, they would have had built into them the implicit assumption that arises from the fact that sequence bespeaks priorities. If "this" precedes "that," there must have been a reason; obviously "this" is more important. But God had to make clear that with regard to His law, it is not so. How does one eliminate the erroneous interpretations arising from the limitations of speech? "And God spoke *all of these words* saying,"—God said them all together to confirm what would subsequently be the message of Rabbi Yehudah HaNasi in the Mishnah: Be as scrupulous in performing a minor mitzvah as you are with a major one, for you do not know the reward given for mitzvot.

We have come full circle. The "Ten Commandments" seemed to suggest a refutation of our principle that all mitzvot are equal. The ten concepts or categories, further reduced to one thunderous simultaneous shout of 172 separate words, teach that the Torah, which may be subsequently broken down into many parts, is ultimately and fundamentally—just like its Author—one.

5

Why Were the
Ten Given?

ut why did God have to give these ten categories?
Why single out one type of law over another when it
could lead to misinterpretation?

We must go one step further to fully comprehend the role of
the Decalogue in Jewish thought—and to understand how this
defines the uniqueness of Judaism and differentiates it from all
other religions.

Why does a Jew believe in God? Why does a Jew believe in the
divinity of the Torah? Some might respond: Because Moses gave
us the Torah in the name of God, and we trust that he was telling
the truth, that he was in fact transmitting what had been handed to
him directly from the Almighty.

Why should we believe Moses more than any of the others who
claimed to have received entirely different messages from God?
For the Jewish believer, what makes Moses more trustworthy than
Jesus, Mohammed, or a host of others? If the Jew says, "I cannot
accept Jesus, I believe in the Old Testament rather than the New,"
is so important a decision based solely on the relative merits of one
charismatic figure over another?

Jewish philosophers were deeply concerned with this issue. It

was Maimonides who made the most startling observation of all in
this regard. The gist of his comments in the eighth chapter of his
halakhic code *Hilkhot Yesodei ha-Torah* in *Yad ha-Ḥazaqah,
Mishneh Torah,* is this: The Jews do not believe because of Moses.
Built into the Bible is a warning concerning the possibility of fraud
spoken in the name of God. The Almighty knows that there will
always be people who might prevail upon others because of certain
talents. Charisma convinces some; magic has power over others.
What if an accomplished soothsayer, diviner, or psychic would
claim that his or her abilities confirm divine stature and partnership? There have always been people who can say "God told me
directly" in a convincing manner.

What is the religious safeguard for all of this? How does God
ensure that no one speak in His Name and use the credentials of
Doug Henning—style witchcraft? The answer is given at numerous
points in the Bible. "You shall not allow a sorceress to live"
(Exodus 22:17); "Do not turn to ghosts or to familiar spirits; do
not seek them out and be defiled by them. I am the Lord, your
God" (Leviticus 19:31); "When you come to the land which the
Lord, your God has given you, you shall not learn to do like the
abominations of those nations that preceded you in the land.
There shall not be found among you anyone who makes his son or
his daughter pass through the fire, [or] one who uses divination, a
soothsayer, or an enchanter or a sorcerer, or a charmer, or one
who consults a ghost or a familiar spirit or a necromancer. For
whoever does these things is an abomination to the Lord and as a
result of these abominations, the Lord, your God, is driving them
[the Canaanite nations] out from before you. You shall be wholehearted with the Lord, your God" (Deuteronomy 18:9–13).

Most significant of all: "If there arises in your midst a prophet
or a dreamer of dreams, and he gives you a sign or a wonder, and
the sign or the wonder comes to pass whereof he spoke onto you,
saying, 'Let us go after other gods that you have not known, or let
us serve them,' you shall not listen to that prophet or that dreamer
of dreams, for the Lord your God is testing you to know whether
you love the Lord your God with all your heart and with all your
soul" (Deuteronomy 13:2–4). In other words, even if someone

uses a miracle to confirm that he speaks in the name of God, you may not listen to him. It is merely a test of your faith.

How then does one come to believe in God? Aren't miracles the most fundamental source of our religious convictions? Absolutely not. In the words of Maimonides: "Moses our teacher was not believed by Israel because of the signs that he did. For one who believes on the basis of signs or miracles has in his heart doubt. For it is possible that these signs or miracles can be done by means of magic or witchcraft" (*Yesodei ha-Torah* 8:1).

Miracles prove nothing. Miracles can be what the French call *trompe-l'oeil* (fool the eye, a reference to optical illusion). Miracles can be deceptive. In the realm of medicine, they may be nothing more than psychosomatic cures or placebos. One dare not use miracles to verify contradictory claims of faith because, as it has well been said, if miracles could be used to prove the truths of one religion, they could similarly be used to prove the truths of all religion, for every religion has miracles within its catalog of convincing arguments. Hence, if miracles prove all faiths, which in fact contradict one another, they must be rejected as proving none.

Here is a fundamental distinction between Judaism and Christianity. The Gospels record the miracles performed by Jesus at length, and miracles play an extremely significant role in Christianity. The wondrous acts of Jesus, such as reviving the dead, healing the incurable, and transforming water into wine, are meant to serve as cogent evidence not only of his divine authorization but of his divinity. The virgin birth and the resurrection are not only major events but also fundamental articles of belief; this, despite the specific warning in Deuteronomy that "if there arise in your midst a prophet or a dreamer of dreams, and he gives you a sign or a wonder" and that sign or wonder is used as a rationale for rejecting any part of the Torah, then the "miracle" must clearly be rejected. In Christianity, miracles were sufficient to warrant the replacement of the Old Testament by the New, the message of Moses to be superseded by that of Jesus.

A remarkable story in the Talmud serves as a revealing contrast. Rabbi Eliezer once tried to convince his colleagues of the correctness of his opinion. He performed a number of miracles to prove his point. When he miraculously moved a carob tree a hundred yards as "proof" of his opinion, the rabbis shrugged it off with the observation that "One does not adduce proof from a carob tree." When he caused water to flow backward and even the walls of the house to incline, they were still not convinced. When finally a heavenly voice proclaimed that he was right, the Sages would have none of it. Quoting the passage from Deuteronomy (30:12), they said: "It [the Torah] is not in Heaven" and added, "The Torah was given to us on Sinai, and so we pay no heed to a Heavenly voice" (*Baba Mezia* 59b).

Judaism is not preoccupied with miracles. What then was their purpose, if not to serve as a basis for belief? Maimonides answers clearly:

> All the miracles that Moses performed in the desert were done only for a specific purpose, not in order to bring proof for prophecy. If it was necessary to drown the Egyptians, the sea split and they were swallowed up within it. If we required food, God caused the manna to descend. When they were thirsty, He brought water from the rock. When the group of Qorah and his followers rebelled, the earth swallowed them. And so, too, all the other signs and wonders. [*Yesodei ha-Torah* 8:1]

Maimonides has given a list of events that occurred early in our history and clarified that they were miracles of pragmatism, not of persuasion. They came to fill a need, not to foster faith.

But don't some miracles seem to negate this principle? For example, when God first spoke to Moses, He showed him a burning bush that was not being consumed. Wasn't the purpose of this miracle to inspire awe in Moses so that he could believe it was God who was speaking to him? The commentators long ago wondered why God would choose this particular "miracle" to demonstrate His presence. Various explanations have been offered, but perhaps the most beautiful one is that of Rabbi Avraham Ibn Ezra. The bush was a symbol to Moses. The man who escaped to the haven of Midian, but who always worried about his brethren whom he left behind in Egypt; the man who named his own son Gershom (Hebrew for "I was a stranger there") because he wanted a constant reminder that he was a "stranger in a strange land"; the man who knew that his people were in the "fire of Egypt," which would some day be paralleled by the crematoria of contemporary history—to that Moses was shown, in the first communication from God, that "the bush may burn, but it will not be consumed." The Jewish people may be in flames, but contrary to the laws of nature, they will never be destroyed. *Am Yisrael Ḥai,* "the Jewish people will live forever," was the metaphorical message that served as the true purpose of the miracle of the burning bush. The burning bush was more than a miracle; it was a message.

Maimonides' principle is accepted as a basic tenet of Judaism. Miracles are not meant to convince anybody. They dare not serve such an important purpose. If they did, other faiths would claim them as well, and people seeking ultimate truth would be forced to evaluate the greater magic or convincing power of one trick over another.

God would not allow His existence and His will to rest on such flimsy foundations.

Miracles therefore *must* be rejected as the basis of belief. So why do we believe in Judaism? Why should we accept the words of Moses in the name of God? And how can we be sure that his message is truer than that conveyed by countless other "prophets" and "spokesmen"?

This is a basic religious problem. To resolve it, the answer of Maimonides, speaking for all Jewish sages and philosophers, must be understood: "And on what basis did the Jewish people believe in him [Moses]? On the basis of what they saw at *ma'amad har Sinai*—standing at Mount Sinai, where our eyes saw and not those of a stranger, where our ears heard and not those of another—the fire, the sounds, the torches, and He drew near the dense fog. And the Voice spoke to him and we heard" (*Yesodei ha-Torah* 8:1).

Judaism differs from all the other religions that begin with one person saying, "God told me to tell you." How can we be sure that this is so? How could God ensure that no charlatan or self-deluded "Messiah," using charm, charisma, or powers of persuasion, would speak falsely in His name? By commanding us at the outset to reject every human claim in His Name; because God will not entrust something so important as the expression of His will to a messenger who may or may not be lying.

Judaism begins with an experience witnessed by close to two million people (600,000 males between the ages twenty and sixty, plus those who were younger and older, making for a male population of about 1,000,000; and an equal number of females for a total of about 2,000,000 people).

We heard God speak. We were there. The Midrash teaches us that the souls of all future generations were present at Sinai. To be part of that commitment means that we had to be present. That would explain why every Jew responds so strongly to the message of Sinai. For if the conscious mind does not recall, then what Freud would call the subconscious, what others might refer to as the psychic memory, what we refer to as the *neshamah,* the soul, cannot forget that it, too, shared the most memorable moment of history as God descended and let an entire people hear: "I am the Lord, your God."

It is fascinating that the declaration of faith recited twice daily by every Jew, *ShemA Yisrael Hashem Eloqeinu Hashem EhaD,* is written in a special way by every scribe who pens a Torah scroll. The Ayin in the word *shema* is enlarged to show that, although the word *shema* means "hear" and today we can only listen to the message, the big Ayin—a letter that means "eye"—reminds us that we originally beheld the Revelation that today makes us believers. In combination with the enlarged final letter of the last word, i.e., the Dalet in *ehaD,* we have the Hebrew word for "witness." This is precisely the principle that Maimonides explained is at the heart of Jewish belief. We are not simply naive, starry-eyed dreamers living out our lives committed to the words of God as transmitted by one man. Rather we are heirs to a heritage that claims credence because every one of our ancestors, as well as all of our souls, could apply the word "AiD" to a shared experience. The phrase *Shema Yisrael* therefore contains not only what we believe, but also why. We believe because we were witness.

שְׁמַע יִשְׂרָאֵל יְהֹוָה אֱלֹהֵינוּ יְהֹוָה אֶחָד

Dalet [*ehaD*]   Ayin [*shemA*]

Let us state more simply why this is so important. All religions based on the claim of a person as representative of God face the same dilemma: if that person lied, the religion is null and void. The word "lied" has many meanings. It may be a conscious distortion of truth for the sake of personal gain, but it may also have other definitions. I have known at least half a dozen people who think they are "Messiah," "Son of God," and, in one case, God Himself. What amazes me is not that people have a capacity for madness, but rather that madness may go hand in hand with other areas of sanity. All these individuals function in society—they are not institutionalized—but they have one area of irrationality. It has become clear to me that people may be self-deluded. Bearing this possibility in mind, Judaism posits that had Moses simply come to the Jewish people and said: "I have a message from God; He spoke with me and told me to tell you that you are to observe the following laws," then the Jewish people would have had every right and perhaps even the obligation to say to Moses, "If God told you, then that's your affair. If you perform miracles, they mean nothing to us. We cannot accept a religion based on a revelation to one person."

The enlarged consonants that encase the *Shema Yisrael,* spelling the Hebrew word for "witness," make all the difference. "Seeing is believing" goes the expression, and indeed we saw. That is why we believe.

Some might say that the claim of Revelation to two million is not that significant. Just as other religions fall by the wayside if one person, the source, either lied or was self-deluded, Judaism is not true if Revelation is not true, or if two million people created an imaginary tale for the generations.

Consider the ramifications of this question. Other faiths never claimed corroboration of Revelation by even one witness; Jews have transmitted an undiluted tradition of a simultaneous, identical Revelation whose words have never varied, a Revelation accepted by prophets of countless different religions. How long ago was Sinai? People often exaggerate the time period. If one considers the generations involved, the 3,200 years requires only eighty generations or transmission periods of forty years each $(80 \times 40 = 3,200)$. This means that there were only eighty parent-to-children eras in which the account of Sinai was described and transmitted. That transmission has never varied. Imagine so large

a number of people describing an event told to them by their fore-
bears. To challenge the truth of that claim is to say that two million people at Sinai or at some later time suddenly came together
to fashion one great lie—a lie of an event they were able to piece
together in such a manner that no one's telling of it differed from
that of another. That would indeed have to be the greatest miracle
of all.

God did not want to limit the Revelation to one person, and so
He spoke to the entire Jewish nation. When a Jew rejects Jesus, it
is not because he favors the personality of Moses or even prefers
his message. It is because the issue is not the credibility of two
people, but rather the plausibility of a Revelation to one, as
opposed to a Revelation to two million. When a Christian who
accepts the historic reality of the Revelation at Sinai tells a Jew to
reject everything heard at Sinai because God subsequently told
Jesus of a new covenant, the Jew can only respond that had God
really wanted to undo what He initially commanded in the presence of the multitude, He certainly would have gathered all of us
together again to experience a second Revelation. Indeed, the
words of the Torah and the 613 mitzvot are called "an everlasting
statute" (ḥuqat olam) because never again were the multitudes
privileged to hear a message from God.

The Jew cannot accept the New Testament since it is the words
of one man intended to undo what the Creator had shared with all
of His children.

Our analysis has convinced us that Revelation is the only valid
source for acceptance of religion. We believe because we heard
with our own ears. We do because God commanded us. That
equation required God to perform a Revelation incorporating two
distinct elements.

Jews must believe in His existence. We must also commit ourselves to follow His commandments. To accomplish the first, it
would have been sufficient for us to have simply heard God proclaim His presence. Jews would have left Sinai knowing that God
is. They would have been confident that they had been chosen for
divine closeness and some special mission. But what was that
mission to be? If they would then have had to rely on the words of

Moses as their sole intermediary between themselves and God, the commitment would have been lacking. How could one man speak to all people for something that would involve obedience by all future generations? The Revelation demanded more than Revelation of God's existence. It also required Revelation of His will. Theoretically, it might have been ideal for God to reveal himself directly to all the Jewish people at great length and teach them the entire Torah, so that whenever a Jew fulfilled a mitzvah he would be certain that it came from the God he heard addressing the Jewish people in totality. However, realistically that could not have been. It took Moses, who was on an almost angelic level, forty days and forty nights to learn all he needed to know. Revelation to the entire people would have taken a lifetime, if not more. And where could one find human beings who were both deserving and religiously suitable for such a long encounter with God?

Thus God was, so to speak, faced with a quandary. How to meet with the Jewish people for a short period of time, and still ensure that after this encounter they would know that everything Moses said in His name really came from Him? The solution was the *Aseret ha-Dibrot,* the Decalogue, expressing those principles they would be certain issued directly from God. And whenever Moses would teach the Jewish people a new law, he would explain it as a clear and logical extension of the concepts that had originally been proclaimed at Sinai by the Almighty Himself, rather than as a "new" man-made mitzvah.

Constitutional law today fills thousands of libraries and millions of volumes as its basic principles have become the source for decisions in cases around the country. When in doubt, it is the Supreme Court that serves as arbiter of last resort. Its function is to clarify what the Constitution had intended. Law is not newly created but rather applied in such a manner that it does not contravene the intent of the founding fathers. One might perhaps even go further. The Constitution itself is an outgrowth of the tenets of the Declaration of Independence. If all men are created equal, if we hold these truths to be self-evident, then the rest of the Constitution must follow.

Similarly, the role of Moses after Sinai was not to transmit new laws to people who had been present at Sinai, but rather to explain the countless legal applications to the categories they had witnessed.

The "ten" were therefore not a pleasant way of introducing the Jews to some laws. Instead, they would serve for all time as the ultimate proof of Divine Revelation for every single mitzvah which, if understood correctly, is a logical derivative of what was stated by God for all.

Understanding this is to know why the ten categories, or principles, had to be given, and why the ten had to summarize the 613 mitzvot. When God wrote the ten on the tablets, he was conveying the unity of the Torah. When God uttered the 172 words simultaneously, although they were incomprehensible, they achieved freedom from the limitations of sequence. In that way God let us know for all time that not only were all the laws of the Torah divine, they were also indivisible.

Part III

The First Exception

6

Why Did God
Give Us Two Tablets?

he exception proves the rule. The familiar adage implies that if a rule has an exception, then that is a test of its legitimacy. There is an exception to the rule that "all mitzvot are created equal," which proves its validity. To find our first exception, let us examine a division of Jewish law suggested in the very physical structure of the ten "categories" as they appear on the tablets.

The Torah tells us that the Decalogue was given on two tablets of stone. Surely God had the ability to condense all the words onto one tablet. What was the purpose of placing them on two separate pieces of stone? To answer this question properly, we must first clarify what appeared on each of the stones according to Jewish sources.

Many people are unaware that Catholics, Protestants, and Jews do not agree on which commandments make up the Decalogue. One would think that this would be one area of total agreement, since the "Ten Commandments" come from Chapter 20 in Exodus and are repeated in Chapter 5 of Deuteronomy. How can there be disagreement if we are dealing with direct quotes?

The answer is that the "commandments" were not numbered in the text, and some verses contain more than one. The different religions disagree about how to number these "commandments" and which ones make up the Decalogue.

Catholics and Protestants are perplexed by what would appear to be the first of the commandments. Jews count the opening words "I am the Lord, your God, Who brought you out of the land of Egypt, the house of bondage," as number one. Catholics and Protestants cannot understand how this can be a commandment, since its wording clearly reads as a statement rather than a directive.

It is an interesting aside that for the Jews this would not have caused any difficulty, since the list is not a list of commandments, but rather of sayings, categories, or principles. "I am the Lord" is indeed a master principle whether or not it is a commandment. Still, most commentators agree that it is a mitzvah as well as a statement. It is a commandment to accept God as well as to verbalize this acceptance. Its fulfillment, Naḥmanides (the RaMBaN, Rabbi Moses ben Naḥman, 1194–c. 1270,) says, is expressed in the principle of *qabalat ol malkhut shamayim,* accepting the yoke of the kingdom of heaven, through the daily recitation of the Shema. Ibn Ezra further explains that the first commandment teaches us that every mitzvah must be performed with an awareness that its source is divine.

Nevertheless, Catholics and Protestants both assert that "I am the Lord" is not a commandment and then number the balance of the sentences so that the required ten indicated by the Torah can be reached.

Catholics count our second commandment, "You shall have no other gods before Me," as the first and continue one commandment short until they reach the end. When they come to "You shall not covet your neighbor's house," they have only counted nine commandments. What is their tenth? "You shall not covet your neighbor's wife," the balance of the statement, which for us as Jews is obviously part and parcel of the same category (see below).

Catholic Ten Commandments

1. You shall have no other gods.
2. You shall not take God's name in vain.
3. Remember the Sabbath.
4. Honor your father and mother.
5. You shall not murder.
6. You shall not commit adultery.
7. You shall not steal.
8. You shall not bear false witness.
9. You shall not covet your neighbor's house.
10. You shall not covet your neighbor's wife.

The Protestants have a different way of solving the problem created by the elimination of "I am the Lord" as the first commandment. What for the Jews is the second category—idolatry—becomes for the Protestants two separate laws: "You shall have no other gods before Me" is the first and "You shall not make for yourself a graven image, you shall not bow down unto them or serve them" is the second. Having split our second commandment into two, the Protestants now continue, beginning with the third, with the same numbering system as the Jews.

Protestant Ten Commandments

1. You shall have no other gods.
2. You shall not make a graven image.
3. You shall not take God's name in vain.
4. Remember the Sabbath.
5. Honor your father and mother.
6. You shall not murder.
7. You shall not commit adultery.
8. You shall not steal.
9. You shall not bear false witness.
10. You shall not covet.

The "Jewish set" appears as follows:

1. I am the Lord your God.
2. You shall not have other gods before Me.
3. You shall not take the name of the Lord your God, in vain.
4. Remember the Sabbath to keep it holy.
5. Honor your father and mother.
6. You shall not murder.
7. You shall not commit adultery.
8. You shall not steal.
9. You shall not bear false witness against your neighbor.
10. You shall not covet.

Let us return now to the original question. Why did God choose to divide these laws and place them on two separate tablets? Our Sages drew a fascinating distinction between the first five "categories" and the second. It is a distinction underscored by the presence or absence of certain highly significant words.

If one looks at every one of the first five categories, one sees, in some form or another, the name of God. Conversely, if one looks at the second set, what is glaringly absent is the name of the Almighty in any form. How do we explain this peculiarity? Jewish commentators agree that it is meant to teach us the two different areas of concern of the Decalogue and of the Torah itself.

God placed the summary of Jewish law on two tablets because the law itself has a dual concern. Judaism teaches that all of law may be divided into two categories, our relationship with God (*bein adam la-Maqom*) and our relationship with people (*bein adam le-ḥavero*).

The fourth "commandment"—to remember the Sabbath—is correctly placed on the first tablet because Sabbath observance is a way of demonstrating our belief that God created the world and took us out of the bondage of Egypt. The fifth commandment, honoring parents, would seem to belong to the second category—laws regulating behavior between one person and another. What is it doing on the first tablet?

To phrase it differently, in a manner whereby the question itself will lead us to the answer, why should obligations to our parents be side by side with our obligations to the Creator? The word "Creator," the key to the claims of the first tablet, allows us immediately to understand the answer. In the words of the Talmud (*Kidushin* 30b): "There are three partners to the creation of Man—mother, father, and God." The text is clarifying the extent to which we owe gratitude to our human progenitors. The first tablet can therefore be summarized as our obligations to Creator/creators. The second tablet (prohibiting murder, adultery, theft, bearing false witness, and coveting) defines the parameters of our daily existence as we involve ourselves with other human beings. The importance of this duality cannot be underestimated. Religion can only be considered full, viable, and complete if it acknowledges the existence of these two claims on our behavior. Religious schizophrenia is an all too common disorder to which this duality of the tablets addresses itself. As a rabbi I am often asked, "How can you explain the fact that I know people who are religious and yet when one enters their places of business, one sees the most corrupt of practices? They are religious and yet they steal. So what good is religion?" To which I invariably respond, "But you have contradicted yourself in the very wording of your question. You tell me that you know people who are religious. But in their rejection of a major tenet of the second tablet, they have made clear they do not accept the word of God." Long ago when the Puritans came to these shores, Cotton Mather, the famous preacher, reflected on this very problem when he noted the lack of ethics among those who proclaimed their religious piety. "Woe to those," he said, "who pray with all their hearts to God on Sunday and then prey upon their fellow man throughout the rest of the week." Orthodoxy would be well advised to be extremely careful of those who believe that religious fanaticism in the arena of their Godly relationship allows them greater leeway to do as they see fit and to ignore ethical strictures in the area of person-to-person relationships. The Israeli cartoon of the bank robber, with his loot in one hand and gun in the other, who shifts his weapon to the left so he can kiss the mezuzah with his right hand as he departs, is a biting commentary on the perception that there are those who rationalize the worst crimes as long as they continue to "kiss" the symbols of God.

Schizophrenia may be found among secularists in equal measure. Those who loudly profess their religious piety because of their commitment to the tenets of the second tablet are equally in error. The world needs God, and the first tablet makes demands upon our subservience to the Creator. Religion, we were told at Sinai, cannot be split. To defraud while posing as a religious person is criminal. To violate the Sabbath or to worship idols is to negate the source of sanctity that allows for the spiritual perfection of the universe.

God gave us two tablets. Jewish law is sensitive to the demands of both.

Let us pose a crucial question. Granting their equal legitimacy, if these two demands come into conflict, which one takes precedence?

7

Who Comes First,
Man or God?

he following story comes from the Torah. It occurred
immediately after Abraham circumcised himself,
marking his covenant with the Creator as the very
first Jew.

"And the Lord appeared to him [Abraham] in the groves of
Mamre as he sat in the tent door in the heat of the day. And he
[Abraham] lifted up his eyes and looked, and three men were
standing directly towards him; and when he saw them, he ran to
meet them from the tent door and bowed down to the earth. And
he said [to their leader], 'My lord, if now I have found favor in
your sight, please do not pass by your servant. Let a little water be
fetched [so that you can] wash your feet, and you rest under the
tree. And I will fetch a morsel of bread and you will eat to your
heart's content; then you shall pass on, for this is the reason you
passed by your servant'" (Genesis 18:1–5).

God had come to visit Abraham. According to our Sages, God
was fulfilling the mitzvah of visiting the sick. It was three days
after Abraham had undergone his circumcision, and he was in
great pain. Yet he sat at the door of his tent in the heat of the day,

hoping that he might be able to fulfill the mitzvah of hospitality to strangers (*Hakhnasat orḥim*).

Each one of our forefathers exhibited one unique and very special trait. The Mishnah in *Ethics of the Fathers* (1:2) tells us that "the world rests upon three basic principles: on Torah, on sacrifice, and on showing kindness to one's fellow man." Jacob, "the perfect man who lived in tents," would demonstrate the pinnacle that could be reached by the study of Torah. Isaac in the supreme moment of his life, bound to the altar on top of Mount Moriah, would demonstrate readiness for sacrificing his very life. Abraham always demonstrated the greatness of showing kindness to others.

Our Sages constantly stressed that the deeds of our ancestors are a sign for us, their descendants. We are to learn from them. And on the simplest level of all, the story we cited from the Torah portion of *Vayeira* (Genesis 18:1–5) is meant to show us that, even though Abraham did not know that the men he was approaching were angels (as far as he was concerned, they could have been idol worshipers), he rushed to take care of them. It was his mitzvah, his mission.

But consider an additional aspect of the story. Abraham was not simply running to bring water to passing strangers. He was, after all, hosting a Guest. Abraham was in the middle of the most important meeting imaginable for any human being, an encounter with his Creator. That, too, is a mitzvah. "Standing before the Lord" entails the duty of prayer (hence the term "Amidah," which means "standing," refers to the Eighteen Benedictions recited in a standing position).

Abraham therefore was not merely fulfilling the mitzvah of hospitality. He was *leaving God to take care of Man.* He made a decision concerning priorities. God was in attendance, man was in need. Abraham was ready to overlook the former in order to deal with the demands of the latter. The Talmud in *Shabbat* (127a) derives an important conclusion from this biblical incident. "It is a greater mitzvah to take in strangers than to receive the Divine Countenance" (*Gedolah hakhnasat orḥim mi-qabalat penei ha-Shekhinah*). What the Talmud contrasted was not simply one specific mitzvah against another. It was a confrontation between the two categories. Both God and Man beckoned. Abraham understood that when faced with a conflict between the two, he must choose Man rather than God.

It is the same conclusion that Hillel the Elder reached in the famous story of the heathen who came to convert and asked to be taught "the entire Torah on one foot." The renowned scholar Shamai chased the man away, but Hillel responded by rephrasing the famous verse "You shall love your neighbor as yourself" (Leviticus 19:18). What did the prospective convert mean when he asked to be taught the entire Torah "on one foot"? The standard interpretation is that he wanted a brief response. It has been suggested, however, that he was alluding to something else. The Torah also has two "feet." At the Seder, we sing: "Who knows two?" "I know two. Two are the tablets."

We have already identified these two foundations as commandments regulating the person—God relationship and those regulating the person—person relationship. "Teach me the entire Torah on one foot" may well be the very same question we posed regarding priorities within Judaism. If God is concerned with two dimensions, which one is more basic? Is God there for humanity or is humanity there for God? Shamai refused to entertain the question. It is enough for us to know that both areas exist, that both obligations are incumbent upon us. Hillel, however, would not dodge the challenge.

When Hillel reiterated the words "And you shall love your neighbor as yourself"—the words that would serve as the most fundamental principle in the Torah—he was saying that love of humanity is the "one foot" to choose over any other commandment of love in the Torah.

Hillel could just as easily have selected the verse recited twice daily immediately after the *Shema,* "And you shall love the Lord, your God, with all your heart, with all your soul and with all your might" (Deuteronomy 6:5). But he didn't. He chose the obligation to love our neighbor (Leviticus 19:18). We must recognize that the most significant dimension of this famous talmudic story is not just what was said, but what wasn't. If a choice must be made, then just as Abraham did, leave God and take care of a human being in need.

What rationale is there for this decision? Isn't God more

important than anyone? Why is welcoming guests more important than receiving the presence of the Divine Countenance? Two answers suggest themselves readily. The first refers to need. A person may be hungry, starving, or even on the verge of death. These needs do not apply to God. Since human need is so much greater, God ordained that we leave Him for the moment to take care of another person.

That certainly must be the intent of the talmudic passage describing the *hasid shoteh,* a pious fool. Who is a pious fool? According to the Sages (*Sotah* 21b), it is one who, standing at the seashore, engrossed in prayer, refuses to heed the call for help of a drowning man because he is "in the middle of his service to God." To allow a human being to drown because you are busy telling God how much you care about Him and His world is the ultimate hypocrisy.

There is another, more concise and scientific reason for why our response to human need takes precedence over our response to God. Maimonides puts it well when he explains that every ethical act of goodness and kindness to another person is intrinsically a mitzvah. Every observance of religious ritual, being commanded by God, is also a mitzvah, a deed assuming its religious identity because God demanded it. The divine imperative invests it with sanctity. Likewise, every law governing person-to-person relations is also an expression of the will of God and consequently a divine imperative. The mitzvah towards others is thus doubly blessed. It comes from God and it achieves good for others. A commandment on the first tablet is a "plus one." It is good because God said so. But a law on the second tablet is a "plus two," because it relates to both our relationship to other people and our relationship to God.

This striking distinction has several other significant illustrations.

The Two Generations of Evil

At the beginning of human history we learn of two times when God was angry with the human species. In collective terms they represent the two occasion illustrating "original sin." In Jungian terms, our Sages long ago recognized them not simply as events but as archetypes; the first two rebellions in history serve as paradigms for the ways in which humankind can go against the will of the Creator.

The first rebellion was staged by the generation of the Deluge. "And the earth was corrupt before God, and the earth was filled with violence. And God saw the earth and behold it was corrupt for all flesh had corrupted its way upon the earth" (Genesis 6:11–12).

What is the "violence" (*hamas*) to which the Torah makes reference? The Talmud (*Sanhedrin* 108a) clarifies: "Their fate was not sealed except on account of theft." The Torah also states, "The earth was corrupt *before God*" to tell us that although they acknowledged God, they rejected the interpersonal ethics and laws that would later be known as the second tablet. The Midrash fills in countless details of what life was like in those days. They reveal a prevailing corruption and violence, in which no one cared about his or her neighbor.

A second, very different rebellion appears in chapter 11.

> And the whole earth was of one language and of one speech. And it came to pass as they journeyed east, that they found a plain in the land of Shinar and they dwelled there. And they said to one another, "Come let us make bricks and burn them thoroughly." And they had brick for stone, and slime for mortar. And they said, "Come let us build a city and a tower with its top in Heaven and let us make us a name, lest we be scattered abroad upon the face of the whole earth." [Genesis 11:1–4]

This was, according to the commentators, a critical moment in the history of the world. It was the turning point from the age of the farmer to the age of the builder, from the pastoral society to the era of science and "enlightenment."

Until the Tower of Babel, humans had only planted and sown, reaped and harvested. Farmers are dependent upon nature and, in their dependency, turn to God. Builders, however, seek to control nature. And in their sense of might they tend to overplay their own role and at times to believe that they are no longer dependent on God. "Come let us build a city and a tower with its top in Heaven" (Genesis 11:4). The Talmud adds (*Sanhedrin* 109a): "We will build a tower that reaches so high that we will be able to come to the very throne of the Almighty and topple him." The metaphor is profound. The scientist says if we build high enough, if we indicate our ultimate strength, if we reach the skies and soar to the very Heavens, then we, too, with Yuri Gagarin, the first Russian cosmonaut, can say with unbounded egoism, "There is no God, because I was in the Heavens and I did not see Him." "Let us make us a name" was the cry of the first technological wizards. "We will dethrone God." And so they built the Tower of Babel.

Two paradigms of evil. At Sinai they would each be addressed in a different manner. When God would bring law to the world, He would recall the dual capacity for sin. The first tablet would be directed to future generations that would try to duplicate the crime of the Tower of Babel builders. The second would address itself to the men and women of violence of all ages who long ago perished in the flood.

The archetypes of sin are meant not only to teach us of possibilities and potentials. The two stories, in their glaringly different conclusions, serve also to convey a lesson on the relative levels of sinfulness.

When His human creations became corrupt and violent, God wiped them off the face of the earth. The wicked were destroyed; only the righteous were allowed to survive. For had God allowed things to go on as they were, in a short time the wicked would have overwhelmed all the others and evil would have triumphed. Sins committed by one person against another were punished by death. It was the only way God could save His world.

The Tower of Babel had a radically different outcome. "Come let us go down and confound their language, that they many not understand one another's speech" (Genesis 11:7). Each one began to speak a different language. The age of technology ended with babbling; hence, the Tower of "Babel."

A threat to humanity is real. A threat against God is humorous. The first is dangerous and must be dealt with severely. The second is ludicrous and its proponents are simply "scattered abroad upon the face of the earth" (Genesis 11:9).

A "Met Mizvah"

There is a special category of the dead known as *met mizvah*, a reference to a corpse that is not attended to properly. The peculiar expression relates to a law that is incumbent upon every Jew. Normally death places an obligation upon the closes relatives—spouse, parent, child, sibling—to bury and to mourn. They are called *onan* until burial and subsequently *avel*, mourner. No one else has any obligation to the deceased. But if a corpse is found in the field and there are no known relatives, then the Jewish people become the relatives of the deceased. Such a corpse is called a *met mizvah*, for it is the duty of every single Jew to be involved with his or her burial.

The Talmud (*Berakhot* 19b) outlines a number of situations in which this law applies even for those whom we might assume would be exempt: a father on the way to circumcise his son or to slaughter his Paschal offering; a *Kohen* (priest) on the way to a sacrificial service; or even a *Kohen gadol* (High Priest) on the way to perform the services on Yom Kippur. If any of these individuals saw a *met mizvah* in the field, he must interrupt his journey in order to bury the dead, even though this will make him spiritually unfit and unable to perform his mission. *Met mizvah* comes first.

What happened to the halakhic ruling that a person engaged in the performance of one mitzvah is exempt from another? Why wasn't that applied here? Why didn't Abraham apply it when he was in the middle of his mitzvah of speaking to God?

Clearly, the man who was en route to redeem captives was told to ignore the holiday of Sukkot and continue on his way because the conflict pitted the laws governing human relations against those governing the human–divine relationship. In such a case, one proceeds with redeeming the captive and does not choose the sukkah. The exemption applies only if the conflicting laws are from the same category. But if one is in the midst of fulfilling a duty toward God—the sacrifice of a Paschal lamb in the Temple, etc.—and is confronted with the pressing need of another person, then of course one would have to be a "pious fool" to proceed with the service to God and ignore the pressing need of a human being who, unlike the Deity, is not self-sufficient.

Mitzvot without Blessings

Does a mitzvah have a blessing? Of course it does. Before we listen to the shofar, or sit in the sukkah, or put on phylacteries, we make a blessing acknowledging the divine source of the law and thanking God for giving us the opportunity to fulfill His will. Yet we know there are many mitzvot that do not have a blessing recited before them. We visit the sick, give charity, and invite strangers without making a blessing. Clearly there is something that these acts have in common that do not demand words of praise to God. Halakhah has made the following distinction: Only person-to-God mitzvot require a blessing. Person-to-person obligations do not. Why not? One beautiful explanation emerges in a moving story. A Sage was once approached by a poor man begging for food. Before responding, the Sage continued with his religious duties. The starving indigent was so far gone, however, that he died before help was offered. The rabbi spent a lifetime trying to atone for his sin. We learn from this that to take time to utter a blessing while another human being is in need is to commit the crime of the pious fool, who pays attention to God while ignoring those in desperate need. In not reciting a blessing before any kind and holy act in the arena of interpersonal duties, we dramatically state that we are so anxious to get to the deed, that God will forgive the renunciation of His praise.

The Destruction of the Two Temples

Twice we reached great heights of spirituality. Two times in history we were able to build the Temple. Both times, on the very same date, the ninth of Av, these Temples were destroyed.

A Jew does not believe that the destruction of the Temples came about principally because of the Babylonians and the

Romans. The month was Av—which means father, because our Father in Heaven was involved. The day was the ninth of Av because on that day, during their wanderings in the desert, the Jewish people sinned in the incident of the spies, when they cried and said, "We cannot go to Israel." Sin was responsible for the destruction of both Temples, because the spiritual symbol deserved to exist only so long as spiritual reality existed among the people.

But the specific crime of the Jews was different on each occasion: two Temples, two sins, two tablets, two archetypal sins going back to the story of the Generation of the Flood and the Tower of Babel.

The First Temple was destroyed because the Jews worshiped idols; humankind rejected God. The Second Temple was destroyed because of needless hatred between Jews (*sinat ḥinam*), a most horrible conclusion to the incident of Kamtza and Bar Kamtza. The Talmud relates that a man mistakenly invited his enemy to a lavish banquet and then humiliated him by ordering him to leave. The disgraced guest, angry that leading rabbis who observed the incident had not objected to his humiliation, exacted revenge by turning Caesar against the Jews, setting into motion the destruction of the Temple.

Jews do not deserve a Temple if they reject either tablet totally. But let us compare the severity of punishment in these two major events of our history. The First Temple lay in ruins for seventy years; God was ready to forgive and allow it to be rebuilt. The Second Temple, however, touched upon a far more fundamental area. Jews hating fellow Jews brought about a catastrophe whose effects have lasted from the year 70 C.E. to this very day.

Which is more severe? The length of punishment gives us the answer. God is prepared quickly to forgive transgressions against Himself. But the lack of unity and the lack of love among fellow Jews, the rejection of the commandment to love one's neighbor as one's self, is a far more serious matter.

Yom Kippur

This is precisely what the holiest day of the year has to teach us. Yom Kippur is a day of atonement and forgiveness. It has tremendous power to bring about rapprochement. We are after all human, and "there is not a righteous man upon earth who does only good and does not sin" (Ecclesiastes 7:20). God understands us and forgives us. But even Yom Kippur with its tremendous power can only achieve its end in one domain and not the other. As stated in the words of the last mishnah in tractate *Yoma*: "Sins between man and God, Yom Kippur atones for; sins between man and his fellow man, Yom Kippur does not atone for, until he appeases his friend." That is why *The Code of Jewish Law* is so strict with regard to the preparations for this holy day; one may pray to God the entire day, fast, weep, and be contrite and yet still not have the day serve any meaningful purpose. If a person comes on this day to be at peace with God while still warring with parent, spouse, child, or friend, Yom Kippur becomes meaningless.

I will never forget the moment as a child when I was asked to be part of a most moving ceremony. I had just turned bar mitzvah and my father, a rabbi, asked me to come with him together with eight other people to the cemetery. There was a Jew in his congregation who had been at odds with another man. They had been friends who became enemies and then the "enemy" died. Yom Kippur was coming and the man could not face entering the holy day without ending his quarrel. Jewish law allows for a situation such as this, where one of the antagonists has passed away. *The Code of Jewish Law* (131:5) states: "If someone whom you wronged died, then you must bring ten people to his grave and declare: 'I have sinned against the God of Israel and against such and such a man.'" This is what we did. We went to the grave site and one Jew asked another for forgiveness. If he could not ask him in body, he would at least ask his soul. But a Yom Kippur without human reconciliation was recognized as a travesty.

The *Haftarah* for the Holiest Day

The selection of the *haftarah* (a chapter from the Prophets, read after the portion from the Pentateuch) for Yom Kippur morning makes this vividly clear.

Why is a *haftarah* read every Sabbath and holiday? It goes back to a time when the Jewish people were not allowed by the law of the land to read the proper section from the Torah itself. Guards were stationed in the synagogue to ensure that the Torah would not be taken out of the Ark and that the Scriptural reading from the Five Books of Moses would not be recited.

Jews found an alternative, still in use, which is based both on the concept of maintaining tradition as well as the awareness that, in the Diaspora, similar decrees are always possible. A section was chosen from another portion of the Bible, comparable in content to the original required reading. In the case of the Sabbath, every *haftarah* contains a reference to what our Sages felt was the most important idea of that week's Torah portion. In the case of a holiday, the Sages selected a reading that captured its single most crucial idea.

The *haftarah* is therefore the most powerful "fixed sermon." When a rabbi is faced with the formidable task of selecting an idea for weekly discussion, it obviously varies from year to year. The Sages, however, had to choose one idea that would permanently serve to summarize the message of the particular day. Its importance can therefore not be underestimated.

And what did the Sages choose as the reading for Yom Kippur morning? It is one of the most moving sections in the Book of Isaiah (57:14–58:14), where the prophet addresses himself to the question Jews often asked with regard to God's apparent unresponsiveness. Why doesn't the Almighty pay attention to our fasting? If we are pious, why is there no proper Heavenly response? How to explain the punishment visited upon those who seem perfect in their fulfillment of the laws and responsibilities toward God?

Isaiah responds: (Chapter 58)

1. Cry aloud, spare not,
   Lift up thy voice like a horn,
   And declare unto My people their transgression,
   And to the house of Jacob their sins.
2. Yet they seek Me daily,
   And delight to know My ways;
   As a nation that did righteousness,

And forsook not the ordinance of their God,
They ask of Me Righteous ordinances,
They delight to draw near unto God.

3.   'Wherefore have we fasted, and Thou seest not?
Wherefore have we afflicted our soul, and Thou takest no
       knowledge?'—
Behold, in the day of your fast ye pursue your business,
And exact all your labors.

4.   Behold, ye fast for strife and contention,
And to smite with the fist of wickedness;
Ye fast not this day
So as to make your voice to be heard on high.

5.   Is such the fast that I have chosen?
The day for man to afflict his soul?
Is it to bow down his head as a bulrush,
And to spread sackcloth and ashes under him?
Wilt thou call this a fast,
And an acceptable day to the Lord?

6.   Is not this the fast that I have chosen?
To loose the fetters of wickedness,
To undo the bands of the yoke,
And to let the oppressed go free,
And that ye break every yoke?

7.   Is it not to deal thy bread to the hungry,
And that thou bring the poor that are cast out to thy house?
When thou seest the naked, that thou cover him,
And that thou hide not thyself from thine own flesh?

8.   Then shall thy light break forth as the morning,
And thy healing shall spring forth speedily;
And thy righteousness shall go before thee,
The glory of the Lord shall be thy reward.

9.   Then shalt thou call, and the Lord will answer;
Thou shalt cry, and He will say: "Here I am."
If thou take away from the midst of thee the yoke,
The putting forth of the finger, and speaking wickedness;

10.   And if thou draw out thy soul to the hungry,
And satisfy the afflicted soul;
Then shall thy light rise in darkness,
And thy gloom be as the noonday;

How can religious people not find favor in the eyes of God? If they restrict their understanding of religion to the first tablet and ignore the second? What good is it to Me, asks the Almighty, if you pile up a plethora of good deeds towards Me, while at the same time you strike with a Godless fist against another human being?

Which are more important—commandments relating to people or those relating to God? On Yom Kippur day, the day that only has power to absolve us of our sins against God but not against others, we read the *haftarah* in which the prophet clearly and powerfully proclaims the correct answer.

8

Aren't All Mitzvot
Created Equal?

e have found an exception to the aforementioned rule. What about the original mishnah in *Ethics of the Fathers*? Its principle—"be as scrupulous in performing a minor mitzvah as you are with a major one, for you do not know the reward given for mitzvot"—was the basis for our conclusion that all mitzvot must be treated in exactly the same manner. Why doesn't the mishnah note this crucial distinction between person-to-God and person-to-person commandments?

It does. Let us return to the mishnah and read it in its entirety.

> Rebbe asked: "Which is the right course that a man should choose for himself? That which is glorious in the eyes of the doer, and in the eyes of his fellow man. Be as scrupulous in performing a minor mitzvah as you are with a major one, for you do not know the reward given for mitzvot. Reckon the loss that a mitzvah entails, against its reward; and the benefit gained from a sin, against the loss it brings. Contemplate three things and you will not sin. Know what is above you: an eye sees; an ear hears; and all your deeds are recorded in a Book." [2:1]

The question Rebbe asked seems to be the fundamental problem discussed by all philosophers. Which is the right course in life? What should our goals be? Socrates, Plato, and Aristotle, each in his own way, deliberated on variations of this theme. Shall we pursue wealth, fame, power, honor, glory? Do we live for this world or the next? Do we live for ourselves or for our children? How people should live is certainly an appropriate question for any secular philosopher.

But it seems totally out of place for a rabbi, especially one of the stature of Rabbi Yehudah HaNasi. How shall we live? What should our goals be? The answer is all too obvious. We are duty-bound by the covenant at Sinai. We are to live for God in accord with the laws of the Torah. What shall we choose? From the moment we accepted the Torah at Sinai, isn't the answer self-evident?

Surely Rebbe did not mean to ask what others have asked. The answer to that is all too obvious. It is rather within the confines of obedience to Torah law that the question must have been raised. What if there are moments when laws come in conflict with one another, when we are forced to choose between them? The real question is, are there choices *within* the Torah? The Mishnah gives two answers. The first says, yes, choose what is glorious in the eyes of the doer and in the eyes of other people as well.

The commentators explain that this is a clear allusion to one category of law over another. A person can do mitzvot that are only glorious to the doer, but not seen as such by others. What are these mitzvot? Imagine a man who is scrupulous in the way he puts on his phylacteries or fulfills the mitzvah of eating matzah; he may be a fine and superpious Jew, but his act does not benefit any other human being. He is to be commended, because he clearly heeds the commandments of God. But he surely cannot be placed on par with a man who, even as he obeys his Creator, brings glory to other human beings. The latter are the mitzvot of charity and hospitality, of care and concern for others.

"Glorious in the eyes of the doer" is the mishnaic way of referring to laws between a person and God. As identified previously in the words of Maimonides, they are a "plus one." "Glorious to the doer as well as to fellow man" is a synonym for a person-to-person mitzvah. Rebbe himself, at the beginning of the mishnah dealing with the question of choice in Jewish law, makes clear that there is a possibility of selection. If the question of observance is between a person-to-person commandment and a person-to-God obligation, then one has to choose the former.

It is only after that statement has been made that Rebbe continues with the phrase we have already analyzed. "And be as scrupulous with a minor mitzvah as with a major one." Having acknowledged the distinction between the two categories of law, each placed on its own tablet, the binding principle remains that all mitzvot are created equal.

9

Why Is God First
on the Tablets?

e have established that in the choice between humanity and God, human beings come first. God doesn't
need us, but people do. Every commandment concerning others is not only intrinsically good, but comes from the
Almighty Himself and therefore carries a dual reason for
observance.

But if that is true, how do we explain the structure of the Ten
Commandments? The two tablets, we have explained, represent
the duality of our obligations. The first five encompass our responsibilities to our Creator(s,—including our parents); the second
five, the way in which we are obligated to deal with others. In that
case, shouldn't the order have been reversed? Wouldn't it have
been proper first to receive those commandments that reflect the
Almighty's greatest concern?

The structure of the tablets does in fact follow a very significant order. Although the verse "And you shall love your neighbor
as yourself" is ultimately more crucial than "And you shall love
the Lord, your God, with all your heart, with all your soul and
with all your might," the laws between person and God must come
first. To understand this is to grasp a cardinal principle of
Judaism.

Let us make our first step in solving the problem by introducing a remarkable insight found in the Jerusalem Talmud. Earlier we clarified that there are no Ten Commandments, but rather ten basic categories or principles. They are the ten that serve as the core of the 613 mitzvot. The bottom line of Jewish law, it would therefore appear, may be summarized by ten ideas.

But the Jerusalem Talmud goes a step further. The most significant number of all is not really ten but—since the "categories" appear on two separate tablets, each of which contains five principles—the most basic number is five. Indeed, there are five fundamental ideas, each of which has an application in the concerns of both tablets.

To be more specific, the following diagram illustrates this basic idea, which might be termed "linkage."

1. I am the Lord your God. ←——→ 6. You shall not murder.
2. You shall not have other ←——→ 7. You shall not commit
   gods before me.   adultery.
3. You shall not take the ←——→ 8. You shall not steal.
   name of the Lord your
   God in vain.
4. Remember the Sabbath to ←——→ 9. You shall not bear false
   keep it holy.   witness against your
                                      neighbor.
5. Honor your father and ←——→ 10. You shall not covet.
   mother.

One word or phrase describes the connection between each set of partners. To demonstrate this concept, let us begin with commandments two and seven: "You shall have no other gods before Me" and "You shall not commit adultery."

Numbers Two and Seven

Long ago, God used a crisis in the life of a prophet to make a point that perhaps only He could have made. Hosea was told to marry a certain woman whom he deeply loved. Subsequently he found out that she had been unfaithful. Hosea was shattered. His life did not seem worth living. The one nearest and dearest to him had not lived up to a commitment they both made under the canopy. God said to the prophet: "Now you will at last understand how I feel when the Jewish people are unfaithful to Me" (Hosea 3:1).

God and the Jews enjoy a relationship of lovers. When the Song of Songs was the subject of an intense debate over its suitability for inclusion in the Bible, it was Rabbi Akiva who justified acceptance and proclaimed, "If all the rest of the Torah is holy, then this is the holy of holies" (*Yadayim* 3:5). He was not troubled by the many direct allusions to love that seemed to refer to the passionate feelings between man and woman. Nor are we, who have indeed included the Song of Songs into the holy books and even recite it every Friday evening before the "Sabbath bride" enters. Man and woman as lovers symbolize the highest demonstration of love possible, the love between God and His people.

The Midrash did not hesitate to dramatize this concept in the most striking manner. Tradition has it that when the Jews came to Sinai to receive the Torah, God lifted the mountain over their heads. Different interpretations are given. According to one, God was enacting a scene readily recognizable to every Jew. The mountain served as the *hupah,* the divine canopy, which turned the Jews' commitment to accept God's law into an everlasting union of wedded bliss and harmony.

The Sages seek complete parity between mortal marriage and marriage with the Almighty. But if a Jewish marriage consists of two states—*qidushin* (engagement, or consecration), legitimized by the placing of a ring on the bride's finger, followed by *nisuin* (marriage), achieved under the canopy, where was our "engagement"? The answer: On Shavuot, when the Jews received the Torah, the mountain served as the canopy and we were fully wed. On Passover, when God redeemed us from Egypt, he gave us the mitzvah of phylacteries, and to this very day as we wind the straps around our fingers, we say the words, "And You are betrothed to me forever."

The Jews and God are lovers. We "met" in the spring, and Passover must ever remain *hag ha-aviv*—the holiday of spring—the season of the Song of Songs, when our thoughts turn to the object of our passion. Marriage demands commitment and ever-

lasting fidelity. If on the tablet dealing with our human relationships we are told, "You shall not commit adultery," the parallel in
our relationship to God is "You shall have no other gods before
Me." Idolatry and adultery are not far apart; both forsake a loved
one and ignore a promise of mutual honesty and fidelity.

The key word for the "partnership" between the commandments prohibiting idolatry and adultery is therefore faithfulness.
Similarly, each of the "category commandments" contains a basic
idea that links the words on either side of the respective tablets.

Numbers Three and Eight

"You shall not take the Name of the Lord in vain"—"You
shall not steal." What is the crime addressed in the third commandment? The Sages say it means two things: either swearing
falsely—a lie—or swearing unnecessarily. To grasp the real sin one
must understand the nature of an oath. In Jewish law, an oath is
only administered when there is no other possibility for determining truth. Ideally, two witnesses establish the facts. But what if no
one saw the event? How will we ever know what happened? Only
the parties involved, with their vested interest, as well as the All
Seeing One Above, know what really happened. An oath gives a
litigant, whose objectivity is suspect, credibility via his association
with God. Every oath in effect says, "If you don't believe me, then
I swear to God, i.e., may God strike me dead if I'm not telling the
truth." In accepting an oath the court is saying, "We have no alternative but to trust you when you take God as your guarantor, and
if we err, God will know and we leave it to Him to punish."

The second type of unacceptable oath is when someone says, "I
swear to God that this table is a table." We profane God's name by
turning it into something uttered for no purpose. It is pointless and
therefore profane. It takes the holy and treats it with irreverence.

"You shall not take the Name of the Lord, your God, in vain."
In both types of unacceptable oaths, you are *taking* something—
something that does not belong to you and that you have no right
to use. It is the equivalent of *stealing*. Judaism believes in ownership and personal property. Stealing is wrong because the object
belongs to another human being. Stealing is equally sinful when

the object involved is the meaning, the reputation, and the sacred essence of the Divine Name.

In a word, theft is the linkage between commandments three and eight. Don't take what is not yours.

Numbers Four and Nine

"Remember the Sabbath day to keep it holy"—"You shall not testify falsely against your neighbor."

What is the real purpose of Sabbath observance? If it were simply to rest, to feel physically better, it would be a mere health law and would have no place on the tablet between person and God.

"Remember the Sabbath day to keep it holy, because in six days God created the heavens and earth and on the seventh He rested." When we rest on Sabbath, we confirm that the world did not simply come into existence by itself. There was a creator. The Sabbath testifies to creation.

We stand when we recite the kiddush, the prayer that formally opens the Sabbath, because witnesses are always required to stand when testifying. Sabbath observance is a Jew's weekly testimony to the reality of God's existence and His role as Creator.

A Jew who violates the Sabbath is bringing false testimony. It implies there is no need to acknowledge a Creator; He does not exist.

"You shall not testify falsely—be it against God or against fellow man." Numbers four and nine are linked by truthfulness or valid testimony.

Numbers Five and Ten

"Honor your father and mother"—"You shall not covet."

What does "honor" really mean? A person claiming to honor Israel, but who never gives charity to any need associated with it, is being hypocritical. To affirm that one honors one's faith while refusing to support a synagogue shows that one is merely spouting platitudes. When the rabbis in the Talmud seek the deeper meaning of the command to "honor," they utilize a specific method of linguistic analogy: a word not fully explicated in one place assumes its full meaning by the manner in which it is utilized in another. We are told to "honor" our father and mother, but the implications of the verb are not explained. In Proverbs (3:9) we are taught: "Honor the Lord from your wealth." It is in the latter verse that the Torah clarifies what the implications of true reverence are. Tipping your hat, standing, bowing—all may seem to suggest subservience or respect. But they lack any substantial follow-through. If you really honor God, then you are prepared to make a financial commitment as well. If you honor parents, then you will be ready to "give them to eat and to drink, take them in and take them out" (*Kidushin* 31b). Of course the requirement of filial respect cannot be met only through monetary commitment. The Talmud teaches that one son may feed his parents expensive geese and violate the law; another, a plate of beans and fulfill it to the optimum. The beans may be served with love, the geese flung in the face of the aged parent who is banished to the isolation of a nursing home. That is why the word used is *kabed,* give in an honorable manner.

The fifth commandment, dealing with the respect due to earthly creators, concerns itself with wealth and the way in which it must be shared. One dare not assume that God makes inequitable demands upon its distribution.

The intent of the last "commandment category" on both of the tablets is identical. Accept the fact that all financial good comes from the Heavens, where He disperses it as He sees fit in light of a supreme higher knowledge. Do not covet if someone else has more than you. It is meant to be so. And honor—you, too, are to distribute it in accord with the demands placed upon you, which require your commitment to respect in its truest sense of the word.

Numbers One and Six

"I am the Lord, your God"—"You shall not murder."

We have purposely left the top partners on the tablets for last. They will illustrate a truth not only relevant to their linkage but also to the linkage of the two tablets and the rationale behind their sequence.

Why is murder the mate of the acceptance of monotheism? The following story in Genesis provides the Torah's answer.

And Abraham traveled from there [the groves of Mamre] toward the land of the South and lived between Kadesh and Shur; and he lived in Gerar. And Abraham said of Sarah, his wife, "She is my sister." And Avimelekh, king of Gerar, sent and took Sarah. But God came to Avimelekh in a dream of the night and said to him, "Behold, you will die because of the woman whom you have taken, for she is a man's wife." Now Avimelekh had not come near her and he said, "Lord, will you slay even a righteous nation? Didn't he say to me: 'she is my sister,' and she too said, 'he is my brother.' In the innocence of my heart and the integrity of my hands have I done this." And God said to him in the dream, "I know that you have done this in the innocence of your heart and I also kept you from sinning against Me; therefore I did not allow you to touch her. And now restore the man's wife, for he is a prophet and will pray for you and you shall live; and if you do not restore her, know that you will surely die, you and all that is yours." And Avimelekh rose early in the morning and called all his servants and told them all these things, and the men were afraid. Then Avimelekh called Abraham and said to him, "What have you done to us? And how have I sinned against you, that you have brought on me and on my kingdom a great sin? You have done things to me that ought not have been done." And Avimelekh said to Abraham, "What did you see that caused you to do this thing?" [Genesis 20:1–10]

The reader should recall that Gerar was a highly civilized city. Yet Abraham was afraid and felt it necessary to lie about the status of his wife. Whether or not it was justifiable, and this is a subject of controversy among commentators, Abraham said of Sarah, "She is my sister." Avimelekh, the king, said to Abraham with seeming sincerity and conviction: "What did you see that caused you to do this thing?" How could you have expected us to do you harm, necessitating your subterfuge, when you could readily see all about you a city filled with unparalleled culture? We are fine and civilized people. What prompted you to expect murder in a sane and sophisticated society?

The answer lies in the very principle that links commandments one and six. And Abraham said, "Because I said: 'surely the fear of God is not in this place and they will kill me over my wife'" (Genesis 20:11). Civilized indeed, but one thing is lacking—fear of God. In a society where this is missing, then, in the immortal words of Tolstoy, "Without God, all is possible."

Secular humanists assert that belief in the divine is not necessary in order to act nobly. One can logically deduce morality. Wisdom will bring in its wake correct and ethical behavior. But isn't the negation of this philosophy the cardinal contribution of the twentieth century, which gave the world the Holocaust? The nineteenth century was the age of hope: education was going to bring about the messianic millennia. All people would come to love one another and to understand and to embrace a universal accord, because Gerar would produce godliness, civilization would foster civility.

No one in his or her wildest imagination dared dream that a time would come when the Nazis who had read Heine and Goethe would gas millions to death. Those who gloried in their poets and philosophers, composers and dramatists, could sink to the lowest depths of human depravity.

"And Avimelekh said onto Abraham, 'What did you see that caused you to do this thing?' And Abraham said, 'Because I thought surely the fear of God is not in this place and they will kill me over my wife.'"

Where there is no fear of God, anything is possible.

Bronislaw Malinowski, the social anthropologist, tells the tale of an Englishman on a safari who is taken captive by a group of cannibals. He is placed in a boiling pot and quickly realizes that he is about to become supper for the wild mob dancing around him. Suddenly he sees what he believes will be his salvation. There among the wild, primitive dancers, he spots a man with whom he went to school years before at Oxford University. "Halt," he shouts out. "Aren't you Simba with whom I studied together?" "Yes, I am," Simba shouts back. "Surely you will save me. You could not possibly be part of this group engaged in cannibalism." "No, you are wrong. They are my people." "But tell me, did your years at Oxford teach you nothing? Didn't civilization have an effect upon you and make you change your ways?" "Of course it did," came the reply. "Now when I consume people, I have learned to use only knife and fork."

Romain Gary in *The Dance of Genghis Cohn* wrote: "The ancient Simbas, a cruel, cannibalistic society, consumed their victims. The modern-day Germans, heirs to thousands of years of culture and civilization, turned their victims into soap. That desire for cleanliness, that is civilization."

In the aftermath of Nazi Germany we must once and for all understand that culture and crematoria are not mutually exclusive. Scientific progress does not ensure moral perfection, nor can secular humanism produce saints. People will always find reasons to justify any kind of behavior.

The Tree of Knowledge of Good and Evil

Maimonides understood well the need to link demands for moral behavior with clear commandments from God. For him it explained the meaning of the remarkable story at the beginning of the Bible, in which humankind is cursed for eating of The Tree of Knowledge. At the beginning of *The Guide of the Perplexed,* he raises the following question:

> How indeed could knowledge have been a crime if the pursuit of knowledge remains to this day the cardinal tenet of Judaism? And how could knowledge be the reward for the performance of a sin, as if transgressing Divine Will results in the most precious possible gain?

Maimonides responds by distinguishing between two kinds of knowledge. If the scientist tells us that the sun will rise and set at certain times, that is true, though not necessarily good. The time for sunrise and sunset is true whether we consider it good or not. Likewise when the mathematician tells us the sum of two numbers or gives us the square root, it is true, but not necessarily good. "Good" and "bad" describe the subjective feelings we have toward something; the words "true" or "false" deal with reality, regardless of our feelings.

We can say that $2 + 2 = 5$ is false. Abortion, rape, and murder are bad. There is a difference between false, which is clearly labeled improper by an irrefutable standard, and bad, which is obviously subjective.

It is bad if you think so; but there must be times when it is good. Murder may be bad if the victim is innocent. Suppose, however, he belongs to an inferior race? Suppose he is aged? Suppose I can give you reasons why he does not deserve to live? Bad may at times be good, but false can never be true.

Adam was forbidden to eat of the Tree of Knowledge of Good and Evil, not of the tree of Truth and Untruth, of *emet* and *sheqer*.

Prior to his sin, had you asked Adam what he felt about any moral evil, he would have said, "It is false." Uncompromisingly *sheqer*, false without reservation or qualification, and without distinctions regarding "situational ethics." The objective clarity of this thinking adheres to a terminology, in the moral-ethical realm, identical with the one we use today in the world of science.

But then Adam sinned and ate of The Tree of Knowledge of Good and Evil. In a divine fiat, God had told him, "Do not eat of this tree." For all intents and purposes, the tree was "false," but the text tells us: "And when the woman saw that the tree was good for food, and that it was a delight to look upon and appealing to the understanding, she took of its fruit and ate, and she gave also to her husband, and he ate" (Genesis 3:6). Objectively it was "false." But subjectively—by the standards of esthetics, taste, or personal desire—it was "good."

There are commentators who suggest the very real possibility that there was nothing in the fruit of that tree to cause any change in Adam and Eve upon eating it. It was simply the tree around which the question of knowledge revolved. Is humankind willing to accept divine decree and proclaim standards of truth and falsehood in every area of life? Or will we insist on using human reasoning to determine that, even when God said "no," our own intelligence protests that in this case it is "good." Before eating of the tree, Adam and Eve did not know the categories of good and evil. They simply did not exist for them, because they were guided by a higher standard. Truth and falsehood were scientifically correct for mathematics, astronomy, geology, and even ethical behavior.

The act of violating the commandment regarding the fruit of the tree—an act of disobedience—exposed the human preference to be guided by the "knowledge of good and evil." That was the cause of their downfall, and the expulsion of Adam and Eve from Paradise ensued.

If today we were to return to the ideals of objective right and wrong, *emet* and *sheqer,* we would be back on the road to the Garden of Eden. There is in fact a tree that allows this return. When Adam and Eve sinned, they were told they could no longer eat from the Tree of Life, which offered immortality. Humans who set their own standards above God's do not deserve to live forever. "So He drove out the man and he placed at the east of the Garden of Eden the Cherubim and the flaming sword which turned every way, to protect the path to the Tree of Life" (Genesis 3:24). But the Tree of Life beckons us in a different form—"It is a Tree of Life for those who grasp it" (Proverbs 3:18). The Torah provides the same benefits implicit in that forbidden fruit. It is the antidote to the Tree of Knowledge of Good and Evil. Every time we are called to the Torah, we make a blessing that emphasizes the most important principle behind our acceptance of divine will: "Thank You, God, for giving us a Torah of truth." We realize that our discussions and deliberations on a particular issue will probably be motivated more by personal interest than by the desire for ultimate truth. It has been said that we use our intelligence most often the way a drunk uses a lamppost—for support rather than for illumination.

How was it possible for the Nazis—not just those who were active in the genocide, but the masses as well—to have gone along with the barbarity of the Holocaust? Somehow they were able to convince themselves that it was "good" to destroy an inferior race, good to reverse the process of Germany's downfall, good to build an empire that would last forever. Rationalizations are cancerous, they breed unchecked.

The entire purpose of Torah was to present humanity with laws that would be universally applicable no matter what the situation, no matter what the personal prejudice. If fidelity is merely "good" and adultery "bad," then if she is beautiful, if my wife is sick, if . . . the possibilities are endless. Bad may become good, but false can never become true. Sinai served to clarify reality in the

world of ethics—just as science does in the physical world—with
the precision of mathematical formulae.

Not eating of the Tree of Good and Evil would have ensured
that morality remain independent of human rationale. So, too,
there is only one way to make certain that the commandment
"You shall not murder," as well as the other categories that follow
on the second tablet, remain inviolate: by accepting the higher,
God-given source of the laws governing relations between one
human being and another.

The counterpart for "You shall not murder" is "I am the Lord,
your God." There is a God, and we are created in His image. To
destroy one is to destroy a little of the other. "You shall not
murder" cannot be qualified, compromised, or questioned.

When Noah steps off from the ark, and God seeks to rebuild
humankind so that there will never again be a need for a Deluge,
God commands: "He who sheds another man's blood, his blood
shall be shed, for in the image of God made He man" (Genesis
9:6). Here is the very correspondence between commandments one
and six, appearing in a biblical text. Humanity and God are related. Indeed, "without God, all is possible." With God, only *emet,*
ultimate truths of human behavior as expressed on the second tablet, are permitted.

Why does the tablet enumerating our obligations to God precede the one concerning our obligations to people, if the latter is
more important? The answer now becomes clear. Perfection in
human relations may be our goal, but the only way to fully reach it
is through love of God.

The very first word of the Ten Commandments is "I" (*anokhi*),
referring to God. The very last word is *le-re'ekha,* "to your neighbor." God requires that we accept Him; not because He needs us,
but because our neighbor does. And when the day comes that
"God will be king over the entire world" (Zechariah 14:9), no one
will ever again find reasons or rationalizations to proclaim war;
the sword will be broken into a plow share, the spear into a prun-
ing hook, and justice will cover the earth as the waters cover the
seas.

Part IV

The Negative Commandments

10

The Three Kinds
of Punishment

e as scrupulous in performing a 'minor' mitzvah as you are in performing a major one, for you do not know the rewards given for mitzvot." Rebbe made the statement only after he allowed for one choice that did take into account priorities within Jewish law. "Which is the right way that a man should choose? That which brings glory to the doer and glory to him from fellow man" (*Ethics of the Fathers* 2:1). Laws that relate to the second tablet take priority over those on the first; they are "doubly blessed," achieving a benefit for someone else while fulfilling a commandment of God.

Reading the words carefully, however, we discover that there is another exception to the rule that all mitzvot are equal. This one is not based on the distinction drawn in the structure of the two tablets, but rather in the very wording used for each of the 613 laws of the Torah.

There are two kinds of mitzvot. There are 248 positive commands, which the Sages link to the organs of the body. Every part of our being is attached to some positive demand. But the remaining 365 laws are phrased in the format of "You shall not." Every day of the solar year carries a warning against divine disobedience.

Goodness is a matter of knowing the parameters both of our obligations and our prohibitions. Holiness has its commitments as well as constraints.

Note carefully the words that Rabbi Yehudah HaNasi used to impress us with the need for avoiding distinctions in Jewish law: "for you do not know the rewards." Rewards refer to the world of good deeds. Sins are followed by punishment. Furthermore, although it is true that we do not know the specific rewards for our actions, for they are not stated in the Torah, punishments are in fact listed, and we know precisely what the relative ranking of every sin is, based on the severity of the punishment expressing divine displeasure.

Jewish law sets down three categories of punishment. Their degree of severity allows us to recognize how much God abhors the crime that was committed.

The Torah teaches us that the punishments, ranging from least to most severe, are *mamon*—monetary or financial penalties; *malqut*—lashes; and *mitah*—death. The death penalty may be further subdivided into death by the hands of Heaven and death through the agency of human beings (the court).

Each one demands elucidation. At the heart of all of them we will discover a profound principle that clarifies the biblical purpose of punishment and differentiates Jewish law from other legal systems.

Mamon—Monetary Penalties

What should the legal response be to theft? Jail? But what good does that do to the person from whom money was stolen? Well then, let the stolen item be returned. However, that would simply mean that the thief did not succeed this time. What will stop a thief from trying again? Where is the punishment? Where is the deterrence?

It is crucial in understanding the Jewish legal system to recognize the principle of "measure for measure." It is used by God in His dealings with the world and is also a major principle in our legal system.

The Mishnah in *Sotah* affords a number of illustrations in which we see divine manifestations of the "measure for measure" concept.

> The way that a person acts, is the way that God acts toward him in kind. The suspected adulteress dressed herself up for sin, so God commanded that she be dressed shabbily in the Temple; she acted immodestly for sin, so God commanded that she be deposed in shame before the public. . . . Samson [the Judge] went after his eyes [telling his father that he wanted to marry for beauty], and so the Philistines poked his eyes out; . . . Absalom was conceited about his long hair, so he was hung by his hair. . . . Also for good . . . Miriam waited for Moses for an hour [after he was placed in the Nile River as a baby] and so the entire Jewish people waited a week for her [when she was exiled from the camp of Israel with leprosy for having spoken ill of her brother]. . . . Joseph merited to bury his father, and in turn his reburial in Israel was later attended to by Moses. [*Sotah* 1:7–9]

It is in this light that we understand the remarkable law of *Kefel,* which states that one who steals must pay back "double." But what does double really mean? The thief who stole a hundred dollars sought both to gain the sum illegally for personal benefit as well as to deprive the other person of it. The mere return of the stolen amount would not be a punishment. But to deprive the thief of an extra hundred dollars, in other words, to force the return of the stolen sum and an additional one hundred dollars, gives a thief a dose of his or her own medicine.

If the thief steals something that is crucial for the victim's livelihood ("If a man steal an ox or a sheep and kill it or sell it") such as an ox, essential for plowing and farming, or a sheep that gives wool—"he shall pay five oxen for an ox and four sheep for a sheep" (Exodus 21:37). The law is tougher on the criminal when the crime has direr consequences for the victim.

But monetary punishment is only applied to the first level of sin. This type of punishment is still external; it does not cause physical pain or affect personally. However, when the crimes are such that the doer is called a *rasha,* a wicked one, then a more severe punishment, thirty-nine lashes, is required.

Malqut—Lashes

"If there be a dispute between men and they come to court to be judged, and the judges justify the righteous and condemn the wicked [*rasha*]: If the wicked man deserves to be beaten, then the judge shall cause him to lie down and be beaten in his presence according to the measure of his wickedness by number. He shall not exceed forty lashes, for if he were to continue to beat him beyond these great beatings, then your brother would be degraded before your eyes" (Deuteronomy 25:1–3).

Lashes are the "middle" punishment between financial penalties and the death sentence. There is some controversy as to which one of the extremes this middle punishment is more comparable. On the one hand, death is final, it extinguishes life. Lashes do not. On the other hand, taking one's money has no effect on one's physical person, lashes do. Lashes may perhaps be called a mini-death, injuring tissues and cells so that they are never quite the same.

Lashes are, however, a biblically ordained means of punishment. What contemporary liberalism would consider abhorrent finds acceptance in the eyes of God. It is interesting to analyze how our Sages viewed the viability of this law, as opposed to the contemporary ideal of prison for criminals.

Whereas the modern Western mind considers physical punishment too cruel and prison compassionate, biblical thought posits the exact opposite. Prison, it says, is not a viable option for punishment, because confining a person and depriving him or her of freedom negates the very ideal of the first commandment. "I am the Lord, your God, who took you out of the land of Egypt, the house of bondage." God removed us from slavery because we were created to be free. Free to make our own choices, to become what we can, and to utilize our time in the manner of our choosing.

True, a Jew may be sold into slavery in order to earn sufficient funds to pay back a stolen amount. Such a person's rights, however, will not be totally abrogated. The Talmud teaches us that when a Jewish master acquires a Jewish slave, it as if "he acquired a master." If a man has two pillows, he must give one to his slave. If he has only one pillow, however, he must give it to the slave, for the latter feels downtrodden enough and should not be made to suffer unduly from a condition of servitude. The Egyptian slave had no rights, while the biblically permitted slave had rights just as the master had restrictions. Most important of all, there was a limit placed on the duration of servitude. "If you buy a Hebrew servant, six years he shall serve and in the seventh he shall go out free for nothing" (Exodus 21:2). What if someone so loved slavery, and was so afraid of personal freedom, that he chose to remain a slave?—"But if the servant shall plainly say, 'I love my master, my wife, and my children. I will not go out free,' then his master shall bring him to God [court] and shall bring him to the door or to the doorpost and his master shall bore his ear through with an awl and he shall serve him forever" (Exodus 21:5–6). He shall have his ear pierced because, the Sages say, "Let the ear that heard on Sinai, 'I am the Lord, your God' and 'I took you out of the land of Egypt, the house of bondage' and nonetheless chose to continue in servitude, let that ear be drilled because it obviously did not hear the message of Sinai."

Slavery of Jews by Jews may have been biblically countenanced—though it is clear from the first verse that it must end in the seventh year—but it was redefined in such a manner that the slave still had rights. Prison, however, has no place in biblical thought as a means of punishment. It clearly suffers from too many deficiencies.

1. It accomplishes nothing for the victim. The status of slave permitted someone who stole to work off the payment necessary for restitution.

2. Prison places criminals into an environment that will only serve to reinforce their criminal attitudes. Prison has been called a "school for crime," where first-time offenders are trained by hardened criminals. In biblically permitted slavery, the courts send the thief to an approved home, one that would, it is hoped, provide surroundings conducive to rehabilitation.

3. Prison confines a man or women to an all-male or all-female society. Sexual needs are not considered, nor is the fact that separation from spouse punishes the innocent mate as well as the criminal. The biblical slave is assured

that if he is married, the master must also allow the slave's wife to be with him and to be released together with him. "If he be married, then his wife shall go out with him" (Exodus 21:3).

4. Prison is incarceration. It does not teach, because it lacks the immediacy of Pavlovian stimulus response. Touch a hot stove, and God sees to it that we learn it is wrong because of the immediate pain that forces our withdrawal. Parents, too, teach in a similar manner. Halakhah decrees that it is forbidden for a mother to tell a child who has misbehaved: "Wait until Father comes home. He will punish you." Children cannot be punished hours later for an infraction committed now. They won't see the connection between the punishment and what they did to deserve it.

For punishment to be effective, it must be given as quickly as possible after the crime itself. What a devastating commentary on the modern legal system, in which criminals wait for months before sentencing—a sentencing that is never certain in any event—and then may find themselves in jail with no specific physical effect to remind them of their crime.

Lashes may seem severe, but they achieve the following: commit the crime and feel the pain.

Not forty, but thirty-nine lashes were administered, corresponding to the numerical value of the word AHiYKHa ("your brother"): Alef = 1, Het = 8, Yod = 10, Khaf = 20, a total of 39. But a medical examination was given before the lashes were administered. If it was determined that the convict could not withstand thirty-nine lashes, then the maximum would not be administered. Most important, the Torah inserts the word "brother" rather than the pronoun "he" in the verse referring to the potential disgrace of the man whipped. The Talmud's lesson here is that once the transgressor has borne his punishment and dishonor, he must again be considered "your brother" (*Makot* 23a). After punishment there is to be reacceptance.

Lashes may seem harsh, but they are meant to be administered both compassionately and quickly. They are meant to convey the message implicit in the beneficial dimension of pain. We learn to stay away from what hurts. And after the message has been given, there is to be reconciliation.

Mitah—The Death Penalty

A secular legal system knows only one kind of death penalty. It is administered by the courts and carried out by human beings. The Torah, however, teaches us that there are crimes punishable either by the courts or by God Himself.

"And that soul shall be cut off" refers to the punishment of *karet*. There are crimes for which a person dies prematurely.

Death of the young *may* be a divine curse. Death can be an indicator of God's displeasure with someone's actions; but it can also be a blessing allowing an individual to move from the world of pain and suffering to the eternal realm of everlasting tranquility and happiness.

The Midrash describes the story of the student who could not deal with the tragedy of his young colleague's death. He walked with his rabbi and begged him for some kind of explanation. As if totally disregarding him, his teacher pointed in the distance and said, "Look how terribly unfair. That worker is leaving the fields to go home when, as you can see from the sun, it is yet not quite midday." The perplexed student could not understand the relevance of the statement. When he asked the rabbi why he was not answering him, the rabbi said, "But I did. Let your own ears hear the meaning of my words. The man in the fields is returning home simply because he has finished his labor early. It is not unfair for him to do so. It is rather a measure of the man that he was able to do in but a short period of time what others require the entire day to accomplish. So, too, did your colleague leave the fields of this world to return to his final home because he had already completed whatever his mission was here on this earth."

There are many ways to explain death before what we would consider one's time. "And Enoch walked with God and he was not; for God took him" (Genesis 5:24). God took Enoch before his time, because, according to our Sages, God foresaw that were he to live out his days he would have turned astray. God spared him by taking him. That is another possibility.

Even Abraham died before his time, on the day of the bar mitzvah of his grandchildren, Jacob and Esau. He lived to see them grow to accept personal responsibility. But he was spared from watching Esau grow into "the man of the field, the man of the hunt," the one who would put to shame the ideals of his grandfather.

To say that a person who dies at a young age must have sinned a great sin is theologically mistaken. It is, however, possible for death to be a punishment.

There are crimes for which the punishment given in the Torah is death. But even this punishment may vary, depending on the severity of the crime. The Torah lists four types of death penalties. They are halakhically ranked—from most severe to least—in the following order: (1) *Seqilah*—stoning, (2) *Sereifah*—burning, (3) *Hereg*—the sword (decapitation), and (4) *Heneq*—strangulation.

Having already decreed death for certain crimes, obviously for those that are the most heinous, why does the Torah make distinctions between different kinds of death? Other legal systems, once they have determined that death is necessary, decree one method of execution, be it electric chair or guillotine. What need is there for four different ways in which to carry out the same sentence?

The answer to that question will lead us to a more profound understanding of the nature and purpose of biblical punishment.

11

Does Judaism
Believe in
Capital Punishment?

e have discussed the three types of punishment in Jewish law. Money, lashes, and death represent the three possibilities, each dealing with a more severe level of crime. Obviously those sins that are most heinous in the sight of God are crimes that warrant capital punishment. These, too, are arranged in a sequence, with the "lightest" being strangulation and the "strictest" being stoning.

Surely this would seem to be a most inappropriate time to ask the question: Does Judaism believe in capital punishment? Even a cursory familiarity with the Torah makes clear that execution is often the prescribed method for dealing with the perpetrators of many different kinds of crimes. "He who kills a man so that he dies shall surely be put to death" (Exodus 21:12). "And he who strikes his father or his mother shall be surely put to death" (Exodus 21:15). "And he who curses his father or his mother shall surely be put to death" (Exodus 21:15).

Isn't it obvious that Judaism is a strong proponent of the death penalty?

What needs to be addressed is the almost incredible contradiction to this view, which is found throughout the Talmud. Resolving this contradiction will lead to a major distinction between the Written and the Oral Law.

There is a mishnah that teaches us: "A Sanhedrin that issues a death sentence once in seven years is considered a murderous court. Rabbi Elazar Ben Azaryah said it is a murderous court if it pronounced a death sentence once in seventy years" (*Makot* 7a). How could the Sages call a Sanhedrin that carries out the will of God a "murderous court"? How could they criticize Sages who ensure that the will of God is implemented? If the Torah says "yes," how could the mishnah say "no"?

To complicate the problem further, the rabbis deduce from various texts that a number of legal requirements must be met before an execution can take place. Considering them in total, it becomes clear that it is impossible to find a situation in which the death sentence will actually be carried out.

What are the halakhic requirements to prove guilt and carry out the execution?

Two Witnesses—
Circumstantial Evidence Is Disregarded in Jewish Law

The famous story of Shimon Ben Shetaḥ (*Sanhedrin* 37b) illustrates how far this law goes. He swore that he had seen a man chase after his friend into some ruins. He ran after him and found his friend dead and the pursuer holding a sword dripping with blood. Ben Shetaḥ said to him: "Wicked one, who killed this man?—It's either me or you. But what can I do—your blood was not given into my hands, because the Torah says, 'On the basis of two witnesses, he shall be put to death.'" The knife may have been bloody, the man leaving the hovel may be the only one who could possibly have committed the murder. But as long as there were not two witnesses who actually saw the crime, the courts cannot condemn. One must remember that a legal system that acknowledges God as the ultimate Judge is not saying that this man should go unpunished. Rather it means that a mortal court is only commissioned by God to carry out retribution when there is total certainty; otherwise we must leave it to God to see to it that the wicked receive their due.

Requirements for Witnesses

Witnesses must be "kosher." This means, for instance, that they may not be relatives of each other. Even Moses and Aaron would have been disqualified. As far as a Jewish court is concerned, a crime witnessed by two relatives is tantamount to a deed witnessed by no one. The witnesses may also not be *pesulim*—a category that includes a wide range of disqualifications elucidated in the Talmud. Gamblers—according to one view, professional, full-time gamblers, according to another, even those who occasionally place bets—are included in this category.

Hatra'ah—Warning

In Jewish law, no one can be convicted of a crime unless he or she has received proper warning. This means that the two witnesses who see a person about to commit a crime must yell out to the perpetrator both the biblical text prohibiting the deed as well as the punishment for that particular infraction.

Tokh Kedei Dibur ("in the midst of conversation")

A warning is not sufficient if given more than four seconds before the crime is committed. (Halakhically this interval is defined as *tokh kedei dibur;* literally "within speaking," a reference to the amount of time required to say the four words *shalom aleikhem rabi u-mori,* "Peace be upon you, my teacher, my master.") The specifics of this time unit have relevance elsewhere in Jewish laws as well. It is conceivable that the perpetrator may have forgotten the warning or no longer taken it to heart if more than four seconds elapsed between warning and crime!

Qabalat Hatra'ah—Acceptance of the Warning

The last requirement is probably the most "outrageous" and "illogical" of the series. For all of the above to have any validity, the villain about to commit a crime must verbally indicate that he or she has heard the warning and has chosen to ignore it. Only if the criminal responds, "In spite of this I will do" (*af al pi khen*) can the courts proceed in their deliberations for the death penalty. Little wonder that the Mishnah called a Sanhedrin that issued a death sentence once in seven or seventy years a murderous court. The strictures placed on the courts prevent them from giving the death sentence. The standards we have explained—from the requirement of two witnesses through acceptance of warning—are all biblically derived. Yet the Bible itself in no uncertain terms mandates *mot yumat,* "He shall surely be put to death." What, then, is God's will? If He wants the villains to die, why does the Oral Law make it impossible to carry out the sentence? If He doesn't want a Sanhedrin to be murderous, why did the Torah teach us *mot yumat,* "He shall surely be put to death"?

To answer this seeming contradiction we must understand a remarkable insight into the purpose of Jewish law. It is a concept implicit in the opening verse in Exodus, which introduces the entire legal system of Judaism: "And these are the ordinances which you shall set before them" (Exodus 21:1). Having recorded the Decalogue, the ten categories-principles in the previous portion, the Torah now proceeds to elaborate on the law. The words "before them" in the aforementioned verse (in Hebrew, *lifneihem*) present us with a difficulty. Ordinances, known as *mishpatim,* are meant to be given "to them" (*lahem*) not "before them." Why does the Torah use a different and longer word to explain how these laws are to be transmitted to the people?

The famous preacher, the Magid of Dubno, responded with a parable: "The Wise Men of Chelm," known throughout the world for possessing a wisdom that illustrates the stupidity of mankind, were faced with a serious problem. One of the roads in their town had a very steep incline at the point where it veered around a mountainside. There was no protective curb. And so when horses and carriages came barreling down at top speed, unable to make the turn, they hurtled down to the bottom of the cliff and were severely injured.

What was the city of Chelm to do about this terribly dangerous situation? For twenty-four hours they sat and deliberated. A sharp curve, no protective guardrail, people, horses, and carriages constantly falling off and being hurt. What to do? What to do? And then the answer, in a flash of brilliant insight, came to them. The city of Chelm agreed, in a unanimous vote, to build a hospital at the bottom of the cliff.

The world has often shown the Chelm response to its problems. An outbreak of crime? Build more prisons. A plague of drugs? Initiate more methadone programs. Violence, wickedness, corruption? Build the hospitals that deal with the effects, but never the causes.

Legal systems invariably are set up to tell us what to do *after* crimes have been committed. Lawyers and judges study the law so that they can respond properly after the fact. But Jews are told from early childhood to study the Torah; not because it is hoped that they will become lawyers or judges and will be required to know what to do with criminals after they have done wrong. Every Jew must know the law because "These are the ordinances which you shall set *before* them"—before, not after. Jewish law is meant to be studied by everyone because the essence of Jewish law is preventative rather than punitive.

When the Torah states, "He who strikes his father or mother shall surely be put to death," or "He who curses his father or mother shall surely be put to death," it is not describing a post facto procedure to be implemented once these horrible deeds have been committed. It is rather a "before the fact" educational doctrine, to be internalized through constant repetition and study, proclaiming that if anyone smites or curses a parent, in God's view that person deserves to die. Read these verses regularly; review the Torah from year to year. Understand how much God abhors these sins and you will never come to do them.

Why does God say "He shall surely be put to death" if the Oral Law makes it clear that He never intended the sentence to be carried out? Because the Written Law deals with what should be, the Oral Law with what is. The Written Law is God speaking "before them"—hoping that we learn a value system that prevents us from doing wrong. The Oral Law communicates what the Sanhedrin and the courts need to know when the moral principles of law have not been mastered.

How do I convey to my child the degree of severity implicit in different types of wrong behavior? If my son disturbs me with slight noise I say, "Stop it." If he, unawares, plays with a screwdriver and begins to put it into an electrical socket, I scream with all my might and perhaps say, "If you ever do that again, I'll kill you." The threat is obviously not meant to be taken seriously. Its purpose is to ensure that what I said doesn't happen, because I don't want him to lose his life. So, too, God screams out in the language of ultimate love and concern, "If you do any of these things, *mot yumat,* you shall surely die." But then these words are followed by God's admonition to the court, "And the court shall judge and the court shall save" (Numbers 35:25), commanding judges to do everything in their power to see to it that once a crime has been committed, the verdict should be "not guilty."

This concept explains another seemingly incomprehensible passage. The Torah states, "an eye for an eye" (Exodus 21:24). Much has been made of the apparent cruelty of this verse, an apparent throwback to the ancient code of Hammurabi. Our Sages explained in the Talmud that the Oral Law has always understood that this phrase was not to be taken literally. "An eye for an eye" indeed meant the value of the eye; the compensation was in fact monetary.

It is reassuring to be told that we are not to be as cruel as the perpetrator. God did not mean "an eye for an eye." But the question remains, if God did not want us to gouge out the perpetrator's eye, why did He say it? We may accept the validity of Oral Law, but why is there a discrepancy in this case between the Written Law and its real meaning? If God meant money, why didn't He say so?

The answer is obvious. The alternative would have been for the Torah to state, "money for an eye," and there is no such thing. Just imagine a very wealthy person who hates another man. He says, "I will knock out that man's eye. Let him be blind forever. What is my punishment? The Torah says, 'money for an eye.' I can afford it. I will gladly pay the price."

No, it is not money for an eye. The Torah says "an eye for an eye" because the Written Law always speaks in the language of what should be. Someone who takes another's eye out deserves to have his eye taken out. Compassion will mitigate the actual punishment. The Oral Law will translate that into monetary terms, but the text has made clear what the crime actually means in the sight of God.

Now we can understand why God chose to transmit a Torah of dual identity, both Written and Oral Law. God is in fact One, but he has two names by which He is known. Our Sages explain the difference between *Adonai,* Lord, and *Elohim,* God, as conveying the two-fold aspects of His personality as we perceive them. When the Lord appears to us as loving, kind, good, and gracious, He is *Adonai,* the Merciful One. When we perceive Him as being strict, harsh, and unyielding, He is *Elohim,* the God of Law. Of course, God in essence is one and the same, always gracious and kind, loving and compassionate. It is only our perception that changes. The biblical verse "Hear O Israel," affirming our faith—*Shema Yisrael Adonai Eloheinu Adonai Ehad*—teaches us this truth. The "Lord" of mercy and the God of law are one *Adonai,* the attribute of mercy. In order to be merciful, He must at times be "cruel"; when He seems "cruel," he is in fact, on a deeper level, merciful.

Both aspects exist and define His essence. They gain expression in the two parts of the Torah, the Written and Oral. The *Zohar,* the master work of kabbalah, Jewish mysticism, puts it this way: "Written Law is the voice of strength and severity [*dina qashya*]; the Oral Law communicates His compassion [*dina rafya*]." The Bible begins with *bereishit bara Eloqim,* "In the beginning Eloqim created," i.e., the world was first created via strict law. The Oral Law tells us how the Lord embraces us after we have sinned and says, "I screamed at you not to do it, but once you transgressed, let Me bring you to My bosom and try to draw you closer once again with love."

The Case of the *Mamzer*—The Illegitimate Child

This concept, counterbalancing the strictness of law with the compassion of love, allows us to understand another seemingly incomprehensible biblical decree. In Deuteronomy 23:3 we are taught: "A bastard [*mamzer*] shall not enter into the assembly of the Lord, even to the tenth generation shall none of his enter into the assembly of the Lord." The word *mamzer* as used in the Bible is not the equivalent of the English "bastard." It does not refer to someone born out of wedlock, but rather to the child of an adulterous or incestuous relationship. When the verse tells us "tenth generation," the Talmud deduces that this child may never "enter into the assembly." This illicit child, the innocent product of a vile sin, suffers an entire lifetime by being unable to marry another Jew. Such offspring are restricted in choice of a mate to those born under similar circumstances; in other words, to another *mamzer* (illegitimate male) or *mamzeret* (illegitimate female).

How harsh a punishment for one who committed no crime! To begin with, we must put the punishment into perspective. God after all did not say that a *mamzer* may not marry. He limited, albeit severely, the pool from which the *mamzer* may select a mate. A priest (*Kohen*) also has a smaller range of possibilities from which to choose a mate, since he may not marry a divorcee. A High Priest is further restricted, as he can only marry a virgin. Diminishing the number of potential candidates for marriage is not necessarily a cruel thing. In any event, God, the matrimonial matchmaker par excellence, is responsible for determining who marries whom and will see to it that two compatible souls find each other. The priest serves God in many ways. One of them is to demonstrate that though Judaism allows divorce, the legal dissolution of a marriage nonetheless has some severe consequences. The fact that a priest may not marry a divorcee teaches us that divorce may be permissible, but "the very Altar sheds tears when man and woman dissolve their union" (*Gittin* 90b). The High Priest must sacrifice his ability to marry anyone who is not a virgin in order to demonstrate the sanctity attached to virginity. Diminishing the choice of mates serves an educational function. So, too, the constraints of the *mamzer* and *mamzeret* proclaim that there are everlasting and terrible consequences to adulterous unions.

What strikes some people as bizarre, however, is the rabbinic response to the problem of *mamzerut* (illegitimacy). In many instances the rabbis have sought to undo the effect of this law by finding a circuitous route through which such children may be allowed to marry without restriction.

If the biblical definition of *mamzerut* includes only someone who is a product of an adulterous union, it may be possible to remove the label if the mother was not halakhically married at the time of conception. Great effort is often expended to find a legal means for dissolving the marriage. Were the witnesses kosher? Was every detail of the wedding service punctiliously observed? Was the marriage document, the *ketubah,* written without a single error? If the mother's marriage can be shown to have been halakhically defective, then, though the child was born from an act of sinful intercourse, the problems of *mamzerut* do not apply. The *mamzer* and *mamzeret* would then be free to marry anyone of their choosing.

Why have Rabbi Shlomo Goren, the former Chief Rabbi of Israel, and many others attempted to do this? Shouldn't we say that a biblical law, even if it appears to be extremely harsh, must be observed because God commanded it and it is His will? Shouldn't such legal circumventions be discouraged?

Not if we understand that the purpose of Jewish law is preventative rather than punitive.

When God wrote, "A bastard shall not enter into the assembly of the Lord even to the tenth generation," He was directing His remarks not to the illegitimate child born after the fact, but to the man and woman before they contemplated committing their obscene deed. Is it worth it? asks God of the two consenting adults carried away in the heat of passion. It is not only the lawyers and judges who know the law. Every Jew who has studied from childhood on, and who has heard the Torah repeated every year, will know this verse. And the adulterous couple will know that their moment of pleasure will be followed by an eternity of consequences. And perhaps, just perhaps, the laws "which you shall place before them" will fulfill their purpose.

Jewish law desires most of all that wrongs not be committed. Once the deed is done, there is a totally different approach to be followed: "and the congregation shall judge and they shall attempt to save." When admonitions do not work, then compassion must rule supreme. The role of the legal system is to warn "If you do that, I'll kill you" before the child places the screwdriver into the socket; afterward we can only show our love, do all in our power to see to it that the severity of the transgression is understood, and make sure the child never repeats the crime.

That is why the Torah so often states *mot yumat*. A more accurate translation would be "he *should* die," that is what he deserves. But God does not really want him to be executed. Hence, He teaches the Sages the restrictions and qualifications that must be placed around the law to ensure that a Sanhedrin that kills someone once in seven or seventy years is deemed a murderous Sanhedrin.

Should the death penalty exist? The most compelling rationale for justifying its acceptance is the educational aspect. Let people be gathered into the town square and see what happens to someone who murdered, raped, or committed a crime society cannot accept. Let them see villains hanging from the scaffolds, so that society may proclaim: Thus shall be done to the man who defies our moral and ethical standards.

But Judaism found a remarkable alternative to capital punishment. Indeed, gather the people into the town square every Monday and Thursday morning as well as on the Sabbath. Let the square be the synagogue. Instead of actually hanging or guillotining, electrocuting or axing, let the people hear the words of God Himself. He who does such and such shall surely be put to death. Imagine a child who from the earliest days has heard in the name of the Almighty that cursing or smiting parents is a capital offense. Whoever does these things should die. Hard to imagine that such a child would treat lightly the commission of these offenses.

What other cultures do after the fact, via public executions, Judaism achieves "before them," with a methodology of public instruction.

So many times people ask, "Why should my child be taught the Talmud and study what happens if one ox gores another? Why should the ideal be that every person know all the fines, punishments, and legal procedures in cases of torts and damages, injuries, and even killings? Let a few people study so that if the cases come up there will be those who will know how to treat them according to biblical law. Why must everyone know the details of legal consequences?" The answer is, "The goal is not that they know legal consequences, but rather that legal consequences—absorbed almost with mother's milk and continuously part of our spiritual nourishment—will, we hope, ensure that our people are immunized against perpetrating any of those acts we have so carefully studied."

The answer to the question "Does Judaism believe in capital punishment?" is not what we would have superficially responded. Yes, the death penalty exists in the Torah, but it is only there to make us aware of how much God detests every crime—and therefore how much we ought to make certain to avoid them. God teaches us different penalties—not in order to actually administer them, but to make us aware of the intensity of His displeasure. Even in the case of capital crimes, in some way we must be made aware of varying levels. Hence, four different death penalties, clearly defined in terms of severity, are needed. *Ḥeneq,* you ought to be strangled. *Hereg,* you ought to be killed by the sword. *Sereifah,* you ought to be burnt. And if, God forbid, you commit any one of the crimes warranting the worst penalty of all, then know of a certainty, you ought to be stoned, *seqilah.* You ought to be, but of course you will not. In order that the awareness of penalties serve a preventive purpose, God demonstrates His love by making the law seek exoneration rather than execution after the fact.

There is one final caveat, that of *hora'at sha'ah* (emergency measures). If criminals know that they will always get away with it, if biblical punishments are seen to be universally inapplicable, is it not possible that its compassion will prove to be self-defeating?

The Sages were clearly aware of this possibility. Therefore they built into Judaism's legal system a safeguard in case the preventative measure, with its educational emphasis, proved inadequate.

Hora'at sha'ah, the power granted the courts for emergency measures, is the "last resort" in order to compensate for the problem of possible ineffectiveness. There was a time when sexual immorality was so rampant that a couple once publicly fornicated in the fields in full view of all. They were condemned to death, although many of the halakhic requirements for execution were not fully met. How could the Sages have done this? And what about the Mishnah's disdain for the Sanhedrin that executed someone in seven or seventy years? All of this is irrelevant when the Sanhedrin, in its wisdom, recognizes that the times demand a different approach.

If the Sanhedrin were in existence today, who knows what the attitude of its members would be toward drug pushers, child pornographers, muggers, and rapists? One may speculate that faced with the reality of the contemporary scene, their response would have allowed for extreme emergency measures. Yet one may also speculate that if there were a Sanhedrin today and a society governed by it, there would be no need for emergency measures. A world exposed to the teachings of Torah, and infused with the preventive vaccinations of Torah study, would never have sunk to the depraved depths of our days.

Part V

The Three Laws of Martyrdom

12

For What
Shall a Jew
Be Willing to Die?

ll mitzvot may be equal. But surely all sins are not.

We have demonstrated that the primary purpose of punishment is to indicate the relative severity of the transgression. From fines to lashes to the four kinds of capital punishment, God indicates His concern for a broad range of offenses.

But the Torah clearly considers three sins to be the vilest of all. Until now we have divided the 613 mitzvot in two ways: (a) the division of the tablets into God–person and person–person, and (b) the division of commandments into positive and negative. But there is a third way: 610 laws belong in one category, and three stand alone with regard to a major ruling of our faith.

There are only three sins for which a person must be prepared to give up his or her life rather than to transgress. Three laws alone demand martyrdom in Judaism. They are so important that it is better for someone to die with soul intact than to transgress them. Three out of 613 are governed by the unique rule "better to be killed than to violate" (*yeihareg ve-'al ya'avor*).

Why Shouldn't We Die for Our Faith?

To understand how special is the category of martyrdom, we

must first grasp the operative principle that applies to all other mitzvot. Judaism is profoundly dedicated to maintaining life. One might almost say Judaism is prepared to maintain life at all costs.

What if someone becomes ill on the Sabbath and must be rushed to a hospital to save his or her life? What if fasting on Yom Kippur is too dangerous for a sick person and presents a threat to survival? What if no kosher food is available and the only thing a person has to eat is forbidden? In all these instances, the law is clear. *Piquah nefesh doheh et ha-kol.* A threat to life, i.e., survival, supersedes all else.

The Talmud offers two sources for this ruling. "Wherefore the children of Israel shall keep the Sabbath to observe the Sabbath throughout their generations [*le-dorotam*] for a perpetual Covenant" (Exodus 31:16): The children are meant to keep the Sabbath [*le-dorotam*] in a manner that enables them to observe it throughout the generations. Better to violate one Sabbath in order to stay alive and observe many more in the future. The second source is a phrase from Leviticus 18:5: "And you shall live by them"—to which the Talmud (*Sanhedrin* 74a) adds, "And you shall live by them, and not that you shall die through them." The seemingly simple phrase that suggests that we are to live by the laws of the Torah has a more profound meaning. The Torah is a source of life; it gives us life both in this world and the next. If it is clear that observance of a specific mitzvah will spell certain death, then clearly *in that particular instance* God would not want us to fulfill the law, but rather to opt for the greater good and choose life.

Violating a mitzvah, when not to do so means death, is therefore not an option but a duty. Were a man or woman to fast on Yom Kippur when their body clearly demanded food and they were in danger of dying, then their fasting is tantamount to suicide. This would be sinful, not praiseworthy.

A Jew must attempt always to preserve life. A departure from this rule applies in only three cases: idolatry, immorality, and bloodshed. The three laws demanding martyrdom are not the rule but the exceptions. Normally we ought not to be willing to give up our lives. Why in these three cases does the principle "and you shall live by them and not die by them" not apply?

The Ruling in the House of Nitzeh in Lod

The talmudic passage (*Sanhedrin* 74a) stating the law "better to be killed than to violate" begins in a remarkable manner. Rabbi Yoḥanan, in the name of Rabbi Shimon, son of Yoẓadek, taught that they voted and concluded in the attic of the house of Nitzeh in the city of Lod as follows: "Regarding all sins in the Torah, if one says to another 'transgress so that you will not be killed,' he may transgress and not be killed—except in the case of idolatry, immorality, and bloodshed." How strange that the ruling is prefaced by an indication of the place in which it was given. And indeed what an unusual place it was! The rabbis decided in the attic of a house? Why weren't they in the house of study? What were they doing in someone's home? And why, of all places, in the attic?

The line of introduction to a law that has had serious consequences for Jews persecuted from the days of the Romans through the time of the Holocaust lets us know that it was legislated by rabbis who fully recognized that they themselves might be forced to die on the basis of their ruling. If they were not in the house of study, it was because they were not allowed to be there. If they were in the attic, it was because they were forced into hiding. Any student of history recognizes the allusions to an age of horrible persecution, in which Torah study was forbidden and observance of Jewish law often resulted in torture or death.

For what shall a Jew be willing to die? That question could not be answered by rabbis sitting in the security of their own homes or in the safety of a house of study that knew no threats. The source of the laws of martyrdom in the Talmud are the rabbis who knew that they might well be forced to become martyrs.

They analyzed, discussed, debated, and came to the conclusion that has guided Jews during the Crusades, the Inquisition, and in the concentration camps.

One who is told "violate this commandment so that you will not be killed" must indeed violate and not be killed. The reason? Rashi, the prime commentator on the Talmud, explains with the verse: "And you shall live by them and not die by them." When the Nazis commanded their charges to work on the Sabbath, when they insisted that the holidays be violated, or made it necessary to disregard laws of kashrut, the rabbis in Auschwitz and elsewhere commanded their disciples in accord with this talmudic ruling, "violate and live."

But there are three moments when we know that Jewish life cannot go on unless we are willing to die.

1.   Sexual immorality (*gilui arayot*). The Nazis were wont to set up sexual scenes for their pleasure. They would demand that a Jew have sexual relations with his daughter or with a dog. Shall I transgress and live, asked those so ordered? The halakhic answer is "better to be killed than to violate."

2.   The shedding of blood (*shefikhat damim*). Murder in Hebrew is not bloodshed, but rather blood*s* shed. This can be traced to a commentary on the very first murder in history. Cain had killed Abel, and God came to him and said, "What have you done? The voice of your brother's bloods [*demei aḥikha*] cry out to Me from the ground" (Genesis 4:10). The Sages asked why is "bloods" in the plural? The voice of the bloods? The response is profound. It is not simply Abel who was killed but all of his potential descendants. Imagine how many millions of people might have been born were it not for the fact that one of the first two children in the world committed fratricide. Every murder is not merely the shedding of blood, but the shedding of bloods.

What if someone commands me to murder or be killed? It was a question raised frequently at the Nuremburg trials. How can you condemn me for what I did if I had no alternative? Not to follow orders meant that I would have been killed myself. It was the life-and-death choice that confronted countless people during the Holocaust. Kill or be killed. And here, too, the Jewish response is "better to be victim than villain."

3.   Idolatry (*avodah zarah*). There were many times in Jewish history when we were offered a choice. Let Hannah's

seven sons bow down to the idol and they will be spared, said Antiochus. Accept another God and you will not be slain. Shall we renounce our very reason for living in order to be granted life? Here, too, the law speaks clearly: die with *Shema Yisrael* (Hear O Israel) on your lips rather than live a life separated from the Almighty.

These three sins are clearly the three ultimate crimes of the Jewish religion. Life is meaningless if these laws cannot be observed. Yet only two of the three seem readily comprehensible based on principles we have established.

The two tablets demonstrated for us the distinction between laws establishing our relationship to God and those dealing with our fellow human beings. Idolatry and bloodshed can be understood simply as the gravest expressions of rejection in each of these categories. If one were to imagine a line on which were placed the various possibilities for sinning against another person—hitting, shaming, striking—the worst of all would have to be murder, the total elimination of another. A similar line for the category of person—God would include many infractions that impinge on our total acceptance of His divinity—not worshiping, not heeding, not offering proper respect—but the ultimate would be idolatry, total rejection.

Bloodshed and idolatry are logical extensions of accepted categories. But to what category does sexual immorality correspond? In what is this the ultimate sin? Why must one ignore the principle of "and you shall live by them" when immorality is the issue?

The Three Pillars of Human Existence

It is interesting that just as there are three "ultimates" in Jewish law, there are also three conditions for the continued existence of the world. In *Ethics of the Fathers* we learn: "The entire world rests on three principles: on Torah, sacrifice (and/or prayer), and acts of kindness." Were it not for the ongoing observance of these three, the world would be destroyed.

These are so crucial that our Sages utilize them to explain why there had to be three forefathers, Abraham, Isaac, and Jacob, before the creation of the Jewish people. Preceding Sinai and the acceptance of the Torah, there were three paradigms of perfection for each of these master principles.

Abraham was devoted to kindness and hospitality to others. If he saw strangers whom he assumed to be Arabs walking in the heat of day, he rushed to invite them and offer his hospitality even though he had just been circumcised. Such evil places as Sodom and Gemorrah were the objects of his concern and compassion. He pleaded for their survival even though his mission in life was to travel from one end of the land to the other to nourish people both physically and spiritually. If Abraham represented kindness, then Isaac represented sacrifices. "If a man offers from you [*mikem*] an offering" (Leviticus 1:2)—the Sages explain that the greatest offering is an offering of one's own person, *mikem*. The animal is merely a substitute, conveying the idea that there but for the grace of God go I. Isaac was ready not only to make an offering, but to be an offering. His was the life of sacrifice. He was the paradigm for *Avodah,* the sacrificial system later instituted in the Holy Temple.

Jacob was the righteous man who sat in the tents and studied Torah. He became for all times the symbol of the Jew dedicated to learning and self-perfection.

In examining the Mishnah concerning the survival of the world and the example of the three Patriarchs, we are confronted with a similar question about categories. It is obvious that the tablets have their conceptual correlates in two of the groupings. Sacrifice clearly links humanity to God—a reference to laws concerning the person–God relationship. Lovingkindness links one human being to another—a reference to the interpersonal laws. Abraham is the second tablet, Isaac is the first. But who is Jacob? What major ideal does he represent? And what need has the Torah of a third pillar if we have already established our links to God and humanity?

It was the Ga'on of Vilna, intellectual giant of the eighteenth century, who posited the existence of a third major relationship, the key to all groupings of three in our religion. It is obvious that we have a relationship to God. That may be illustrated by an arrow pointing from self to the heights above, a vertical line. The second is person to person; that is an arrow extending outward, horizontally. But these do not yet exhaust the areas of responsibility. For even as we must strive upward and outward, there remains inward dimension—the relationship to the self (*bein Adam le-azmo*).

What is the real meaning of the three pillars on which the world rests? Of course lovingkindness is directed to people, sacrifice to God. But the greatest purpose of Torah is to allow us to realize our potential to the fullest. Be true to yourself. Be what you can be. Jacob, who represents the paradigm of Torah, was therefore "whole and complete," an *ish tam* (Genesis 26:27).

The High Holy Days highlight yet another grouping of three. In the famous prayer of Rabbi Amnon, we are told that all is decreed at the beginning of the year in accord with our actions. But "Repentance, prayer, and charity [*teshuvah, tefilah, zedaqah*] may avert the evil decree."

Here, too, we find three ultimates, three ways in which everything inscribed for us may be changed for the better. Prayer clearly involves our relationship to God. Charity involves us with people. What is *teshuvah,* the word used for repentance? According to its root meaning in Hebrew, *teshuvah* refers to nothing other than a return. The movement describing the countless people returning to God and to Torah in contemporary times is called the *ba'al teshuvah* movement. It has been asked, how we can speak of these newly pious as "people of the return"? To what are they returning? Quite the reverse, they are breaking away from their past. Most often they are forsaking their backgrounds. To what, then, are they coming back? The answer is implicit in the very words that form the mitzvah of repentance in the Torah: "And you shall return to your heart" (Deuteronomy 30:1). "Teshuvah" is a return to one's inner core. Repentance means going back to one's essence. It means reaching for the third, inward dimension of *bein Adam le-azmo.*

The calendar also expresses this three-fold grouping. The historic holy days relating to the birth of our people are Passover, the Pentecost (Shavuot), and the Festival of Booths (Sukkot). There is clearly something significant about their combined number, because they are mentioned as a group, the *shalosh regalim,* or the Three Festivals. What is the purpose of each?

On Passover, when we left Egypt, we were able finally to achieve the goal of belief in God: "And Israel saw the great work which the Lord did upon the Egyptians, and the people feared the Lord; and they believed in the Lord and in His servant, Moses" (Exodus 14:31). The very first commandment of belief in God is therefore a direct result of the Exodus experience—"I am the Lord, your God, who took you out of the land of Egypt, the house of bondage." On Passover, the Jew discovered the link between humanity and God.

On the other end of the annual trilogy, on Sukkot, the Festival of Booths and of the Harvest, Jews are duty-bound to strengthen their link with others. Leave the precincts of your own house and break out of the barrier that separates you from your neighbor. Wave the *lulav* (palm branch) and *etrog* (citron) to the four corners of the world to understand that you are a part of a larger universe. Read as the Torah portion for this holiday the section of "Tithe, you shall surely tithe" (Deuteronomy 14:22f), so that at a time when your granaries are overflowing, you remember you are not alone in this world. Offer seventy sacrifices corresponding to the seventy nations of the world, so that you acknowledge you must give on their behalf as well. Finally there is the beautiful ritual of *Ushpizin,* inviting guests into the sukkah, in order to fulfill person-to-person commandments.

But what is in the middle of these two? What is central to the proper acceptance of these two responsibilities of life? The answer is Shavuot, the time when the Jewish people received the Torah—as in the grouping of Torah, Sacrifice, and Lovingkindness, which refers us to that all-important dimension of self. Indeed, how can we relate to God and to others and ignore what for us must be our prime responsibility on earth? "And you shall return to thine own heart," be true to yourself, do not forsake the divinity, the image of God in which you were created. That is the very essence of your being.

The Three Cardinal Sins

It is the third category, the inner dimension of self, that allows us to solve the riddle of the third law of martyrdom. We understood bloodshed and idolatry as the extremes of those laws pertaining to our relationship with humanity and God. We wondered, what room was there for sexual immorality? What could possibly be the conceptual area of its concern?

Secular law has made clear those areas that cannot be part of its domain. Law is meant to protect people from each other. That is why individuals may turn to the courts and say, "This was solely between us. We were adults and consenting partners." Indeed if a man has sex with an animal, he may claim "I wasn't hurting anybody." If by "anybody" only another human being is implied, that defense is justified. If, however, as Jewish law maintains, we must be concerned not only with what we do to God or to others, but even to ourselves, then sexual immorality is, in fact, the ultimate desecration of the divine image in which we were created.

Woody Allen might have thought it the height of humor in his movie *All You Ever Really Wanted to Know About Sex* to portray bestiality. In Jewish thought, that may well be the worst sexual crime of all—not because of what it did to the victim, but because of what it did to the human being who will never again be as "human" as he was before.

On the seventh commandment, which we have already indicated subsumes all the sins relating to the category of "Thou shalt not commit adultery," the commentator Ibn Ezra offers a fascinating opinion of Rabbi Sa'adyah Gaon (892–942 C.E.). Sexual sins, according to Sa'adyah Gaon, are graded in accord with the following principle: The more difficult it is to render an illicit sexual act permissible, the more heinous it is in its essence. The "simplest" sexual sin is that committed between an unmarried man and woman. Their crime consists of not having sanctified their union. Yet clearly it could readily have been rendered permissible through the mitzvah of marriage. Next in level of severity is for a man to have relations with his wife while she is menstruating and in the state of impurity. Sexual relations are then forbidden, but this remains a relatively low level of crime inasmuch as the passage of a short period of time and the use of the ritual bath would have turned this act into a permissible one. More severe than the two just mentioned is an illicit union between people married to others. Their act of sex is not permissible, nor will it ever be permissible, unless divorce or death allow them subsequently to sanctify their mating. These are neither automatic nor in their own hands. Hence, this level of sin transcends the crimes previously listed. Sex with someone not of our faith would be a severer sin still. Here the forbidden could only become permitted if the "stranger" would convert, an action tantamount, according to Halakhah, to actual rebirth. One may ask at this point, how could there be sins worse than these? On a scale of sexual severity, what supersedes adultery and the others already listed? By the system of Sa'adyah Gaon the answer is homosexuality and bestiality—because both of these are sexual acts that have no way of being transformed from sinfulness to legitimacy.

How striking that precisely those two sexual areas, which contemporary morality seems to suggest are beyond the pale of ethical concern, are in fact used as illustrations of the very worst sins. The fact that homosexual partners may be consenting or that in bestiality the "consent" of the animal is mute, is irrelevant. Obviously the rationale for illicit sex in Jewish law transcends the category of "harming another."

Harming oneself is a valid concern of Jewish law. If someone were to watch pornographic films around the clock, the crime involves not simply a waste of time. It is far more severe. It is the demeaning process of exposing one's inner sanctity, one's innate Godly essence, to an experience that equates human life with animal behavior.

What is a human being? But a little lower than the angels. Jewish law strives to make us remember this truth. If a person is ready to forget it, then sexual immorality is granted a unique status—one of the three major laws of Judaism—so that we are reminded: better to die than to destroy your own self.

13

The Torah Source
for Idolatry
and Martyrdom

ow do we know? A Jew must always ask not what do you think, but how do you know. It isn't enough to have an opinion, one must back it up with a biblical source. An opinion is right not because I think it is, but because God said so.

When the rabbis in the house of Nitzeh in the city of Lod gathered in the attic and voted on the categories demanding their readiness for martyrdom, they did not trade viewpoints, but rather texts.

Let us follow them to determine how they concluded that these three mitzvot were in fact different than all the others. Where does the Torah itself teach us that, although normally to choose death over transgression is suicide, in these three instances it is saintliness?

The source for idolatry offers us an insight into a major prayer of Judaism:

We have learned, Rabbi Eliezer says, "You shall love the Lord your God with all your heart [*levavkha*] and with all your soul [*nafshekha*] and with all your might [*meodekha*] (Deuteronomy 6:15). If it says "with all your soul," why does it say "with all your might"? And if it says "with all your might," why does it say "with all your soul"? If there be a person whose body is dearer to him than his wealth, therefore it says "with all your soul." If there is a person whose money is dearer to him than his body, therefore it says "with all your might." [*Sanhedrin* 74a]

Before we can analyze the talmudic text properly, it becomes evident that the translation of *ve-khol meodekha* as "with all your might" is not what the Sages meant. Indeed, "might" has nothing to do either with the context or the root of the Hebrew word. Furthermore, if we are given degrees of love necessary for our relationship with God and are told on the second level "with all your soul," meaning unto death, what room would there subsequently be to be told "and with all your might"?

What does *meodekha* refer to? "If there is a person whose wealth is dearer to him than his body—therefore it says *ve-khol meodekha.*" *Meod* in Hebrew means very, excessive. Wealth is excess. The Talmud perceived a remarkable series of steps implicit in the love relationship between the Jew and God.

The Problem of "And Thou Shalt Love"

Jewish philosophers long ago recognized the difficulty posed by the vaguely worded commandment "And thou shalt love." It was not simply the poet E. B. Browning who asked, "How do I love thee, let me count the ways." Love, after all, is an emotion, Judaism is concerned, as we have indicated, with Halakhah, a way of life, with deed and with action. What should the practical response to the command "And you shall love the Lord, your God" be?

The text itself defines it by means of three phrases. Three, of course, is a significant number in Judaism, as we are taught at the conclusion of the Hagadah in the famous prayer linking major numbers to basic concepts. "Who knows one?" asks the text, and responds, "I know one. One is our God in the heavens and on earth." One always stands for the Almighty. The number two is associated with the tablets on which the Decalogue was given; the number three with our ancestors Abraham, Isaac, and Jacob. It is indeed striking that Rabbi Ya'aqov Ben Asher (1270–1340), the biblical commentator known as *Ba'al HaTurim,* suggests that the very word *VeAHaVTa* (that you shall love), with its letters re-arranged, spells the Hebrew word HaAVoT—the Fathers.

ואהבת = האבות

Hence, the Hebrew command contains the solution to the problem of its vagueness. How shall you love? Precisely because the mitzvah is unclear, God gave us three paradigms, or Patriarchs, to define the ideal love relationship. It is to them that the three phrases apply, in proper sequence. "With all your heart" was Abraham. "With all your soul" was Isaac. "With all your wealth" was Jacob.

The Love of Abraham

The prayers a Jew recites every morning offer a brief review of Jewish history. We begin by quoting a section from Nehemiah (9:6–7), in which he recounts the founding of our faith with the story of Abraham. "You are the Lord alone. You created the Heavens and the Heavens of Heavens and all their hosts, the earth and all that is upon it, the seas and everything that is in them. And You bring life to all and the hosts of the Heavens bow to you. You are the Lord, God, who chose Avram and took him out of Ur Kasdim, made his name Avraham. And You found his heart faithful before you."

When the Bible chooses to identify Abraham's greatest virtue, the unique trait that earned him the name change from Avram to Avraham (the latter defining his mission as the father of many nations), the phrase is "And You found his heart faithful [ne'eman] before You." For the heart is the source of faith. The Bible constantly relates the two: *lev ne'eman,* a faithful heart.

Abraham was the one who grew up in the home of Terah, the idol maker. He witnessed paganism first hand. Yet he destroyed the idols of his father and traveled from place to place to bring personal witness to the reality of monotheism.

To worship God and to love Him, it is obvious one must first believe in Him fully. It is not enough to suggest that there may be a God. Total commitment demands unwavering certainty. If you

proclaim "Hear O Israel, the Lord our God, the Lord is One,"
then you must love Him "with all your heart." What is involved?
A love as powerful as the one shown by the Patriarchs. The first
one, Abraham, is the living illustration of the command to love
God "with all your heart."

The Love of Isaac

There are illustrations in biblical books of the Binding of Isaac,
the scene in which Abraham brings Isaac to be sacrificed on
Mount Moriah. Some picture an old man carrying an infant in his
arms to be brought up for slaughter. That image is not true. Our
Sages relate that Isaac was 37 years old when that incident took
place. Hence, it was not simply Abraham who was tested. Isaac
was already a thinking adult capable of choosing his actions; Isaac
knew that he was being taken to serve as a personal sacrifice to
God. When the Torah tells us "And the two of them walked
together," the implication is they walked as one, in mutual recognition of what would transpire, both equally prepared for acceptance of the incomprehensible commandment, "And bring him up
there as a sacrifice."

True, the Torah introduces this story with the words "And it
came to pass after these things that God did prove Abraham"
(Genesis 22:1). Why call it "The Test of Abraham" if Isaac was the
one who knowingly and willingly would have to offer his own life?
The answer is a profound and yet simple truth: Jewish thought
teaches that it is a far greater test to force Abraham to kill than to
ask Isaac to be killed. Isaac would die once. Abraham, had he been
allowed to carry out the commandment, would have subsequently
spent a lifetime of everlasting pain, for which death would have
been a far preferable alternative.

Be that as it may, it was still Isaac who had to be prepared to
die. He was ready to do so. Thus, in the biblical sequence illustrating the Patriarch's love of God, if Abraham was able to believe
with his entire heart, then the next step is a love "with all your
soul," i.e., a readiness to offer one's soul back to the One Who
gave it. Simply put: if you believe in something fully, you must be
prepared to die for it.

When Rabbi Akiva, one of the Ten Martyrs selected by Rome

for public execution, knew that he faced his last moments on earth, he smiled even while enduring the most painful torture. When his students asked him how he could possibly accept his affliction in such manner, he said, "I rejoice because all my life I recited the words *U-vekhol nafshekha* [with all your soul] and could not be certain if ever the time came for me to demonstrate my willingness to fulfill them, that I would be able to do so. I thank God that I have found within myself the spiritual power to demonstrate my love for God, with all my soul." With his last breath, Rabbi Akiva recited the *Shema,* and at the word *Eḥad* (one) his soul left the earthly sphere to be rejoined with the Creator.

The Love of Jacob

Believe in Him. Be prepared to die for Him.
And what else?

Jacob made a great discovery. According to our Sages it happened on Mount Moriah, the very spot on which the Temple would eventually be built.

Jacob made the discovery when he fled from home in fear of his brother Esau, who had threatened to slay him.

> Jacob went out from Beersheba and went toward Haran. And he lighted upon the place and tarried there all night because the sun was set; and he took one of the stones of the place and put it under his head and laid down in that place to sleep. And he dreamed, and behold a ladder was set up on earth, and the top of it reached to Heaven; and behold the angels of God ascending and descending on it. [Genesis 28:10–12]

What is the meaning of that remarkable dream of a ladder, a ladder rooted in the earth, and its top reaching to the Heavens? The Baal HaTurim suggests a fascinating correspondence in the numerical value of the word for "ladder" in Hebrew, SuLaM [סלם, ס (Samekh) = 60, ל (Lamed) = 30, מ (Mem) = 40 = 130]. Two other Hebrew words have precisely this total. MaMoN [ממן, מ (Mem) = 40 × 2 = 80, נ (Nun) = 50 = 130], wealth and SiYNaiY [סיני, ס (Samekh) = 60, י (Yod) = 10, נ (Nun) = 50, י (Yod) = 10 = 130]. What a remarkable trilogy. What could they possibly have in common?

The answer is the symbolic content of the dream. On the very spot that would one day become the site of the Holy Temple, Jacob was taught that the essence of Judaism is the merging of earth and Heaven. Humanity's role is not, as in Christianity, to forsake this world. "My Kingdom is not of this world" is the teaching of Jesus. Judaism commands that it is our role rather to sanctify the world. A man does not become a saint if he takes a vow of poverty. He becomes holy if he uses his wealth to enhance and sanctify the presence of God on earth. The angels of God ascend and descend the ladder—the very ladder numerically equivalent to wealth and to Sinai itself. For Sinai means to find a way in which to bring the angels of God up and down in a mutual interchange between earth and Heaven.

What is money, holy or profane? The Midrash gives us the answer in the explication of the verse concerning God's commandment to Moses: "This they shall give, everyone that passeth among them that are numbered, half a sheqel, after the sheqel of the Sanctuary" (Exodus 30:13). God stressed *this* they shall give, illustrating with the actual coin, because Moses was baffled by a command he did not understand. Yet what was so difficult about that commandment? Why did it cause confusion in Moses' mind? Our Sages explain that what Moses could not grasp is that for the construction of the Sanctuary itself, God commanded something as seemingly secular as half a sheqel. How could money be introduced into the Holy of Holies?

"God then showed him His sheqel, a coin of fire." What does the Midrash mean? How can a coin of fire solve a problem? And did Moses have to be shown the picture of a coin in order to know what God was talking about?

The explanation is profound. If you, Moses, cannot believe in the relevance of a coin, then let me illustrate with a coin of fire. Fire is to be the symbol of money. Fire destroys, but it also creates. Fire may burn, but it can also cook, warm, and serve the most beneficial purposes. So, too, is wealth. Precisely because it has this quality, it becomes doubly holy. When we choose to use a potentially destructive object in a positive and productive manner, we have learned the secret of true holiness.

It is a concept we find similarly expressed through a symbol used on the High Holy days. Why is the shofar the vehicle for bringing us to repentance? What is there about the horn of an animal that may be linked to spiritual rebirth? The horn is one of the four major causes of damage produced by animals. We, too, may at times allow ourselves to be possessed by our animalistic nature, but the shofar tells us to take the potentially destructive horn and transform it, thereby to become holy.

Hasidim have suggested that the word for coin, MaTBeiA (מַטְבֵּעַ), may be read in Hebrew as MiTeVA (מִטֶּבַע), which means nature. It is the world around us. When God told Moses "Take a coin of fire," He taught us that we may find opportunities for great holiness from and in the world about us. Like fire, a coin may be creative or destructive. The potential for both exists; the choice is in our hands.

Symbolically, Jacob's dream is also about Sinai and the proper use of material blessings. The metaphor of the ladder at Mount Moriah unites these themes. The Christian crucifies the flesh in order to rise above it. The Jew sanctifies the flesh in order to elevate it. The Christian, at least in theory, condemns wealth and takes a vow of poverty. The Jew controls wealth and seeks to utilize it in a way that will make the world a better place by spreading the message of Sinai.

Jacob had the dream and immediately after that: "And Jacob vowed a vow saying, 'If God will be with me and will keep me in this way that I go, and will give me bread to eat and raiment to put on, so that I come back to my father's house in peace, then shall the Lord be my God; and the stone which I have set up for a pillow shall be God's house, and of all that Thou shalt give me I will surely give the tenth unto Thee'" (Genesis 28:20–22).

The concept of tithing (ma'aser) comes from Jacob. It appears immediately after he had the vision of the ladder. Why would he speak of something as mundane as money immediately after experiencing the most sacred vision of his life? Because that very vision enabled him to comprehend that one can serve God and one must serve God even "with all your wealth."

Money should not be renounced. It should be used correctly. Wealth is not to be rejected; rather, it should be used for its capacity to strengthen God's presence.

All this Jacob understood. All this is the necessary third step in the proper expression of love between humankind and God. A Jew must love God with a full heart, be prepared to die for Him, and even be willing to live for Him. The greatest challenge of all is to give not only of one's self, but even of one's possessions.

The Three Love Mitzvot

In the *Shema,* the very same paragraph that commands love and illustrates it with three phrases corresponding to the Patriarchs, concludes by demanding we perform a number of specific mitzvot:

וקשרתם לאות על־ידך והיו לטטפת בין עיניך: וכתבתם על־מזוזת ביתך ובשעריך:

"And thou shalt bind them for a sign upon thy hand and they shall be for frontlets between thine eyes and thou shalt write them upon the doorposts of thy house and upon thy gates" (Deuteronomy 6:8–9). If we love God we will fulfill these laws. How many are there? We might be tempted at first glance to say two: phylacteries (*tefilin*) and mezuzah. Yet careful reading indicates that there are in fact three, because the phylacteries are divided into two parts. There is the part placed on the head and the other placed on the hand. They are in fact viewed as separate commandments. If one cannot for some reason put on the *tefilin* for the hand, one must nevertheless use the one for the head.

The very same passage that teaches us we must love God in three ways concludes with the requirement for three rituals. Why three? And why precisely these three? Because it becomes obvious that these three are directly linked to the three methods of indicating one's love and allegiance to God.

"And thou shalt bind them for a sign upon thy hand." The Talmud deduces that the hand meant is the left one. And exactly where is the placement to be? Again, tradition teaches us, "on your hand opposite the heart" (*keneged ha-lev*). Indeed, was not the first of the three love expressions "with all your heart"?

First we bind a small box, halakhically called a *bayit* (house)—a metaphor for the site where family love is expressed—opposite the heart. It is the first step.

Second, another box is attached to the forehead: "And they shall be for frontlets between thine eyes." This corresponds to the command to love God, "with all your soul," not simply to believe but even to die for one's object of love.

The phylacteries for the head are not placed directly between the eyes. That would have been on the bridge of the nose. The Oral Law, however, teaches us that the proper place is in fact on the hairline between the eyes, i.e., positioned in the center, moving upwards from the point of the bridge of the nose to the top of the skull. It is halakhically referred to as the place where, in an infant, we can feel the throbbing and movements of the brain (*maqom she-moho shel tinok rofes bo*).

How do we know that the words *bein einekha* do not actually mean "between the eyes"? The Sages employ a method of analogy known as *gezerah shavah*, a principle allowing us to understand the true meaning of the text in one place from its amplification in another. The phrase "between your eyes" does appear elsewhere in the Torah. It is in connection with a law concerning an improper response to death.

"Ye are the children of the Lord, your God. Ye shall not cut yourselves, nor make any baldness between your eyes for the dead" (Deuteronomy 14:1). Pagans would rip out their hair when they were confronted with the incomprehensible tragedy of death. To this very day, tearing one's hair at the roots is symbolic language for total frustration. If something makes no sense and there's nothing we can do about it, ripping the hair from our head gives vent to our impotence and intellectual limitations.

Jews are not permitted to rip the hair from their head. To do so would mean a surrender to pessimism, anger, and finally a disagreement with the will of God. "Ye are the children of the Lord, your God." A child must understand that parents never willingly harm their children. Death may be incomprehensible to us. But if you believe that you are children of the Lord, then He must surely love us. He is wiser. And on that very spot where our brain first begins to indicate its movement, and where human capacity for thought is demonstrated, we place a symbol of God's presence to show that God is above human intelligence. For that reason, on the very place where pagans rip out their hair as a sign of both frustration and condemnation, the Jew places his phylacteries in recognition of a Superior Intelligence who rules the world.

There is nothing more incomprehensible than the moment of death. It is incomprehensible when God tells Abraham to take Isaac and offer him as a sacrifice. It is incomprehensible that Rabbi Akiva faced torture and death at the hands of the Romans. And yet "with all your soul" means that a Jew must be prepared to demonstrate a love for God even in the most incomprehensible way of all, by giving up one's very soul.

"With all your soul" really means "even when it doesn't make sense, even onto death." The phylacteries placed upon the head make the same statement. We thereby declare that God is wiser than we are, that whatever happens has a purpose.

"And thou shalt write them upon the doorposts of thy house and upon thy gates." A house is not only a man's castle, it is the most potent external definition of his wealth. We may live in a slum or a suburb. We may own a hut or a mansion, a hovel or an estate. Whatever we have as our haven must be marked by a mezuzah at its portal. A mezuzah makes a powerful statement. Not only myself, but everything I own, is subservient to God. In the final analysis everything really comes from Him.

If phylacteries demonstrate the allegiance of my heart and my mind, my readiness to believe and even to die, then the mezuzah visibly illustrates my third major commitment, "with all your wealth."

The three ways to love God are suggested paradigmatically by the three Patriarchs. They are more clearly given halakhic form by the three mitzvot that conclude the "love" paragraph: phylacteries of the hand, of the head, and the mezuzah.

Which Is the Source for Martyrdom?

We are now prepared to analyze the laws of martyrdom, determined in Lod by talmudic sages centuries ago, more carefully.

Which phrase of the three—"with all your heart, with all your soul, with all your wealth,"—is significant for the rabbis sitting in the attic in Lod and trying to determine the mitzvot for which one must be prepared to give up one's life? Clearly, the only one of the three is "with all your soul."

Why didn't the Talmud simply quote this phrase to show that there are times when we must be ready to die? Why did the Talmud continue with a discussion including "with all your wealth"?

The Talmud was obviously troubled by the sequence that seems to give the lie to our interpretation of "with all your soul." If, in fact, the second phrase teaches us that we must be ready to die for our belief in God, how could there conceivably be a third? What more need be added to convey the extent of our commitment? If one has to die for God, is it conceivable that yet another commandment is required to take it further?

The talmudic answer recalls the most famous laugh ever recorded in the history of radio. When the robber breaks into the home of Jack Benny and confronts him with the line "Your money or your life!" the response is a considered silence—silence that leads the audience to laughter progressively intensifying as recognition dawns that Jack Benny could not make up his mind which one to choose. It is laughter that confronts a profound psychological truth. There are in fact people ready to die for a cause, but not to live for it. There are people who treat their money with more care than they treat their health, their bodies, or their life itself.

I will never forget the emotional high of the days in 1967 when Israel fought for survival and then succeeded in retaking Jerusalem. Members of my congregation came to me in the opening days of the Six Day War and begged to be allowed to find some way to join the Israeli Army. They were ready, they told me, to die for our people. I pointed out that untrained civilians could not fight in the war. They could, however, give financial support. They could give of their wealth, if not their bodies. Strangely enough, that was more difficult to achieve. The very people who had been willing to offer their all with regard to life were not prepared to sacrifice financially in a significantly comparable manner.

Can *bekhol nafshekha* really mean "with all your soul," i.e., unto death, if there is still a phrase after it? Yes, indeed, replies the Talmud. "If there is a person whose body is dearer to him than his wealth, therefore it says 'with all your soul.' If there is a person whose wealth is dearer to him than his body, therefore it says 'with all your wealth.'" Both phrases are necessary in addition to "with all your heart," the commandment for total belief.

Belief alone is insufficient. One may believe in many things with "all one's heart" and not be affected by that belief in the slightest. Belief requires application not simply in one area, but in two. Be prepared even to die for God. More importantly, be prepared to live for your faith with all your possessions.

But Why Idolatry?

One thing remains difficult in our analysis. The biblical text, it is true, has now spoken clearly to us, demanding readiness even to die. But the Talmud has taken that to apply only in one specific situation. The text is not used to demand martyrdom for every mitzvah. We still maintain the operative relevance of the biblical commandment "you shall live by them, and you shall not die through them" for the majority of the commandments.

What made the rabbis in Lod relate the phrase "with all your soul" to idolatry? How can we be sure that if the Torah mandates martyrdom, it is to prevent our worshiping other gods? Rashi clarifies this by relating the phrase to its specific context. "With all your soul" is a followup to "You shall love the Lord, your God." Love implies faithfulness. As Rashi writes: "And you shall love the Lord, your God," this means that you not exchange Him for idols.

"With all your soul" is associated with this total commitment to God, to the exclusion of other gods. Be prepared to die so that you properly fulfill love of the Lord, your God. Therein lies the Torah source for the first of three major laws declaring that it is better to be killed than to transgress.

"Hear O Israel, the Lord Our God, the Lord is One." That phrase cannot remain a mere verbal affirmation. It is always followed by a magnificent paragraph explaining the deed implicit in the creed. To love God is to imitate Abraham, Isaac, and Jacob. It is to put on the phylacteries of the hand, the phylacteries of the head, and to attach the mezuzah to the doorpost. It is a total commitment of belief, a willingness to offer our wealth and possessions, and a readiness to give up our lives rather than forsake our Lord.

14

The Torah Source
for Immorality
and Martyrdom

artyrdom is not to be taken for granted. Quite the reverse. Without a specific exclusion, the prohibition of idolatry would have been treated like any of the other mitzvot bounded by the law of "and you shall live by them, and you shall not be required to die through them." "With all your soul" taught us, however, that with regard to the love of God, death is preferable to a life desecrated by service to a false deity.

But the rabbis in the attic in Lod taught us there were two other mitzvot for which one must die, rather than transgress. How did the Sages know that sexual immorality and murder also belong to this distinctive grouping requiring martyrdom?

These two are, in fact, linked in a most remarkable manner. The Torah itself makes clear that they share a halakhic affinity. If we are to comprehend the text requiring one to choose martyrdom over sexual immorality, we must acquaint ourselves with a biblical chapter of law as well as a concept of Torah analysis known as the *heqesh*.

The Difference between Rape and Seduction

In Deuteronomy (22:23–27) we are presented with two cases of

sexual crimes that differ fundamentally with respect to the consequences for the woman involved. They constitute the master cases
of biblical law for both seduction and rape. The first case reads as
follows:

> If there be a damsel [*na'arah*] that is a virgin betrothed unto a man
> and the man find her in the city and lie with her, then ye shall bring
> them both out onto the gate of that city and ye shall stone them
> with stones that they die; the damsel, because she cried not, being in
> the city; and the man, because he hath humbled his neighbor's wife;
> so thou shalt put away the evil from the midst of thee. [Deuteron-
> omy 22:23–25]

The Talmud and Oral Law have amplified the case and clarified its application. Let us summarize some of the most salient
points. "If there be a damsel"—the Hebrew term *na'arah* alludes
to a minimum age requirement. The word *qetanah* refers to a
minor, a girl below the age of twelve who cannot be held accountable for her actions owing to her immaturity. As a first prerequisite
for the death penalty that follows, the woman involved must be
one who by virtue of her maturity can be held accountable for her
transgressions.

Second, although adultery is, of course, a sin in any situation,
the penalty for sexual contact with a betrothed virgin is stoning—
the severest of all the four death penalties—because the woman
has had her very first sexual experience with someone other than
the man to whom she is betrothed and has professed fidelity. To
betray one's mate at the very start of a marriage is enough to
render the standard punishment for adultery, strangulation, insufficient. The couple is therefore stoned to death.

The translation of *meorasah* as "betrothed" suffers because
there is in fact no proper English word to convey the religious
standard involved. An explanation is in order. Jewish marriage
consists of two stages, *erusin* and *nisuin*. We may, for the purpose
of proceeding, do our best to distinguish between the two by trans-
lating *erusin* as betrothal and *nisuin* as marriage. In fact, however,
erusin means far more than the English equivalent, engagement.
Engagement, which serves as a prelude to marriage in today's
society, merely reflects a public announcement of a decision that

will become formalized and effective at a later date. Those engaged may still "break off" without any legal consequences. There may be emotional pain, but it will be coupled with thanksgiving for the knowledge that "at least they weren't married yet."

Erusin, however, creates a status of marriage with but one qualification. The *erusin* formally and legally binds the future bride and groom. The "betrothed" woman is halakhically deemed an *eshet ish* ("wife of man"). Furthermore, *erusin* can only be dissolved through divorce. What is the one restriction that only *nisuin* removes for the union to be complete? The *erusin,* also known as *qidushin* (sanctification or consecration), declares man and woman to be husband and wife for everything except sexual union. They are married, but they may not cohabit. Indeed, in the days of the Talmud, there was a "waiting period" between *erusin* and *nisuin,* which usually lasted for approximately one year.

At first glance, one is perturbed by this peculiar law. How can one call them husband and wife and yet not allow sexual activity? How can we speak of marriage without sex? Isn't the very purpose of a wedding permissibility for intercourse? How can Jewish law say they are wed while prohibiting sexual consummation?

Precisely through this preparatory period of *erusin,* the Torah stresses that marriage is more than sex, that before man and woman unite physically, they require a period of time when they learn the emotional components of togetherness. They learn to merge their minds and souls before they allow their bodies to express this linkage of persons. If in contemporary society it is normative that men and women mate before they really know each other and use sex as a prelude to further acquaintanceship, Jewish law requires precisely the reverse. How fascinating that the very first time sex is alluded to in the Torah, it is by way of the word *Yada,* "he knew." "And the man knew Eve, his wife" (Genesis 4:1). It is only when one truly knows one's mate that sex has meaning. The sexual act thus becomes the ultimate and final knowing of another human being. In ancient society where dating was unknown, *erusin* preceded *nisuin.* Getting to know the other person as an individual, before initiating sexual contact, would ensure that we follow the sequence implicit in the Seven Blessings recited under the canopy, where we bless bride and groom as "friends and lovers" (*re'im ahuvim*). First be friends and only afterward become lovers.

It is during the time of *erusin*—the courtship period when the couple is nominally married but not yet physically close—that adultery and infidelity assume the direst proportions. *Erusin* then is the third requirement, in addition to virginity and age, that will permit the law to come into effect with all of its stringency.

If the woman had sexual relations with a man other than her husband in a city, then both were stoned—the man for committing the deed and the woman for not screaming out. The Sages clarify that the word "city" is shorthand reference for a specific situation. It refers to a place where, had she screamed out, she would have been heard; her silence condemns her. Of course, even in a city there might be places where it would be clear that shouting would be of no avail, screams would not be heard. In those cases, the law of "city" would obviously not apply. The text is stating that a woman who clearly cooperated in an act which, although perhaps not of her initial choosing, proved satisfactory to her, is equally culpable. Both are to be punished "so that thou shalt put away the evil from the midst of thee."

The law changes dramatically, however, if the case is not that of "city" but of "field."

> But if the man find a damsel that is betrothed in the field, and the man take hold of her, and lie with her, then the man only that lay with her shall die. But unto the damsel thou shalt do nothing; there is in the damsel no sin worthy of death; for as when a man riseth against his neighbor, and slayeth him, even so is this matter. For he found her in the field; the betrothed damsel cried, and there was none to save her. [Deuteronomy 22:25–27]

In the field the girl is not liable. She did scream or she may not have screamed. Perhaps there was even no point in her screaming, for she knew at the outset that none would hear her, no one would be able to come to her aid. She is presumed innocent until proven guilty. Nor do we assume that rape in every instance implies a stigma upon a woman who must have dressed provocatively, acted suggestively, flirted, inspired, and flaunted so that in fact "she was really asking for it." We do not ever suggest that if a man was murdered he was "clearly asking for it." Rape is compared to murder. "For as when a man riseth against his neighbor, and slayeth him, even so is this matter."

The Meaning of *Heqesh*

The Torah not only taught us a law but included within it a legal comparison. That comparison has a name and serves a specific halakhic function. God is not simply suggesting that rape is "like murder" in some abstract way. When two cases are linked in such a manner—"for as this, so is that"—this is legally termed *heqesh* and tradition teaches us that its function is to create a double comparison. This means that each one of these two cases already has a "known" halakhic ruling; but because of the *heqesh,* the halakhah of one is transferred to the other.

The Talmud in *Sanhedrin* amplifies: "The case of murder is compared to the betrothed maiden, for just as the betrothed maiden is given over to be saved by his soul, so, too, is the murderer given over to be saved by his soul." What is the meaning of that strange phrase "given over to be saved by his soul"? Halakhically it refers to the right given to others to kill the assailant if that proves to be the only effective way to prevent the crime.

This is a "known" in the case of the betrothed maiden. "The betrothed damsel cried and there was none to save her." The implication is: If there was someone to save her, the witness had an obligation to do so. But how? Is the Torah implying that the witness do no more than verbally suggest that the rapist not continue? Of course that is absurd. In suggesting that the woman had "none to save her," the implication is that any witness to the scene is obligated to intervene, and if the only effective mode of intervention is slaying the assailant, then that, too, is permissible.

We are permitted to save her "with his soul," i.e., by taking his life. The Tosafists on this passage in the Talmud are struck, however, by a seeming grammatic inconsistency. To properly express this thought, the text should have read "to save *her* with his soul," i.e., by taking his life. The text, in fact, states that permission is granted "to save *him*." Why? He, the rapist, is the one we have permission to kill before he acts on his desire. In a profound theological and ethical comment, the Tosafists suggest that permission is given to save the rapist's soul by slaying him before he becomes guilty of committing the crime. Of course we protect her from being raped. But even more significant, we protect his soul from violating the law that touches upon the very "image of God" in which human beings are created.

This, therefore, is the first step of the *heqesh* equation. The law deduced from "and there was none to save her," granting the right for intervention by any spectator, is thus transferred to the case of a murderer. If one sees someone about to slay an innocent person, the halakhah is the same. Stop him or her at all costs, even if you must take the potential assailant's life. The right is given to save with the taking of life.

But a *heqesh* always has an arrow pointing in both directions. That is to say, the transference of law must go both from Case A to Case B and from Case B to Case A. What does murder have to teach us concerning the case of the betrothed maiden?

The Talmud draws the following analogy: Just as in the case of murder we know the law teaches "better to be killed than to transgress," so, too, in the case of the betrothed maiden, it is better to be killed than to transgress. Hence, we deduce that one must choose martyrdom over sexual immorality by comparing the latter to murder. The second in the series of three codified by our Sages in Lod has as its source the third, which leaves us with the obvious question immediately asked by the Talmud: "and murder itself how do we know?" In other words, what is the biblical source that teaches us it is better to be killed than to kill an innocent other? The answer deserves a section to itself.

15

The Torah Source
for Murder
and Martyrdom

e have made much of the fact that law in Judaism must come from God. Otherwise it represents nothing other than our own prejudices. People can rationalize almost anything, which is why divine legislation is so crucial. It transcends the limitations of our own perceptions. For every law we have therefore always asked, what is the biblical source? Where did God tell us it is so?

In that light the final response of the Talmud to the question of how the Sages in the attic in Lod knew that murder, too, is part of this unique trilogy, seems most remarkable.

"Murder itself, how do we know [that it, too, is a case of 'better to be killed than to transgress']. It is logical. A man came before Rabah and said to him, 'The master of my estate told me, "Go and kill so and so and if not I will kill you."' He [Rabah] said to him, "Let him rather slay you than that you should commit murder; who knows that your blood is redder? Perhaps his blood is redder."' You have no right to murder him to save yourself; his life is no less valuable than your own."

What is the meaning of the phrase "It is logical"? So many things may be logical and yet they do not become law. In this instance in particular, we are already dealing with a clearly stated law: "And you shall live by them, and you shall not be required to die through them." Why shall I not murder in order to live? Have I not been taught that life, my continued existence, is my first priority?

The answer is simple. It is logical not that we create a new law, but rather that we have no right to change an existing one. It is logical because the Torah has already commanded us, "Thou shalt not murder." To seek to live at the expense of another is to declare dramatically that "Thou shalt not murder" does not apply in this instance because my life is at stake, and God could not have wanted me to observe the restriction against murder if my existence is imperiled. I know how much God treasures life. Therefore, let me murder *him* so that *I* live. That line of thinking is logically absurd. Who is to say, "Your blood is redder than his"? What entitles you to commit a crime in order that your life be the one spared rather than that of another human being? Are you permitted a value judgment with regard to the worth of human existence?

All Men Are Created Equal

Note carefully how the law is phrased: "Who is to say that your blood is redder than his? Perhaps the blood of that person is redder." Perhaps? Why not weigh the worthiness of their respective lives and come to a conclusion based on the specifics of the situation? Is one a man, the other a woman? Is one a Sage, the other an ignoramus? Is one young, the other old? Surely there must be standards. Certainly the law ought to have hundreds of qualifications.

The truth is there are no such standards. Never may someone murder another human being. Who says your blood is redder? Life is given by God and every person on this earth has a reason for being. No one may judge the relative worth of another's existence. "All men are created equal" is a halakhic principle that finds fullest expression in this law. Kill another person—a fool, an old man about to die anyway, a sick or poor person whose life in any event is filled with pain and suffering. Kill them and you will be spared. Kill them so that you may live.

No. The source? It is *logical* for a Jew to conclude, based on every value that comes to us from the totality of Torah, that

"Thou shalt not murder" cannot be compromised so as to transfer the right to life from one human being to another.

But what about the classic case concerning the "two men in the desert"? The Talmud in *Sanhedrin* seems to have clearly stated that if a choice of life is to be made, I have no right to pick my own. Yet this seems to contradict the famous passage in *Baba Meẓia* (62a), where the conclusion of the Sages suggests that my life takes precedence.

> If two are traveling on a journey [far from civilization], and one has a pitcher of water, if both drink, they will [both] die, but if one only drinks, he can reach civilization.—The son of Patura taught: It is better that both shall drink and die, rather than that one should behold his companion's death. Until Rabbi Akiva came and taught: "that thy brother may live with thee:" thy life takes precedence over his life. [With "thee" implies that your life take first place, but that the other also has a right to life after yours is assured.]

The case is often quoted as a controversy between our Sages. A careful reading, however, shows that at the end of the matter there is no disagreement. The son of Peturah is quoted as suggesting "Let them both share and drink so that one not be forced to see the death of the other." This view prevailed "*until* Rabbi Akiva came." This means the view propounded by the son of Peturah was only accepted until he, as well as the other Sages, heard Rabbi Akiva's opinion. It was then that unanimity prevailed. Rabbi Akiva won the day. As noble as it may appear for two people to share the one flask and, in an act of supreme love, avoid a decision that would allow only one of them to live, the truth is that would spell mutual suicide.

"And your brother shall live with you" is the operative halakhic text. We do have obligations to our brothers, but they stem from an initial responsibility to ourselves: "Your life takes precedence."

Perhaps Rabbi Akiva had in mind the phrase that he believed contained the single most important concept of the Torah: "And you shall love your neighbor as yourself." Contemporary psychologists have spoken of the need for an appreciation of self as a precondition for love of others. It has been suggested that violence and hatred are manifestations of an inability to come to terms with oneself. Indeed, the precondition for love of others is love of self. The Bible is obviously telling us that without self-love one cannot come to care and show concern for other people.

Love in that connection is an all-encompassing law. "And your brother shall live with you" (*ve-hai ahikha imokh*) is more specific, since it mandates assistance to another as well as self-preservation. The law does not categorically state that you shall cause your brother to live, but that your brother shall live *with you*. Proper priorities dictate that you must first ensure your own survival and then take care of others in a similar manner.

This then is the conclusion of the Talmud in *Baba Mezia*. The man with the flask of water is to drink it and save himself, although the other person will then surely die.

Should one not ask the question that would appear to contradict this ruling? How could he choose his own life over his neighbor's? Who is to say his blood is redder? Perhaps the blood of his friend is redder! The case of the two men in the desert suggests that you come first. The case of the man commanded to murder teaches that the other comes first.

What is the resolution of this apparent contradiction of law? The resolution, in reality, is not difficult to grasp. The two cases are totally dissimilar, because they deal with different problems. In the story of the two men in the desert, no crime will actively be committed by either party. The question merely revolves around who is permitted to drink the water that ensures survival. The answer: If the water belongs to you, then God has placed means for life at your disposal. Drink it and save yourself. Suicide is forbidden. Even if the other person will surely die? He may die at the hands of God. I will not have killed him. This necessitates a passive acceptance of the will of God rather than an active violation of law that I am duty-bound to observe at all times and in all situations.

"Thou shalt not murder" is God's decree. Shall I actively transgress in order to save my life? Rashi brilliantly explains the logic used by the Talmud: "It is logical that one is forbidden to destroy another innocent life where there would be two wrongs committed, loss of life and sin [murder], for the sake of preserving one's own life, in which case there is only one [wrong], i.e., loss of life, but one will not actively transgress. For when did the Torah tell us to transgress laws because of the principle 'You shall live by them'? Only because the soul of a human being is dear in His eyes, and here in the case of murder; since in any event there is loss of life, why would it be permissible to transgress? Who knows whether his soul is dearer to his Creator than the soul of his friend? Therefore the word of the Almighty is not given to be negated."

Rashi has explained the logic of the law with almost mathematical precision: "I am threatened with death or I must murder another innocent human being. One death will result in either event. If I choose to be victim rather than murderer, my life is taken but I have not added the commission of a terrible crime to my soul. However, if I choose to save my own life, then again another innocent person dies and, added thereto, is my act of murder. Two tragedies are worse than one. It is far better for me to die in purity."

To us, the reasoning is so logical and irrefutable that it has become part of our national psyche and ingrained within our people. Even those not known particularly for religious piety express the concept, probably without even being aware of its talmudic source.

How moved the world was when Golda Meir summed up her feelings in the aftermath of the wars for Israel's survival: "We can forgive the Arabs almost everything. We can even forgive them for killing our children. We cannot forgive them, however, for turning our children into killers."

Better to be killed than to kill.

It is a concept that serves our Sages as the explanation of a seemingly strange redundancy in the Torah. Jacob knew (Genesis 32) that his brother Esau was coming toward him with four hundred men. He feared for his life. The last time they had met, Esau threatened him and told him that as soon as their father would be out of the way, he would slay him. The meeting was imminent. "Then Jacob was greatly afraid [va-yira] and was distressed" [va-yeizer lo] (Genesis 32:8). In terms of sequence, the second word is always more significant than the first. "Distressed" conveys a higher level of fear. What were these two fears? And why was the second stronger than the first?

Rashi quotes the Midrash. "He was afraid [*va-yira*] lest he be killed" and "He was sorely distressed [*va-yeizer lo*] that perhaps he be forced to become a killer."

One of the most moving tales from the Holocaust records the last words of a rabbi before he was brutally slain by a Nazi guard. A survivor witnessed the scene. The Nazi had randomly selected the rabbi for extermination. He pointed his rifle at him and, as he did so, the rabbi began to mutter something under his breath. For whatever reason, we will never know why, the Nazi was intrigued and asked, "Jew, what are you saying?" The rabbi responded, "I am reciting a blessing." What kind of blessing, wondered the Nazi, would the rabbi be uttering moments before his death? "What are you thanking God for now that you know you have but a few seconds to live?"

"I am reciting the blessing, 'I thank you, O Lord, for not having made me a *goy,* a heathen.' I cannot fully express my gratitude to the Almighty that He has made me, *me,* and not *you;* that I have maintained my dignity as a human being and that I am not the beast that you, the German, have become. I will be murdered but I have not become a murderer."

Presented with the choice, it is self-evident that, if between two people one must die no matter what, I as a Jew will not compound the crime by committing the foul deed.

The lyrics of the famous song, *El Condor Pasa,* are not in accord with what Jewish theology teaches: "I'd rather be a hammer than a nail, yes, I would, I really would, if I only could" may reflect the musings of Paul Simon. But if to be a hammer means to murder innocents and to be the nail means to die in purity, with a soul unblemished and unstained, I'd rather be a nail than a hammer and meet my Maker with a blessing on my lips, thanking Him for having allowed me to live my life as a Jew and not as a heathen.

16

But There Is
a Time to Kill

s it really always better to die than to kill?

It is time to amend the talmudic conclusion "better to be killed than to kill" to allow for three major qualifications. There are, in fact, times when we not only may kill, but we must. For what the Talmud taught us as a result of "logic" is simply that it is better to be killed than to murder an innocent person. There are those, however, who clearly demonstrate by their actions that the phrase "Who is to say your blood is redder than theirs?" does not apply.

The Case of the Break-In

In Exodus we are taught: "If a thief be found breaking in and be smitten so that he dieth, there shall be no blood guiltiness for him" (Exodus 22:1). The last three words of the verse, *ein lo damim,* literally mean "there is not to him blood." Who is the "him" referred to? Rashi, quoting the Talmud, tells us that "him" is the thief. "He has no blood" implies that he has forfeited his life. The occupant of the home has a right to slay him. The logic of the verse is as follows: This situation describes a thief breaking in by night, as opposed to the following verse preceded by the phrase "If the sun be risen upon him, then there shall be blood guiltiness for him." At night people are at home. The thief knows he may well confront the master of the house and he nonetheless proceeds. A thief also knows that people will protect their property. He is obviously prepared for this confrontation. The assumption is, therefore, that a thief breaking in at night is ready, if necessary, to kill the owner. The law therefore teaches us the all-important principle "He who comes to slay you, rise up and kill him first." Self-defense is a basic principle of Jewish law.

Christianity teaches that if someone strikes you on one cheek, you are to turn the other. Judaism says that you would in fact be inviting the second blow and incurring indirect responsibility for it. He who is about to strike you—strike him first. Such a person does not merit application of the principle "Who is to say your blood is redder than his?" Indeed, your blood *is* redder, i.e., more valuable and worthier than his. If he is ready to take an innocent life, he does not deserve it as much as you. Entering the house makes him "as good as dead."

It is only "If the sun be risen upon him, there shall be blood guiltiness for him." The commentator, Rabbi Avraham Ben David of Posquières (c. 1125–1198), known as Rabad, teaches that the difference between verse one and verse two is simply a matter of the time involved. By day a thief would assume there is no one home. Hence, he comes only to steal, not to slay. He is not prepared to murder. Consequently, we have no right to kill him. The Talmud takes the entire phrase in a metaphoric sense. If it is "clear as day" that this situation is not one in which the thief is prepared to murder, then we may likewise not do so.

However, where the thief is intent on taking your life, "He who comes to slay you, slay him first." A Jew is obliged to kill someone coming to destroy him. Not to do so is suicide, and suicide is always forbidden.

The Case of the Pursuer

Self-defense has a logical extension. After all, "All Jews are responsible, one for another." If someone comes to kill me, I must stop that person from doing so. If someone comes to kill another and I may prevent that murder, Jewish law teaches that I have an obligation to stop the pursuer.

Much has been made of the first incident recorded in the Torah concerning the life of Moses, our teacher. No sooner are we informed that he has "grown up" (*va-yigdal Mosheh*), than the text tells us, "He went out unto his brethren and looked on their burdens" (Exodus 2:11). Perhaps in the deeper sense, that is the very meaning of the phrase "grown up," for maturity implies awareness of the pain of one's brethren. It was then that he saw "an Egyptian smiting a Hebrew, one of his brethren, and he looked this way and that way and when he saw that there was no man, he smote the Egyptian and hid him in the sand" (Exodus 2:11).

This is the same Moses who would subsequently bring us the law from God at Sinai. This is the Moses who would teach us, in God's name, not to kill. There are those who have asked, how could Moses, who would proclaim to the world "Thou shalt not kill," be guilty of that same crime, and how could the Bible record the killing as the first incident bespeaking Moses' maturity?

It is futile to suggest that it was only later that Moses learned that slaying another is a sin. Even before the Covenant at Sinai, Cain was held accountable for the death of his brother.

Why then is Moses never held to task for violating a commandment that prohibits killing? Because neither Moses nor God ever taught that it is illegal to cause death in any situation. That would, in fact, be the law if the Torah had actually written "Thou shalt not kill." But it does not. In Hebrew "do not kill" would have required the phrase *lo taharog*. *Hereg* implies killing in every conceivable case. What God said at Sinai is *lo tirẓaḥ*, which properly translated means "Thou shalt not murder." The difference between killing and murder is that murder refers only to forbidden slayings. And what is forbidden is made clear by Jewish law. Murder is the slaying of the innocent. Self-defense is not included in its parameters, nor is the defense of another human being, who is about to be senselessly slain and whose death must be prevented at all costs.

What did Moses see? "An Egyptian smiting a Jew." It is the same word used in Exodus 21:12. "He that smiteth a man so that he dieth shall surely be put to death." Smiting is not simply slapping. The Egyptian who was attacking the Jew was beating him in such a manner that were Moses not to intervene, the beaten Jew would have died. Moses had to intervene in order to prevent murder. To do so was not forbidden, but a mitzvah. Moses was wise enough to understand it as an extension of self-defense. For it was part of his self that was endangered. It was a fellow human being. To prevent that Jew's death, Moses killed but did not murder. Justifiable homicide is, in fact, a valid legal category.

Milḥemet Miẓvah—The Obligatory War

If I may kill in self-defense or in defense of the other, how much more so if the "other" who is endangered is not one, but many; not a person, but rather the totality of the Jewish people.

Should Jews be prepared to go to their deaths like sheep to slaughter if there is an alternative? The Talmud is clear that not only is war at times permissible, but it may, in fact, deserve the designation milḥemet miẓvah, a war noble enough to become a divine command. War can represent the collective expression of the Jewish people prepared to fulfill the command: "He who comes to slay you, slay him first."

Of course Judaism is a religion that emphasizes the supreme value of peace. In Hebrew every greeting, both of welcome and farewell, uses the word shalom. The major prayers of our faith conclude with a request for peace. The Eighteen Benedictions conclude with the words "Blessed are You, O Lord, Who blesses His people Israel with peace." The last words of the priestly benediction encompassing the threefold ideals of our people are "May the Lord lift up His countenance upon you and grant you peace." The Kaddish, a proclamation even in the face of death of our hope for a messianic future, ends with the words "He who makes peace above, may He make peace for us and for all of our people."

Yet we make a grievous error if we assume that peace means Neville Chamberlain's "peace at all costs." Judaism is realistic enough to understand that we must love and pursue peace to such an extent that we are even prepared to fight for it if necessary.

When the United States was engaged in an unpopular war in

Vietnam, it may have been very appropriate for protesters to criticize our efforts by condemning specific moral issues. But it was misleading for many spiritual leaders to pronounce it an evil based on religious grounds. "God," they said, "is opposed to war."

That statement is simply a lie. When the Jews crossed the Red Sea successfully and witnessed the destruction of the Egyptians, they sang a song of praise to the Almighty. In it they described God in the following words: "The Lord is a man of war, the Lord is His Name" (Exodus 15:3). The greatest command incumbent upon us is *imitatio dei,* the imitation of God. The Bible commands us "Ye shall be holy, for I, the Lord your God, am holy" (Leviticus 19:2). Even as I am holy, so must you be holy. The very ways in which I express My holiness are the ways in which you are to act as well. The Midrash teaches that since the Torah begins with an act of kindness, God clothing the naked, and ends with an act of kindness, God burying the dead, then, in keeping with our primary obligation to imitate God, we are to clothe the naked and bury the dead as well.

So too, if the Lord is described as "a man of war," then we must acknowledge that, in the words of Ecclesiastes, "There is a time for peace and a time for war" (3:8).

Of course General Sherman was right when he claimed "War is hell." And that is why the verse beginning with "The Lord is a man of war" concludes, "The Lord is His Name." What purpose is served by repeating His identity? It is to make clear that, although war is a necessary evil, the worst thing that might happen to us is that we become insensitive and lose our commitment to compassion and mercy. God, as we have indicated, has two names, Adonai and Elohim. They are the two roles that He must play in His relationships with us. He is the compassionate Adonai, Lord, the appellation designating the divine quality of mercy. He is also, when necessary, Elohim, God, concerned with strict justice and law.

The Lord may be a man of war, or better, as Rashi and the commentators put it, a "master of war," that is, in charge and in control of war's outcome. But no matter what occurs, Adonai shemo, His Name remains Adonai, Lord—sensitive, loving, kind, and compassionate.

In a remarkable book published in Israel in the aftermath of the Six Day War, aptly titled *The Seventh Day,* we read of the discussions held by kibbutzniks following their encounters with killing. What upset them most was their recognition of what even a justifiable need to kill might have done to their psyche. How does one go on after having knowingly taken the life of another human being? How does one continue to be the same loving husband, father, and son as before? To kill may at times be required. To become a killer is anathema to us. Finding the proper balance is the hardest task, but it is implicit in the verse "Hashem is a man of war; Hashem is His Name."

That is why it is dangerous to oppose war on religious grounds or as a conscientious objector because of the poorly translated commandment "Thou shalt not kill." Such a stance would imply every war is immoral and that killing anybody is wrong.

What if I could have killed Hitler? How were Israelis to respond, knowing that Arabs fully intended in June 1967 to "push them into the sea," to murder men, women, and children? Is the response to be the silence of suicide? Or should it not be the biblically approved "He who comes to slay you, slay him first"?

Although the Grace after Meals ends with an allusion to peace ("God will bless His people with peace"), the penultimate phrase is "God [Adonai, the Lord of mercy] will give His people strength." Only through strength can there be peace. Only when those prepared to destroy us know we will defend ourselves is there hope that evil and genocide will not be permitted among civilized nations.

The realization that sometimes even "nice Jewish boys" have to lift up arms in self-defense and do battle against their oppressors is the key to a major story in the Torah, where a Patriarch discovered a principle that changed his name and ours.

17

Why Jacob
Became Israel

t took a traumatic moment in the life of Jacob to finally make him realize that a Jew does not live by the code of "turn the other cheek." That moment became so central to his identity that it was responsible for a biblical change of name. In the Bible, a name is far more than an appellation. It bespeaks the very mission and purpose of a human being's life. It captures his or her personality. When a person changes drastically in a way that alters his or her life completely, then we find several occasions where God Himself intervenes and proclaims, via a name change, that we now have before us a new individual.

Who was Jacob (in Hebrew, *Ya'aqov*)? Before birth, as a fetus, he already epitomized the root meaning of his name *Ya'aqov* (*a.q.v.* is the root meaning "to follow" and its derivative, *eqev,* means "heel"). "And after that came forth his brother and his hand had hold on Esau's heel and his name was called Jacob [*Ya'aqov*]" (Genesis 25:26). Holding on to the heel! Better put, being stepped upon.

The Midrash explains that Jacob actually had been conceived first. He should have been the one to leave the womb before his

brother. Technically, he was the eldest, with all the attendant privileges of primogeniture. His brother Esau, however, pushed himself
forward and forced himself over Jacob. What was Jacob to do?
After all, even in the womb, it seems Jacob knew that "nice Jewish
boys don't fight." And so he allowed himself to be stepped upon.
He was content with simply being *Ya'aqov,* trailing after his
brother, being stepped upon because a religious person has faith
that "God will take care of everything. He will right all wrongs.
There's no need to fight if one believes in a righteous God Who
rules the universe."

The twins grew up different as day and night. Jacob was righteous. Esau was a hunter, a man of the fields who would not hesitate to kill not only game, but human beings who might have stood
in his way.

Yet, "Now Isaac loved Esau because he did eat of his venison"
(Genesis 25:28). Esau was not only a hunter for food, but he
sought also to capture the heart of his father. He fooled him completely, as our Sages point out, by posing questions of a religious
nature as if he were concerned with correct halakhic procedure.
How shall I eat? How shall I bless? Isaac was blind to the truth,
even as his eyesight correspondingly failed him.

Yet the text tells us ". . . and Rebecca loved Jacob." Mother
was not taken in by this sham. She knew the truth. Jacob studied
constantly, and as the unassuming *Ya'aqov,* he was ". . . a quiet
man dwelling in tents" (Genesis 25:27).

The time came for Isaac to pass on the blessing he had received
from his father, Abraham. To whom should he promise the destiny
blessed by God? Isaac was about to make an error that would have
had the gravest consequences for all of Jewish history. He wanted
to bless Esau instead of Jacob.

Jacob was prepared not to say a word. True to his nature, he
would have allowed himself to be stepped upon because "nice
Jewish boys don't fight back. Somehow God will help."

It was only Rebecca, his mother, who pushed him to action so
that the tragedy of undeserved blessing not be played out: "And
Rebecca spoke unto Jacob, her son, saying, 'Behold I heard thy
father speak unto Esau, thy brother, saying, 'Bring me venison
and make me savory food that I may eat and bless thee before the
Lord before my death." Now, therefore my son, hearken to my

voice according to that which I command thee. Go now to the flock and fetch me from thence two good kids of the goats and now make them savory food for thy father, such as he loveth, and thou shalt bring it to thy father that he may eat so that he may bless thee before his death'" (Genesis 27:6–10).

The plan was not Jacob's. It was not his style. It went against all that he was: "My father, peradventure, will feel me and I shall seem to him as a mocker; and I shall bring a curse upon me, and not a blessing" (Genesis 27:12). "And his mother said unto him, 'Upon me be thy curse, my son, only hearken to my voice and go fetch me them.'" His mother insisted, so he went. Thus, the blessing that sustains us to this day was uttered by Isaac to Jacob and not to Esau. But it is crucial to remember that Jacob, left to his own initiative, would have let the opportunity pass.

The story does not end there. An encounter with Esau is not so readily resolved. A victory over a villain of his ilk cannot be so quickly proclaimed.

"And Esau hated Jacob because of the blessing wherewith his father blessed him. And Esau said in his heart, 'Let the days of mourning for my father be at hand, then will I slay my brother Jacob'" (Genesis 27:41). Esau would merely wait a little while, until his father died. And then he would kill Jacob, his brother. Let us see then what good the stolen blessing will do him.

Psychologists tell us there are basically two ways in which we can cope with the world. People are divided into two major typologies: those who favor either fight or flight.

Encountering any difficulty, one can either attempt to cope, grapple, and wrestle with an issue and overcome it, or one can flee, giving up at the outset. Flight may even be rationalized as a correct religious response. Why take a chance, why get involved? Let me not do anything, and if God really desires a certain outcome, let Him handle it to His satisfaction.

What did *Ya'aqov,* the man of the "heel," do in the face of this threat? He "took to heel," he ran away, he fled so that there would be no encounter. That is how he came to the house of Laban, his uncle. And that is where he fell in love with Rachel, Rachel of whom the Torah says, "And Rachel was of beautiful form and fair to look upon (Genesis 29:17).

From the first moment he saw her, he became endowed with

almost supernatural strength. "And it came to pass when Jacob saw Rachel, the daughter of Laban, his mother's brother, and the sheep of Laban, his mother's brother, that Jacob went near and rolled the stone from the well's mouth and watered the flock of Laban, his mother's brother" (Genesis 29:10). With the newfound strength of a lover hoping to demonstrate his manliness to his beloved, Jacob the student, the scholar who had spent his days sitting in the tent, was able to push aside the very stone that all the shepherds could not budge.

It was for Rachel that Jacob was willing to work for seven years. It was because of her that the time "seemed unto him but a few days, for the love he had for her" (Genesis 29:20).

Imagine the anticipation of the wedding day. Jacob endured seven long years of servitude so that finally he could wed the woman for whom he had a consuming passion: "And Jacob said unto Laban, 'Give me my wife for my days are fulfilled, that I may go in unto her.'"

Laban made a feast. He prepared a wedding. But he did not keep his word. He gave him Leah, not Rachel. In the modest behavior of the bedroom, Jacob did not realize the truth until morning. "And it came to pass in the morning, that behold it was Leah." What does Jacob do at this moment of ultimate betrayal? What violence will he wreak? How much anger will he demonstrate? Will he tear Laban limb from limb? Will he fight bitterly at this betrayal?

"And he said to Laban, 'What is this thou hast done onto me? Did I not serve with thee for Rachel? Wherefore then hast thou beguiled me?' And Laban said, 'It is not so done in our place to give the younger before the firstborn. Fulfill the week of this one and we will give thee the other also for the service which thou shalt serve with me yet seven other years'" (Genesis 29:25–27).

What did "Ya'aqov," the man whose very name indicated his readiness to be stepped upon, his unwillingness to fight back, do in response? "And Jacob did so," fulfilling the conditions that Laban had illegally placed upon him.

Jacob still had not changed from his days in the womb. His approach was still to fling his arms skyward, as if to say both

"Well, what am I going to do?" and "God, I leave it in Your hands."

For twenty years Jacob worked for Laban. He made his father-in-law a very wealthy man. In the process, he also achieved a measure of security and riches for himself. It is then that he heard "the words of Laban's sons saying: 'Jacob hath taken away all that was our father's; and of that which was our father's hath he gotten all this wealth'" (Genesis 31:1). Jacob feels the envy. He is sensitive to the animosity. It is clearly time for a showdown. How could Laban and his sons begrudge the very man responsible for all of their blessing?

Something must be done. Following his lifelong code of behavior, he decides there is only one proper solution.

"And Jacob rose up and set his sons and his wives upon the camels and he carried away all his cattle and all his substance which he had gathered in Padan Aram, to go to Isaac his father unto the land of Canaan" (Genesis 31:17). *"Ya'aqov"* would flee once more. He would leave the site of potential confrontation. There was no point in fighting Laban and his sons or in attempting to clarify the issue. *Ya'aqov* sets to heel. "So he fled with all that he had" (Genesis 31:21). Until a moment came when he had to change. And when he changed his ways, then God changed his name.

Returning to Canaan, Jacob knew there was yet one more threat awaiting him. What would his brother do after so many years had passed? Was he still waiting to slay him or had the time gone by softened Esau and perhaps assuaged the anger?

"And Jacob sent messengers before him to Esau his brother unto the land of Sai'ir, the fields of Edom" (Genesis 32:4). The messengers would go bearing gifts, hoping to appease Esau. Jacob divides the people that are with him, his wives, flocks, herds, and camels into two camps. He sends them all before him. He fears the meeting. Before it takes place, we read of an enigmatic, almost incomprehensible encounter. "And Jacob was left alone and there wrestled a man with him until the breaking of the day" (Genesis 32:25).

Who was this mysterious assailant? What was this battle all

about? Our Sages disagree. For Maimonides it was a dream.
Freudian insights allow us to comprehend its meaning on a far
more profound level. The attacker, according to all biblical commentators, was the angelic representation of his brother (*saro shel
Esav*). If it was a dream, how obvious the interpretation. Jacob
feared his brother. The confrontation was imminent. Yet Jacob
sought, by sending his divided camp ahead of him, to prevent war
as long as possible. Yet in the dream, the two finally came
together. In the dream at long last, "*Ya'aqov*" is forced not only to
confront his adversary but to do battle with him.

For Rashi and for many others it was more than a dream. It
actually happened. What an angelic representative is, we do not
know. But the story, dream or reality, means one and the same
thing. This was at last the time when Jacob, the man who until this
moment had constantly fled from moments of conflict, controversy, and confrontation, finally recognized: there comes a time
when you can no longer flee. The man who had lived by the credo
of flight was now forced to finally acknowledge there is a time for
"fight."

Who was the victor in this encounter? At first glance it appears
that Jacob was defeated. "And the hollow of Jacob's thigh was
strained as he wrestled with him" (Genesis 32:26). Jacob was left
limping. The injury was significant, for it leaves us with a halakhah
until this very day. "Therefore the children of Israel eat not the
sinew of the thigh vein which is upon the hollow of the thigh, unto
this day; because he touched the hollow of Jacob's thigh even in
the sinew of the thigh vein" (Genesis 32:33). But if Jacob lost the
fray, how do we explain that he makes a demand upon his
attacker? "And he said, 'I will not let thee go except thou bless
me.'" Indeed, the attacker grants Jacob his wish: "And he said
unto him, 'What is thy name?' And he said, 'Jacob [Ya'aqov].'
And he said, 'Thy name shall be called no more Jacob, but Israel
[Yisrael]; for thou hast striven with God and with men and hath
prevailed'" (Genesis 32:28–29).

Why bless him? And why call him now "Yisrael"?

Because the name *Yisrael* refers to someone who has fought
for his beliefs, someone who has not simply allowed himself to be
stepped upon.

Jacob may have suffered a blow. But he won the greater battle—the battle over his passivity. The battle over his unwillingness previously to engage in combat. Jacob won the greatest victory of all, for he finally managed to conquer himself.

And if he was left limping, what of it? That would simply mean he would *never again be able to run away* from anyone or any place, not even from himself.

A new personality deserves a new name. No longer would Jacob say, "turn the other cheek." Nor would he refuse to face reality or say, "If I believe in God, I will let Him do everything." A Yisrael fights back because he understands that "God helps those who help themselves" is basic Jewish theology.

The phrase "which God created to do" (Genesis 2:3) is explained by the Jerusalem Talmud to imply this very idea. God left the world incomplete so that we might play a role in its perfection. God created us to be a "partner with God in the act of creation." God will not do it all; our dignity requires that we be left with a role to play as well.

A Yisrael does not simply accept the world as it is, rationalizing its inadequacies as the will of God. The very first mitzvah given to a Jew is that of circumcision. The Midrash records how a pagan questioned Rabbi Akiva: How could you Jews take a gift from God, a newborn baby boy, and as the very first act alter a portion of his anatomy and change the way in which God had created him?

That question is asked in many other contexts concerning the permissibility of change as we react to the world around us. Do we have a right to interfere in a world created and managed by God? Dare we heal the sick? Should we feed the hungry? How dare we clothe the naked! If God had wanted any of these things, shouldn't the religious Jew's response be that God would have done them? And the fact that He chose not to would thus imply that things are to remain exactly as they are, for this is how God clearly chooses them to be.

Indeed, if this were a world created in a state of perfection, we would not be allowed to tamper with it. But after Creation, God proclaims "which God created to do." This means that God left it unfinished so that humanity assume a role of partner with Him. The world has imperfections, and our role is to perfect the world.

A circumcision is held on the eighth day because in seven days God created the world. On the eighth day God says to man, *berit*—there is a Covenant and a partnership between us. I have fulfilled My role. Now beginning with Day Eight, you take over. You perfect and improve. You, build a better world.

It is remarkable that the command of circumcision is prefaced by God identifying himself as *Ani El Shadai* (Genesis 17:1), in English "I am God, Almighty." In Hebrew the word *Shadai* has a far more profound meaning. *El* refers to God the Creator. *Shadai,* from the root *dai* (enough), means the one *she-amar dai,* who at a certain point in the act of creation said, "Cease! Enough!" God stopped creation at a certain point and left it unfinished. Were God to have completed everything in accord with His will, there would be no possibility and no right for human beings to alter anything. But God says *Ani El Shadai,* I am the Creator Who left the world in an imperfect state so that "You walk before me and become perfect."

Circumcision captures the theology underlying the concept of "Yisrael." From the moment of birth Jews must recognize that they are to live in a world in which God wants them to act and to alter, to shape and to fashion, to improve and to confront, to fight and to change.

We are not allowed to simply sit back and say, "God, do it all." Nor are we allowed to say that whatever evil exists, from a pogrom to a Holocaust, from persecution to genocide, must clearly be God's will; that if evildoers abound, then I have neither obligation nor the right to oppose them.

That is why the change of name from Ya'aqov to Yisrael was not simply a change of identity for one person, but a new designation destined to become the title of our people, the children of Israel.

Why Did Jacob Retain His Name?

There is a remarkable distinction between the name changes of Abraham and Jacob. The Talmud teaches us a law codifying this difference:

> Bar Kappara taught: Whoever calls Abraham Abram transgresses a positive precept, since it says, Thy name shall be Abraham. R.

Eliezer says: He transgresses a negative command, since it says, Neither shall thy name be called anymore Abram. . . . But if that is so, the same should apply to one who calls Jacob, Jacob?—There is a difference in his case, because Scripture restored it [the name Jacob] to him, as it is written: And God spoke unto Israel in the visions of the night, and said, Jacob, Jacob. [*Berakhot* 13a]

Once Abram became Abraham (*Avram* to *Avraham*), the new title remained exclusive. To call him by his former name is a sin. His name shall no longer be called *Avram*. Yet, although we have seen how crucial was the transformation from Ya'aqov to Yisrael, the Torah does not hesitate oftentimes to refer to him by his former designation. The very last portion in Genesis states: "And Ya'aqov lived in the land of Egypt seventeen years" (Genesis 47:28). There are even verses that combine the two names: "Now these are the names of the sons of Yisrael who came into Egypt with Ya'aqov" (Exodus 1:1). If Abram's name change to Abraham was exclusive, it appears that Ya'aqov to Yisrael was complementary.

What accounts for the difference? To understand the rationale for the change allows us to grasp the answer. When Abram is told to circumcise himself because he has accepted the mission of becoming a Patriarch of the Jewish people, God says to him, "As for me, behold, My Covenant is with thee and thou shalt be the father of a multitude of nations. Neither shall thy name anymore be called Abram, but thy name shall be Abraham, for the father of a multitude of nations have I made thee" (Genesis 17:4–5). If previously Abram could be restricted to a small locality of Aram, the believing Jew must now and forevermore become father of a multitude of nations. His role now is to teach Godliness to mankind until that day will come when "The Lord will be King over all the whole world. On that day the Lord will be One and His Name will be One" (Zechariah 14:9).

Never again must *Avraham* be called *Avram*. Never again shall the mission of universal brotherhood under the kingdom of God be diminished into a dream of only local significance.

The same is not true for Jacob. Ya'aqov would not fight. He had too much compassion, too much faith in God alone. In the face of an Esau, he had to learn to become Yisrael. The Jew, the fighter, although not an ideal, often becomes a necessity. Yet the message of Ecclesiastes must never be lost upon us. There is a time for war, but there is also a time for peace. In simpler terms, there is a time to be Yisrael, but there is also an ultimate dream, a prayer that Yisrael the fighter may return to being Ya'aqov, "the simple man dwelling in tents," leading a life of tranquility and studying Torah.

The Jews who survived the Holocaust learned all too tragically the lesson of that long night when "Jacob remained alone" (Genesis 32:25). They were deserted by all the nations of the world, forced to confront the reality that there is a time when the Diaspora Jew can no longer have faith in flight. So we fought. We returned to our ancient homeland. Was it simply coincidence or was it divine fate that in 1948 (in the Jewish year 5708), those who best understood the theological significance of the transition from Ya'aqov to Yisrael, chose to call their land the State of Israel—*Medinat Yisrael*?

We are no longer those who will allow ourselves to be stepped upon as the "Ya'aqovs" of history. Jews of necessity have become Israelites. But the danger still persists that, having changed our identities with readiness to fight, we will perhaps go too far and alter our total essence. Is it our collective dream that every Jewish child grow up hoping to become a paratrooper? Is our national vision to identify with David, a warrior? No, David had to fight, and David became a hero of our people. However, David's ultimate greatness rested not on the sword but on the Psalms, not on his victories in the battlefield but on his ability to master his evil spirit.

We are blessed by the State of Israel. But our prayers also remind us that we seek "the God of Abraham, the God of Isaac, and the God of *Jacob*." The fact that the last of the Patriarchs, the one who fathered the twelve children who became the tribes of our people, continued to bear two names rather than one has ramifications that touch upon the very name of God Himself.

If Jacob, called "the choicest of the forefathers" by our Sages, maintains a dual identity, it is ultimately because our major mitzvah is *imitatio dei,* the imitation of God. God Himself continues to represent two aspects, as indicated by the two names used to describe Him. One name, represented by the letters YHVH (the Tetragrammaton), Adonai, conveys His dimension of compassion. Grammatically this name has a feminine ending in Hebrew. Elohim has a masculine ending. The latter is the "tough" God, the strict God of law and discipline. The name ELohim is found in the name YisraEL. The fighter contains the Godliness of the strict Deity. When man fights, no matter how noble the cause, he is emulating Elohim; as a Jew he is YisraEL. The love and compassion shown by YHVH, the feminine dimension, is summarized by the phrase "the House of *Jacob*," which our Sages say invariably refers to the women of Israel (see Rashi's commentary on Exodus 19:3: "Thus shalt thou say to the House of Jacob and tell the children of Israel").

The third Patriarch had two names because God has two names. Ya'aqov corresponds to YHVH, Yisrael to Elohim. Had he not become Yisrael, Jacob would have allowed Esau to triumph. Yet the Jew who recites "Hear O Israel" has learned the necessity of doing battle. In the *Shema,* God is called both by His names of compassion (YHVH) and harsh law (Eloheinu), but the prayer culminates with the words *YHVH Eḥad.* Ultimately Eloqim and YHVH are a unified essence—a final invocation of the God of love and compassion. That is why in a perfect world, the dream we look forward to is "In that day the Lord [Y-H-V-H] will be One and His Name will be One." His Name will no longer be Elohim. He will no longer need to be that kind of God whom we are forced to emulate in our battles against the Esaus of history.

"The saviors will ascend Mount Zion to judge Esau's mountain, and the kingdom will be the Lord's [of YHVH]" (Ovadiah 1:21). When Esau will be eliminated, then we will finally be able to renounce our name of Yisrael and we will evermore worship the God of *Avraham*, the God of *Yiẓhaq*, and the God of *Ya'aqov*, the tranquil scholar and dweller of tents.

Part VI

Life above All

18

Health Is a Mitzvah

e have learned that 610 commandments are ruled by the principle "And you shall live by them and not die by them." The three exceptions to this rule—idolatary, murder, and sexual immorality—have their source and rationale.

What must not be lost sight of is that for almost all the laws of the Torah our guideline is "the preservation of life takes precedence over everything else" (*pikuaḥ nefesh doḥeh et ha-kol*). A Jew may not consider life merely as a fleeting interlude before the far more important reunion with God after death. Life is to be treasured, guarded, and valued as the ultimate good.

Such an orientation makes two major affirmations: that of the body (the value of health and well-being) and that of the world (the value of human existence). The admonition to guard one's health—"Take ye therefore good heed onto yourselves" (Deuteronomy 4:15)—is the theme of this chapter.

Abraham, we are told by our Sages, voluntarily observed all the mitzvot subsequently given at Sinai. His intellect enabled him to share in the wisdom of the Almighty. The truths of Torah were real to him before the Revelation at Sinai occurred. That is why he

157

complied with everything without having been commanded to do
so.

Yet the Sages ask a fascinating question. It is clear that Abraham did not circumcise himself on his own. He waited for God to
tell him to do so. Why is this the one duty Abraham did not do
before God's specific commandment? One answer is relevant for
us. Abraham could voluntarily take any command upon himself
except for circumcision, because that would endanger his health.
Unless commanded to do so, Abraham understood that a Jew dare
not endanger his well-being and, God forbid, hasten his death.

Why the Fear of Death?

The Talmud tells us that when Rabbi Yehudah HaNasi was
critically ill, Rabbi Ḥiya came to visit him and found him weeping.
Rabbi Ḥiya questioned him: "Why are you crying? Are we not
taught that when one dies cheerfully it is a good sign, but when one
dies weeping it is a bad omen?" Why indeed should the greatest
rabbi have been weeping as he confronted death? Does not death
imply release? Does not death mean reunion with the Creator?
Does not death for the pious mean a time of reward and recompense for all the good they achieved on this earth? Perhaps the
wicked should weep, but not the righteous. Is not crying, therefore, a bad sign suggesting sinfulness? Rabbi Yehudah replied, "I
am weeping because of the Torah and the meritorious deeds that I
shall no longer be able to perform" (*Ketubot* 103b).

Death is tragic because it deprives us of the ability to continue
to serve our Master. As the Psalmist wrote it: "The dead praise not
the Lord, neither any that go down in silence" (Psalms 115:17).
Life presents us with opportunities—for blessings, acts of kindness, and other mitzvot.

It may be but a fanciful tale, but there is profound wisdom in
the story of the rich man who came to the other world for his
"final exam" devoid of good deeds on this earth. As he passed
before the Heavenly Judge and saw the procedure enacted there,
he became far less fearful. He noticed that recorded acts of charity
had tremendous influence on the divine decree. Gifts given during
one's lifetime could outweigh many sins. And so, when it was his

turn to stand before the Accuser, he said, "It is true I may have not done all I should while I was on earth, but permit me to take out my checkbook and write out significant sums for worthy institutions and let that be added to my ledger." To which the Heavenly courts replied: "Here we do not accept checks. We only accept receipts."

There is a limited time on this earth to do good. Admittedly, the beauties of the other world far outweigh the happiness of this one. "Better is one hour in the World to Come, than all the goodness of a lifetime here on earth" (*Ethics of the Fathers* 4:17) is the teaching of our Sages. Yet what this earth offers is something the other world no longer has. Here, there is opportunity. There, there is only a final reckoning.

Death is termination of opportunity. Suicide therefore becomes an unspeakable crime, a choice to undo the gift, to willingly give up every chance to do more, every occasion to right one's wrongs, or to compensate for deeds left undone.

If suicide is a sin, hastening one's demise is equally sinful. "Take ye therefore good heed onto yourselves"—we must do everything in our power to see to it that our days on this earth be extended.

Is it strange that Maimonides in his *Code of Law* has a section on how people should eat, drink, and take proper care of themselves? Not at all, because Judaism places health and hygiene within the category of a mitzvah.

The Talmud affirms that laws relating to health are in a category of severity transcending those dealing with ritual prohibitions.

"More stringent are the laws of danger than those relating to the religiously forbidden" (*Hullin* 10a). In the realm of the forbidden (*isur*) and permissible (*heter*), we are taught the concept of "nullification" (*bitul*). If a forbidden food falls into a larger mixture of permissible food, then a ratio of 60 to 1 is sufficient to nullify its effect. Not so, however, if the danger is one relating to health. Here no quantity is considered too small to signal danger.

If the Surgeon General today warns that cigarettes are dangerous to one's health, then the warning may, in fact, be comparable to a label indicating that this product is not kosher. Moreover, the standard of safety supersedes even the forbidden nature of eating pig or mixing meat and milk.

Do Not Crucify the Flesh

Body and soul in Judaism stand in a special relationship. They are partners, jointly enabling us to serve the Lord. No wonder that Jews and medicine have a special affinity. In a sense the ideal professions of our faith cater to health of mind and body. Thus rabbis and teachers take care of souls, physicians of bodies. It is a divine partnership in which both must function properly; each needs the other.

Maimonides, who was both rabbi and physician, was especially keen about this point. He taught that one acts piously by keeping the body healthy and strong, even as one must purify one's soul through study and mitzvot: "Since it is impossible to have any understanding and knowledge of the Creator when one is sick, it is man's duty to avoid whatever is injurious to the body and cultivate habits that promote health and vigor" (*Hilkhot De'ot,* Chapter 4:1).

It is God Himself who makes clear this relationship between body and soul, physician and Sage, observance of mitzvot and maintenance of health, when He proclaimed even before the Jewish people reached Mount Sinai: "If thou wilt diligently hearken to the voice of the Lord, thy God, and will do that which is right in His eyes and will give ear to his commandments and keep all His statutes, I will put none of the diseases upon thee which I have put upon the Egyptians, for I am the Lord that healeth thee" (Exodus 15:26). The concluding phrase may in fact be better translated as "For I am the Lord your Physician."

Judaism and Christianity do not approach the relationship between body and soul in the same way. The New Testament places the spirit and the flesh in opposition. The tension between them cannot be solved by cooperation. The holy man must learn to negate the demands of the body: "Live by the spirit and then you will not need to indulge your physical cravings. For the physical cravings are against the spirit, and the cravings of the spirit are against the physical; the two are in opposition" (Galatians 5:16ff).

When a Christian remembers the Crucifixion, it is not simply a historic event describing the manner in which his deity faced death, but also a theological ideal for his disciples in terms of how properly to live life: "They that are of Christ Jesus have crucified the flesh with its passions and desires" (Galatians 5:24).

Crucify the flesh because it is the enemy of the soul. The ascetic is a saint, and the holy man wears a hair shirt tearing away at the flesh. In Judaism, the ascetic is a sinner. The flesh is the handiwork of God and no less sacred than the soul. Matter and spirit complement each other. Since one cannot exist without the other, it is a crime to despise and degrade the body through which the spirit must manifest itself.

A Jew also wears a special item of clothing. It is called a *talit* (prayer shawl). The fringes, the *zizit*, were originally attached to the standard garb worn by all, a four-cornered garment. *Zizit* have eight strings. One of them was to be blue, the other seven white. The azure *tekhelet* was selected because it "resembles the color of the ocean. And the ocean resembles the sky. And the sky resembles the divine throne" (*Menahot* 43b). That is why the Torah commanded us to wear them so that "when you look upon it you will remember to do all the commandments of the Lord and will not follow your heart and eyes which lead you astray" (Numbers 15:39). But if the blue is what reminds us of God, then why not have all strings be of that color? If the purpose is to remember the Heavens, why should seven other strands represent the purity of whiteness on this earth?

Rabbi Samson Raphael Hirsch of Germany (1808–1888) explains it beautifully. The *tekhelet* represents the soul; it is the reminder of Heaven. But a Jew does not only aspire to Heaven. He takes that one string and winds it round the other seven, representing the seven days of creation, the world as we know it. The material things of this world, the body and the flesh, which we would think at first glance are removed from the Almighty—these are the very things around which we must wind the sky-blue thread of the soul. The thread of blue sanctifies the world. The world and the spirit are not in conflict. They can be made to cooperate.

The hair shirt of the Christian crucifies the flesh. The *zizit* of the Jew, merging blue and white together (like the flag of Israel), teach that body and soul, flesh and spirit, earth and Heaven, can be merged. Jews are not taught to build a fence between them, but rather a ladder. A ladder "rooted in the ground and its head reaching up to the Heavens."

19

Enjoy Life
on This Earth

he body is holy. It is not to be crucified. The world is holy. It is not to be renounced.

The founder of Christianity said "My kingdom is not of this world." Christianity is concerned primarily with life after terrestrial existence. The Torah does not mention life after death clearly, although it is one of the fundamental beliefs of our faith, because the purpose of Torah is to teach us how to live life on this earth. This world is not to be rejected, but perfected. Our mission is to perfect the world in the kingdom of the Almighty. *Shadai,* the Creator who said "enough," refers to a God who created an imperfect world and left it unfinished so that *we* might fashion it, shape it, and bring it to its ultimate utopian destiny.

Holy men of other religions had as their primary function the community's dealings with death. The *Kohanim* (priests) among our people were commanded: "And the Lord said unto Moses, 'Speak unto the Priests, the sons of Aharon, and say unto them, "There shall none defile himself with the dead among his people"'" (Leviticus 21:1). If a priest dare not have contact with the dead, with what then shall he occupy himself? Is that not a primary function of the religious leader? Are not the Kaddish, funerals, and unveilings the chief duties of rabbis?

Obviously, the Torah had a different view. Judaism is to be concerned with life and not with death. Religion is not a preparation for life after this one, but a blueprint for perfecting the world in which God placed us. This world must be lived in and worked upon. Since God created it, He also meant for it and everything on it to be enjoyed.

The Talmud teaches us that at the end of life, every person will have to account for all of his or her actions on earth. There will be questions asked in the Heavenly court. One of the first will demand: "Are there any legitimate pleasures in this world which God created for your benefit that you denied yourself from enjoying?" (*Kidushin* 4, end). God created the world, and every day as He viewed His handiwork, He proclaimed: "It is good." For us to reject the benefits of creation is to declare a contradictory evaluation: "It is bad so I will renounce." The Talmud therefore teaches us that forsaking the world is not saintly, but sinful. Ascetics are not to be commended for their willingness to give up the pleasures of this world. They are to be condemned because God set a table before us of earthly delights, and ascetics willingly and knowingly chose to reject them.

The *Nazir* as Sinner

The Torah describes a person who chooses to come closer to God and is willing to offer personal sacrifices in order to achieve closeness to Him: "When either man or woman shall clearly utter a vow, the vow of a Nazirite to consecrate himself unto the Lord, he shall abstain from wine and strong drink. He shall drink no vinegar of wine or vinegar of strong drink. Neither shall he drink any liquor of grapes nor eat fresh grapes or dried. All the days of his Naziriteship shall he eat nothing that is made of the grapevine, from the pressed grapes, even to the grape stone. All the days of his vow of Naziriteship shall there no razor come upon his head until the days be fulfilled in which he consecrateth himself unto the Lord. He shall be holy. He shall let the locks of the hair of his head grow long" (Numbers 6:2–5). Here is someone of whom the Torah says, his purpose is "to consecrate himself unto the Lord." What he gives up are wine and the cutting of his hair. One symbolizes

personal pleasure; the other social companionship. "Wine glad-
dens the heart of man" (Psalm 104:15). Long hair, even as for the
mourner, represents a desire to avoid human contact.

The Nazirite is willing to do all this "for the sake of God."
When he concludes his period of Naziriteship, the Torah teaches
us that he must bring a sin offering (Numbers 6:14). The Talmud
explains (*Nedarim* 10a): "Were the restrictions found in the Torah
not sufficient for you?" Unnecessary abstention is a sin against
one's own person and against society. What God created for
humanity ought not to be rejected. Furthermore, the Nazirite
becomes a paradigm for Judaism's view of pleasure. "If the Nazirite who abstained only from wine needs atonement, how much
more so he who abstains from all pleasurable things?" is the rabbinic conclusion (*Sifri, Naso,* no. 30).

This conclusion contrasts sharply with the Christian view of
holiness. Saint Anselm (1033–1109) was considered the most pious
of men because he climbed a tree, built himself a little ledge there-
on, and stayed there for the rest of his days. To come closer to
God, he felt it necessary to remove himself from the world, separate himself from his community. Hillel the Elder recommends the
opposite in *Ethics of the Fathers*: "Do not separate yourself from
the community" (2:5). The goal of the Jew is not to remove himself
from earth and reside closer to Heaven. It is rather to bring
Heaven down to earth, to make the teachings of God relevant in
human society. A hermit does not improve the world, he renounces it. A monk does not affect what happens here on earth, he
is content to remain apart from it. Not so a Jew, who is entrusted
with the task of perfecting this world in the Kingdom of God. The
world needs not critical spectators from afar, but active partici-
pants from within.

Sinai itself serves as the most powerful illustration of the difference between these two theological approaches of Judaism and
Christianity. On the very mountain on which God appeared to
reveal His law, Christians have built a monastery. Members of the
order take a vow never to leave that holy site. Those who die there
are buried within. Generation after generation, the holy brothers
have stayed there, ostensibly to fulfill the word of the Lord and live
life as He would have wanted them to do.

No Jew lives on top of that mountain. Jews maintain that the exact spot of Revelation is unknown and purposely so. God did not want us to mark the mountain or to turn it into holy ground, for then the medium would have become the message, Sinai would have become confused with the purpose of Revelation. God asked Moses to come up to Mount Sinai to receive the Torah, but then He told him to go down with it, bring it to humankind, and turn the desert of human existence into holy land. To stay on top of the mountain is to complete only half the journey. Moses had to ascend to receive, and to descend in order to transmit.

Torah is compared to water. Why water? Even as water flows from the top of the mountain down to the lowest valley—watering, nurturing, irrigating, and bringing life—so, too, if Torah is to fulfill its purpose it must descend to the lowest levels of earth and infuse them with the spirituality of God.

Solitude, Celibacy, and Poverty

For the Christian the convent is a holy abode. It is where pious monks and nuns flee from mundane interests and concerns. It is where Sinai is recaptured. For the Jew, solitude goes against the most basic of biblical concepts. If "you shall love your neighbor as yourself" is the major principle of the Torah, then clearly it cannot be performed in isolation. A person must merge with others and dare not withdraw from the community. "All Jews are responsible one for another" implies a relationship of common concern, acceptance of communal responsibility, and living within a social structure where the world is not forsaken as unredeemable, but improved in the hope of bringing about a messianic era here on earth. "My Kingdom is, indeed, of this world," says God to the Jew, "and it is your role to hasten the coming of that glorious era." The Christian must believe that Paradise can only exist in another world because Jesus, having claimed he was the "Messiah," nonetheless left the world riddled with war and hatred. For us Messiah has not yet come. We must help bring him. And we believe that the day can be brought closer if we do God's will here on earth.

That is why a Jew may not take a vow of solitude, nor can a Jew accept the legitimacy of celibacy. God created man and woman to be fruitful and multiply. He wanted this earth "not to be a waste; He formed it to be inhabited" (Isaiah 45:18). God created sex both for procreation and pleasure. How then could marriage be evil, how could sexual relations be against the will of the One who made them possible?

Anyone who is unmarried, according to the Talmud, lives "without joy, without blessing, without goodness" (*Yevamot* 62b). A Jew must categorically reject Paul's instruction to the Corinthians: "To all who are unmarried and to widows I would say this: It is an excellent thing if they can remain single as I am, but if they cannot control themselves, let them marry. For it is better to marry than to be on fire with passion" (1 Corinthians 7:9). A Jew must also reject the disparaging remarks of Jesus: "The people of this world marry and are married, but those who are thought worthy to attain the other world and the resurrection from the dead neither marry nor are married" (Luke 20:34–35).

What the Christian crucifies, the Jew sanctifies. What the Christian renounces, the Jew utilizes in order to render it holy. Sex cannot be sinful. It is the source of all life, and life is holy. Everything created by God must be used for some divine purpose.

In Judaism poverty is not glorified as an ultimate good, nor is wealth an automatic sin, as the New Testament states: "It is easier for a camel to go through the eye of a needle than for a rich man to enter the kingdom of Heaven" (Matthew 19:23).

Wealth is not a curse, but a challenge. "And God blessed Abraham with all things." As a rich man Abraham could invite strangers, feed them, clothe them, and subsequently bring them closer to God. "Poverty in the house is worse than fifty plagues" (*Baba Batra* 116a). The Talmud also teaches: "A poor person is the equivalent of a dead man" (*Nedarim* 76). A Jew may strive for possessions. Once he attains them, let him learn to give charity and to transform his blessing into a blessing for mankind.

The Parable of the Magid of Dubno

It was the famous preacher, the Magid of Dubno, who clarified the ideology of Judaism by means of a simple parable. It is a parable which, in its very simplicity, manages to summarize the three different approaches expressed in the differing outlooks of major religions as well as philosophies of life.

Imagine if you will, said the rabbi, three men seated at a table on which there rests a full bottle of rare and very precious old wine. One of them is an ascetic. He believes that by depriving the body one cleanses the soul and thereby comes closer to God. The second is an epicure, one whose beliefs follow the admonition of Epicurus of old, who taught, "Eat, drink, and be merry, for tomorrow you may die." He believes the goal of life is to enjoy everything in the here and now. Physical gratification is the primary goal. The world should only be viewed from a materialistic standpoint; following natural instincts and desires represents the purpose and function of life.

Joining these two diametrically opposed ideologues is the Jew. He, too, sits down at this table offering wine, symbol of the world and its pleasures. What happens next becomes a paradigm for the three possibilities inherent in our choice for dealing with pleasure.

The ascetic peers at the wine greedily. His drawn, jaundiced face betrays desire. His entire body is pained with unrequited lust. He is attracted to the bottle, feels a hot cloud settling over his mind, but being true to his principles he overcomes the desire that seethes within him. It costs him strength. He knows that it will leave marks upon his health, that these spiritual pains eat into him with consuming desire. But, feeling that if he were to give in to the smallest extent, his desire for greater gratification would then overwhelm him in uncontrollable passion, he prefers abstinence— and tears himself away disappointed and unfulfilled. He has not tasted "the wine of this world." He does not comprehend why God claimed after every act of creation "Behold it was good." He has by personal choice never allowed himself to taste of that goodness, certain that the very God who made the judgment prefers people to be unaware of it in their encounter with the world. For the ascetic, all goodness has proved to be merely unfriendly temptation. Would that the good were not here so that he not be forced to encounter it.

Whether the ascetic faces wine or woman, food or frivolity, wealth or possessions, his response is always the same: he will reject everything so as not to be destroyed by excess. The world is a cruel place for him, tempered only by the knowledge that his asceticism may perhaps be a preferable alternative to the opposite extreme.

The epicure, on the other hand, is repulsed by the sight of a person who rejects the joys of gratification. He cannot understand how anyone could deny himself. And so, he stretches his feverish hand and his fingers, burning with lust, snatch the bottle. In a moment it reaches his lips and loud gulps are heard in the room. The wine flows smoothly into his thirsty throat as his eyes gleam with ecstasy. His face becomes red as hellish fire. His entire body throbs with joy as the wine continues to flow into him. "It is good, very good," shouts his very being. His desire does not become satiated, but rather renews itself in an ongoing orgy of unbridled lust. Because happiness and pleasure are his twin goals, he does not stop to question when his pursuit of these ideals turns them into their very antitheses.

The wine creeps into his mind and inflames him. It arouses within him the urge to destroy everything around him. Pain begins to overtake him. His innards rebel. And soon he learns the most amazing lesson of life. "Too much" produces a reaction just the reverse of what he sought. Wanting to feel good, he now feels miserable. Wanting pleasure, he now experiences pain. Queasiness, hangover, inability to function, embarrassment caused by his actions—these are all the results of his unbridled pursuit of "the good life."

Substitute for wine any worldly pleasure and the conclusion remains the same. Excessive eating brings on ill health. Sexual surfeit leads to boredom.

Those who do not touch the wine at all or those who imbibe from it too freely, the ascetic and the epicure, both leave the "table of the world and its pleasures" feeling unfulfilled. One is in pain because of his abstinence, the other is ill because of his excess. Neither philosophy of life has faithfully served its disciples.

Yet there is one other person sitting at that very table. It is the Jew, the Jew who accepts the doctrines of his religion and lives in accord with the principles of his faith. He, too, looks at the wine, wonders what he will do, and then quickly reviews in his mind the relevant talmudic passages:

To torture oneself by not drinking at all is strictly forbidden
   by God. [*Nedarim* 10a]
Every man will have to account for every [permissible] enjoyment that he denied himself. [*Yerushalmi, Kidushin* 4]
It is like one who, when offered a gift, takes it and throws it
   back at his friend's face. [*Sukkah* 28b]

The Jew knows he cannot reject the wine. It was made by God.
Hence, it can become holy. One may use it for Kiddush. To reject
it is to reject God's work. However, to grab it with animalistic
desire, the Jew remembers, is also forbidden. It is necessary first to
recite a blessing. He must utter a benediction and reflect upon not
only his sense of gratitude to the Almighty, but also his recognition
of the spiritual purpose implicit in all things created.

He will drink, but only after he reflects on God. He will have
sexual relations and renounce celibacy, but only within the sacred
context of marriage. He will bless and enjoy—and then remember
religious law, which imposes limitations to prevent excess.

The Jew blesses and drinks. Then he recalls the passage from
the Midrash describing the moment when Noah planted the first
vineyard in history. It was Satan who happened along at the very
moment when Noah was engaged in the planting. Satan asked:
"What is it that you are planting here?" Noah responded: "A vineyard." Satan offered: "Let us go into partnership in this business of
planting a vineyard." Noah agreed, whereupon the Midrash says
Satan thereupon slaughtered a lamb, and then, in succession, a
lion, a pig, and a monkey. The blood of each as it was killed he
made to flow under the vine. Thus, he conveyed to Noah what the
qualities of wine are: before man drinks of it, he is innocent as a
lamb; if he drinks of it moderately, he feels as strong as a lion; if he
drinks more of it than he can bear, he resembles the pig; and if
drinks to the point of intoxication, then he behaves like a monkey,
he dances around, sings, talks obscenely, and knows not what he is
doing (*Bereshit Rabah* 36:3–4).

The Jew will not be an ascetic, but he will also guard himself
from becoming a disciple of Epicurus, who became synonymous
with the Jewish word for heretic, *Apikorus*. A Jew will drink "only
as much as is necessary for stimulation, for refreshment, and for

waking the napping organs" and he will constantly recall that when he has finished drinking, "his mind must be sufficiently sober to recite his prayers dutifully" (Maimonides, *Hilchot De'ot* 6:3). He will drink enough to rejoice in a world that offers its blessings, and then he will cease because God has decreed that to say "enough" is to imitate the Creator.

Three people have encountered the world. Three people have dealt with the temptation of "wine," symbol of all the goods of this earth that please and satisfy in moderation, but cause harm and grief when taken without limitations. Philosophies of asceticism and epicureanism have throughout history proliferated under many different guises. All have, however, left their devotees unsatisfied.

What is the message of Judaism? Enjoy—wine and sex as Kiddush and *qidushin*; enjoy—wealth and possessions so that you may give charity and know the joy of helping others; enjoy—everything about which God said "Behold, it is good," so that you fulfill the ideal of our faith: "and you shall rejoice before the Lord, your God" (Leviticus 23:40; Deuteronomy 12:12).

Part VII

The Seven Universal Laws

20

Does God Care about Non-Jews?

side from the 613 laws obligating a Jew, our Sages stressed another significant summary of law, the seven commandments given to "the children of Noah" (*sheva miẓvot benei Noah*), God holds all humanity accountable for the Seven Noahide Laws. The 613 devolve upon us because of a specific commitment, predicated upon the "sanctity of Israel," made at Mount Sinai. What is the source of responsibility for the seven universal laws? Not a covenant, but a condition. Not the commitment at Sinai, but the very human condition. We are created in the image of God and that uniqueness, shared by all people, is sufficient to place demands upon everyone.

Cain was not present at Mount Sinai to hear the words "Thou shalt not murder." Yet he was judged guilty and punished for divine disobedience because murder falls under the heading of universal law. It transcends obligations resulting from the covenant accepted at Revelation.

A descendant of Noah is duty-bound to obey those laws that define a person not as a Jew, but simply as a human being. That obligation must be considered first in light of its dramatic meaning vis-à-vis our understanding of the relationship between God and the entire non-Jewish world.

Universalism or Particularism?

Does God care about people who aren't Jewish?

There are two ways in which one might view all of history in the aftermath of the covenant God made with the Jewish people at Sinai. The first is to assume that God, the Creator of the heavens and the earth, sought a people who would believe in Him and follow His ways. All the nations of the world, according to the Midrash, were offered the Torah, but they refused. They were not willing to live by its restrictions. They felt it too confining for their lifestyles and values. Only the Jews said "We will do and we will hearken" (*na'aseh ve-nishma*). From that moment on, it was the Jews who became the sole concern of the Almighty. All others exist merely to be tolerated, or perhaps in light of how they might serve in God's grander scheme for His chosen people.

In this view however, non-Jews forfeited all rights and no longer enjoy any favor in God's eyes. They are written off forever because the purpose of the earth's existence is Torah. Without Torah the world would cease to be. And the Gentiles who do not accept Torah are simply vestigial remnants of ancient times and of peoples who once might have been God's, but who are now consigned to the oblivion of divine unconcern.

Or: God created the entire world and made Adam in His image. That makes all humanity one, at least in some measure, with the Creator. It lends humanity divine dignity. It sets humans apart from the beasts that preceded them in the acts of creation. Human existence is imbued with a level of holiness. Divine stature imposes obligations. These, if mastered, make humans worthy of some measure of immortality. The refusal of non-Jews to accept all of the 613 mitzvot is but a temporary aberration. The goal must be for all descendants of Adam to live as God had intended. Until that time, the human race is incomplete. Yet a human being is almost divine, "little lower than the angels." The goal of history will be to have the Jews serve as a catalyst for the rest of the world, to ensure that what they have already grasped will become the combined heritage of all.

Which is the correct interpretation of the human condition? It is clearly the latter. The very existence of the Noahide Laws implies that God continues to hold all people accountable for their actions.

The Jerusalem Talmud teaches that "The righteous of the nations of the world have a share in the World to Come" (*Sanhedrin* 10:1). A Jew believes that a righteous Gentile, i.e., one who observes the Seven Noahide Laws, still finds room in the Heavenly Kingdom. For God has not disowned anyone. The Jew may reach a higher level and hence be assured of greater proximity to the Almighty in the afterlife, but a non-Jew is not cut off from the Creator. Non-Jews, too, have their "Torah"—a Torah of seven, not of 613. If a non-Jew observes those seven, then he or she is reckoned among "the righteous of the nations of the world" and can find favor in the sight of God. Eternal blessing and reward can await even one who is not a member of our faith community.

Attitudes to Missionizing

The importance of the Noahide Laws helps us understand why Judaism differs so dramatically from Christianity in its approach to conversion. May someone become a Jew by choice? Can one become a member of "the community of Israel" through acceptance of Torah and mitzvot? Most decidedly, yes. Judaism is not a race, but a religion. Jethro and Ruth stand as paradigms, male and female, of pagans who saw the light and became members of our people.

Why did God give the Torah in the desert of Sinai rather than in the Holy Land? Our Sages explain that He wished to demonstrate that the Torah did not belong to one nation alone or even to one country. A desert is halakhically designated "a place free for all, unowned, no man's land," or better put, "every man's land" (*maqom hefqer*). The Torah was not given even in the holy land of Israel, for that would have meant it was to be uniquely the Jewish constitution. It was given in a space owned by all humankind, for it was intended for all. Its purpose is to turn a world without law—which, by definition, is barren desert—into a blooming, fertile, and productive place for human existence.

Yitro (Exodus 18–20) is the name of the biblical portion in which we read the account of the most important moment in Jewish history, the Revelation. Strange that Moses does not receive this honor. Stranger still that the portion has as its title the name of Jethro, someone who was not even born a Jew, but who later in life abandoned his false idols and recognized monotheism. Why choose him? Because he is the greatest illustration of what the Torah is meant to accomplish—to transform idolaters into believers, pagans into worshipers of God.

It is on the festival of Shavuot, which commemorates the receiving of the Torah, that we read not only from the portion of *Yitro* but also the story of Ruth, (in Hebrew, RUT). Why was this Moabite woman called RUT? A fascinating numerologic interpretation explains that her name equals 606 [Resh = 200, Vav = 6, Tav = 400, a total of 606]. Ruth was a convert. She willingly accepted mitzvot upon herself. Prior to her conversion, when she was only obligated by universal law, she was committed to the Seven Noahide Laws. In choosing to be bound by 613, she willingly added 606. How fitting that her name should be "RUT," permanently identifying her greatness as the one who added 606 by personal choice and conviction.

It is Ruth who is the ancestress of David, who in turn is the ancestor of the Messiah. How fitting that the Messiah, whose task will be to make the entire world come under the canopy of the one God, stems from a woman who paved the way for precisely this attitude of acceptance.

We look forward to the day when God will be One and His Name will be One. So significant is this ideal that Rashi explains it as the real meaning of the Shema, our declaration of faith "Hear O Israel, the Lord who is our God will be one God alone." At present, it is only the Jewish people who worship Him. But at some future point in history, He will be the One God, the God of all peoples. With this interpretation we may understand why in many prayer books, following the final line of the *Aleinu* prayer where we recite the verse "And the Lord will be King over the entire world and that day the Lord will be One and His Name will be One," we find the words "as it is written in Your Torah, 'The Lord Who is our God will be the One Lord'" for all.

Judaism accepts the convert fully. Not only are converts granted all rights, but they are admired for stepping forward and acknowledging what others do not yet know, what the rest of the world will require the Messiah to teach them. They are Jews in every sense of the word, even descendants of Abraham, Isaac, and Jacob. Halakhah wonders whether the converts ought read the text of the Eighteen Benedictions in the same manner as "biological Jews." The text states: "Blessed are You, O Lord our God, and God of our ancestors, God of Abraham, God of Isaac, and God of Jacob." Shall a convert say "God of our ancestors"? The conclusion is yes, for they, too, are his spiritual ancestors. Let no one imagine that the Jew is guilty of a chauvinism that excludes all others from joining the Jewish faith. The Jews are not the "Chosen" People as much as the "choosing" people. Our greatness consists in having been wise enough to accept what the other nations of the world rejected. Whosoever acknowledges what we recognized at Sinai becomes a descendant of our ancestors as well, and we are duty-bound to fulfill the command repeated thirty-six times in the Torah: "And you shall love the stranger."

Every convert is a follower of Jethro or of Ruth. Every convert represents a stranger disagreeing with his or her progenitors (who refused the Torah when God offered it to them) and who now willingly re-creates the moment of Sinai. Each convert has hastened the arrival of the Messianic Era. What the messianic descendants of David and Ruth will achieve for all peoples, the convert has understood and acted upon without requiring a messianic intermediary.

Why have the Jews been exiled around the globe throughout history? The Talmud dares to suggest that one of the main purposes of this seeming punishment may have a totally different rationale. Rabbi Eleazar said: "The Holy One, blessed be He, did not exile Israel among the nations save in order that proselytes might join them, for it is said: 'And I will sow her unto Me in the land' [Hosea 2:25]. Surely a man sows a *se'ah* (biblical measure) in order to harvest many *Kor*!" (*Pesaḥim* 87b). Jews must spread the knowledge of one God. The existence of the Jew allows for an awareness of Torah in the greater world community.

In light of all this, why don't we actively missionize? Because we are aware of the difference between the non-Jew's responsibili-

ties to God and ours. This difference has far-reaching implications. "Know before whom you are destined to give a final
accounting" (*Ethics of the Fathers* 3:1). When we will face our
Maker as Jews, we will be held accountable for 613 mitzvot. The
scales will be brought forth. Our sins and good deeds will be
weighed and compared. It is an awesome responsibility, but one
that is rooted in our past and our heritage. The non-Jew who is
judged faces a far simpler test. Seven, not 613, are the extent of his
responsibilities.

Conversion is a tremendous burden as well as blessing. To take
upon oneself a far greater task is a wondrous thing. It is highly
pleasing in the sight of God. But to make a commitment to
Judaism, knowing full well that one will not abide by its laws, is to
assume culpability for countless transgressions that otherwise
would have gone unrecorded. Simply put, to convert someone to
Judaism who will clearly not observe the Sabbath, Kashrut, family
purity, or celebrate the festivals is to make that individual liable to
punishments that otherwise would not have been relevant.

This explains the rabbinic attitude to those who come seeking
conversion. Push them away at least three times, says the law—but
not because we do not want potential converts. We pray that they
view this rejection as temporary and have a will so strong that our
apparent refusal to comply with their conversionary request is
ignored. The convert is cautioned: "Do you know that if you join
our people, you will be joining those who are universally despised?
You will be committing yourself to the observance of countless
laws. Are you sure that you are up to it? Are you certain that you
truly desire to comply?" If the convert responds, "I, too, will be
like Ruth, 'Your people will be my people. Your God will be my
God. His law will be my law,'" then we will embrace the stranger
and be grateful for the addition of a soul whose acceptance will
bring the convert to a higher level of reward in the afterlife.

Christianity begins with a totally different premise. All those
who do not believe in Jesus, all those who are not baptized, are
eternally damned. The damned can be brought to Heaven if they
are taught and believe in the glories of Jesus. From the Christian
perspective, it is crucial to send missionaries to Africa and every
far-flung community to offer grace, salvation, and the gift of eter-

nity to otherwise damned souls. For the Jew that gift already belongs to all. As stated in the Jerusalem Talmud, "The righteous of the nations of the world have a share in the World to Come" (*Sanhedrin* 10:1). They earn this share through observance of the seven universal laws placed upon the descendants of Noah. We will not convert someone to Judaism unless changing seven into 613 offers an opportunity for far greater compliance with the will of God and greater blessing.

The Universal Ideal

Jews could never have converted others at the point of a sword. For moral and theological reasons, a tactic such as the Crusades is one that Jews cannot consider. Judaism dare not be imposed on another person or people.

However, Judaism is not ultimately meant to be the faith of only our people. Our tradition teaches a fascinating combination of particularism and universalism encapsulated in the two paragraphs that form the closing prayer of every daily service. The *Aleinu*, as its very name implies, begins by placing emphasis "upon us." It would appear that we are identifying ourselves as unique, totally different, and pleased with the concept of separatism.

> It is our duty to praise the Master of all, to ascribe greatness to the Molder of primeval creation, for He has not made us like the nations of the lands and has not emplaced us like the families of the earth; for He has not assigned our portion like theirs nor our lot like all their multitudes. But we bend our knees, bow, and acknowledge our thanks before the King who reigns over kings, the Holy One, Blessed is He. He stretches out heaven and establishes earth's foundation, the seat of His homage is in the heavens above and His powerful Presence is in the loftiest heights. He is our God and there is none other. True is our God, there is nothing beside Him, as it is written in His Torah: "You are to know this day and take to your heart that the Lord is the only God—in heaven above and on the earth below—there is none other."

We have made a firm declaration that posits separatism: The Jew is a world apart. *We* are not *them*.

And yet the prayer proceeds:

Therefore we put our hope in You, Lord our God, that we may
soon see Your mighty splendor, to remove detestable idolatry from
the earth, and false gods will be utterly cut off, to perfect the universe through the Almighty's sovereignty. Then all humanity will
call upon Your Name, to turn all the earth's wicked toward You.
All the world's inhabitants will recognize and know that to You
every knee should bend, every tongue should swear. Before You,
Lord our God, they will bend every knee and cast themselves down,
and to the glory of Your Name they will render homage, and they
will all accept upon themselves the yoke of Your kingship that You
may reign over them soon and eternally. For the kingdom is Yours
and You will reign for all eternity in glory, as it is written in Your
Torah: The Lord shall reign for all eternity. And it is said: The Lord
will be King over all the world—on that day the Lord will be One
and His Name will be One.

The second paragraph is a paean of praise to a God of the entire
universe, acknowledged by all.

How can the two paragraphs be reconciled? Indeed Judaism
acknowledges the truth of both. The first, Jewish separatism, is
meant to lead to the second. We must retain our distinctiveness so
that the entire world can be sanctified through the holiness of the
Jew.

We are not to remain one small portion of the world population, possessing the truth and content to allow humanity to remain
in ignorance. As soon as *Avram* understood, his very knowledge
gave him a mission. The one who comprehends God must spread
the word. *Avram* had to become *Avraham,* "father of many
nations."

So, too, when the Jewish people stood at the foot of Mount
Sinai and were prepared to accept the Torah, God defined the
commitment by telling Moses to convey to the people the following: "Now therefore, if you will hearken unto My Voice indeed,
and keep My Covenant, then you shall be Mine Own treasure
from among all peoples; for all the earth is Mine; and ye shall be
unto Me a kingdom of priests and a holy nation. These are the
words which thou shalt speak unto the children of Israel" (Exodus
19:5–6). The commentators are intrigued by the phrase "a kingdom of priests" (*mamlekhet Kohanim*). Surely the Jewish people

will not all be priests. The Twelve Tribes were divided into Priests, Levites, and Israelites; most Jews are simply Israelites. Why does God say that the Jewish people in its entirety will become a kingdom of priests? Yehudah HaLevi explained that even as the priests were to be the teachers and holy leaders for the rest of the Jewish people, so, too, the Jews are to become the holy leaders for the rest of the world. That is the meaning of "Ye shall be Mine Own treasure from among all peoples." Not to be selected "from among" so that all others be discarded. Rather to be the *Kohanim* who will ensure that all others eventually follow, for "*all the earth* is Mine."

The *Shalosh Regalim* in Nature and History

The Exodus from Egypt contained three major aspects that are commemorated in permanently established holidays. Passover, the time when the Jews left Egypt, is identified always as the "Festival of our Freedom." Fifty days later when the Jews came to Sinai and accepted the Torah, Shavuot would always remind us of the "Time of the Giving of our Torah." The forty years' wandering through the desert, leading up to the entry into Israel, would be marked by Sukkot, the "Festival of our Rejoicing."

Each of these festivals is described in a way that recalls its historic component. Yet another aspect is also built into every one of them. The history of our people coincides with specific seasons. These seasons become crucial to the proper observance of the festivals.

The lunar calendar that Jews observe is shorter than the solar by eleven days. Every year, events marked by the calendar would theoretically be observed at an earlier date. Were the lunar calendar to be the only one used by the Jews, Passover in a short period of time would become a winter holiday. That, we are taught, cannot be. Passover is called *Ḥag he-Aviv,* the "Festival of the Spring." To ensure that it is always celebrated as a spring holiday, our Sages determined that a leap month must every so often be introduced into the lunar calendar in order to make it coincide with the solar. To prevent Passover from falling "too early" in the year, a second month of Adar is observed.

The emphasis on season in addition to the historic basis for

Passover is true for the other two festivals in the series. In the Bible and in prayer, Shavuot is referred to as *Hag ha-Bikurim,* the "Festival of First Fruits." Farmers saw the first of their harvest ripen at this time of year. They would take the first fruits that bloomed and bring them to Jerusalem. Sukkot, the last in the series, must always occur in the fall so that its agricultural title applies: *Hag ha-Asif,* "Festival of the Harvest."

Spring, first fruit, and harvest are not simply addenda to the historic moments that these holidays commemorate. By way of metaphor, they offer the most profound insight into the meaning of the historic moments.

To what may Passover best be compared? God finds a people He feels worthy of deliverance. To them He will subsequently give the Torah. They will be bearers of His mission. After the long darkness of historic winter, God's people begin to "blossom." It is spring. Lovers, God, and Israel meet. But the meeting has not yet borne any fruit. Without Torah one can speak of no real fulfillment. Spring is thus the season of promise, projected in terms of budding and blossoming. But it remains for Shavuot, the time of the giving of the Torah, to metaphorically coincide with *Hag ha-Bikurim.* The messages of historic revelation and of nature's sending forth its first fruits are in fact identical. Just as the farmer longs for his fruit to come forth from the seed, so too did God gratefully recognize the spiritual birth of the Jewish people. The world bore its first fruit when the Jew said, "We will do and we will hearken."

Yet that moment of Revelation in nature is not the final harvest. It is merely synonymous with the "Festival of *First* Fruits." How fitting the comparison when one notes the word used by God to describe His people. At the Burning Bush God already informed Moses that he would one day warn Pharaoh about the plague of the firstborn. The reason for the tenth plague was given: "And thou shalt say unto Pharaoh, 'Thus sayeth the Lord. Israel is My son, My firstborn, and I have said unto thee, Let My son go that he may serve Me. And thou hast refused to let him go. Behold I will slay thy son, thy firstborn'" (Exodus 4:22–23).

The firstborn of Egypt were slain because Pharaoh had harmed God's "firstborn"; *beni bekhori Yisrael,* "My son, my firstborn, is

Israel." Firstborn in what sense? Ibn Ezra explains: "They were the first of My children to serve Me."

God has many children. Everyone on earth is, of course, one of His creations. What is the uniqueness of the Jewish people? Not that we are His "only" child, but rather that we are His first. We are, as it were, the first fruits of the Blessed One. How appropriate that at the moment when the first nation appeared on the scene of world history to acknowledge God as Master and accepted His will as law, Nature speaks an annual message and says, "This is the time when my first fruits flower."

First fruits are not the final harvest. Shavuot cannot be the end of the cycle of festivals. How could God, who created the entire world, be content if only a small portion of humanity is dedicated to Him? History must bring about recognition on the part of all; from first fruits we must eventually proceed to a gathering of all the crops in the fields.

Significantly, the readings of the haftarah during the holiday of Sukkot deal with the Messianic Era, when all nations shall acknowledge God and when the kingdom of Heaven will reign on earth. If Passover commemorates the Exodus, and Shavuot the Revelation, then Sukkot speaks of a time that has not yet materialized, the time commensurate with the "final harvest," the epoch when the first fruits of the Jewish people will be followed by all peoples, as symbolized through the seventy sacrifices offered on Sukkot. Passover is the festival of freedom and Shavuot the time of the giving of the Torah; but Sukkot is the time of rejoicing in the fullest sense of the word, rejoicing for the end of history.

When do we observe *Simhat Torah*? Not on Shavuot, when we might have expected it. True, the Jewish people made a commitment at the Revelation. But there could not be complete happiness if the Torah, given in the desert, remained in the realm of "My son, My firstborn." It was still the festival of *first* fruits. The Torah, however, was meant for all peoples. There must be and there will be a Sukkot for all the nations of the world.

The Torah begins with a reference to God's universalism: "In the beginning, God created the Heaven and the earth." That is perhaps why the Scriptures (comprising the Pentateuch, Prophets, and Writings) cannot really come to a close with the verse that concludes the Pentateuch. The last words of the Pentateuch are "in the sight of all Israel" (Deuteronomy 34:12). It was, we are told, the Jewish people who acknowledged all the wonders and signs that the Lord did through His servant, Moses. God, Creator of the universe, was accepted by Israel. There is an imbalance between the opening verse of the Five Books of Moses and their conclusion: The Creator of the universe is perceived only by a small portion of the earth's inhabitants. That imbalance is rectified by the verse that concludes the entire Torah. It was the men of the Great Assembly, in the spirit of prophecy, who recognized the holiness of other works that would be appended to the Five Books of Moses. What is the concluding verse of the Scriptures? It appears at the conclusion of the Second Chronicles: "Thus sayeth Cyrus, king of Persia: 'All the kingdoms of the earth hath the Lord, the God of heaven, given me; and He hath charged me to build Him a house in Jerusalem, which is in Judah. Whosoever there is among you of all His people—the Lord his God be with him—let him go up'" (36:23). When the non-Jewish king, Cyrus, proclaims God as the God of Heaven and of earth, the Scriptures may come to their proper conclusion. The first verse of Genesis has met its counterpart. Even the pagan recognizes that the Lord created the world and acknowledges the right of Jews to build a temple unto Him.

That recognition marks the dawn of that day when the Lord of Israel will in fact be the One God of the entire world, as recited in the prayer "Hear O Israel" for generations.

21

The Source
of the Seven
Universal Laws

hat are the seven universal laws?

They are obviously very special, for they define responsibility rooted not in Revelation but Creation; not in the acceptance of Sinai, but in the reality of humanity; not as a result of accepting the Torah, but as a by-product of the divine image in which human beings were created. Before one can be a Jew, one has to be a *mentsch*. It is the person as *mentsch* that brings with it seven crucial obligations.

Three of the seven belong in the unique category of laws demanding martyrdom. Murder, idolatry, and immorality are basic to non-Jews as well as Jews. To these three one must add four other laws, which can easily be remembered by the mnemonic "Alef, Beit, Gimel, Dalet." Alef recalls *Aver min ha-ḥai*—eating the organ of an animal while it is still alive (vivisection). Beit equals *Barekh et Hashem*. Literally *barekh et Hashem* means "to bless God." The Sages resort to this euphemism to avoid even uttering its opposite—the unimaginable crime of cursing God. Gimel equals *Gezel*—robbery. Dalet equals *Dinim*—the establishment of a judicial system to avoid anarchy and total lawlessness.

One may well ask, how could the world be held liable for these seven commandments if they were never verbalized, transmitted, or clarified? Perhaps we may respond that "we hold these truths to be self-evident." All people, not just Jews, should know better, just as Cain should have recognized the illegitimacy of murder. Our divine image makes us intuitively aware of minimum standards of ethical behavior.

Our Sages, however, tell us there is a far clearer source for these seven laws. They are implicit in the very first communication from God to Adam: "And the Lord, God, commanded the man saying, 'Of every tree of the Garden, thou mayest freely eat, but of the Tree of Knowledge of Good and Evil, thou shalt not eat of it, for in the day that thou eatest thereof, thou shalt surely die'" (Genesis 2:16–17).

On a superficial level the main point of the command appears in verse 17, beginning with the allusion to the Tree of Knowledge of Good and Evil. The Oral Law, however, interprets the first of these two verses, verse 16, in a fascinating manner. Every word of this sentence carries with it allusions to concepts from which we derive the Seven Noahide Laws.

Va-yezav—"And He Commanded"

The biblical word for "commanded"—*va-yezav*—carries with it an implication extending beyond the speaker and the one addressed. The Talmud teaches us that whenever that verb is used, it applies "from now and for all generations." It carries the force of eternity. The root *z.v.h.* forms the word *mitzvah*. Mitzvot are meant not only to be performed, but to be transmitted. The one who accepts carries the burden of ensuring compliance by others as well. When God addressed Adam via the language of *zav,* He made clear that a legal system, for purposes of regulation and enforcement, would be required. In short, the Oral Law makes us aware that the initial divine mandate refers to the establishment of *dinim,* or courts of law, for all times. This is the first of the seven universal laws addressed to humankind long before Sinai.

A word should be said here about the nature of the relationship between the Oral and Written Law. It would indeed be foolish to claim that one may derive a teaching of this sort simply from a cursory analysis of a word. The Oral Law does not maintain that it *derives* its conclusions as a result of pure interpretation. Rather, the Oral Law was always taught in conjunction with the Written. The two were transmitted as one unit. The Written Law leaves us sufficient reminders to reinforce what has orally been taught in conjunction with that verse. One may compare the relationship of Written and Oral Law to a student's notes for a lecture he or she had already attended, where the shorthand summaries offer sufficient recall for the entire discussion previously heard. If one were to object to a student explaining his or her notes: "You are reading far too much into them," the student would reply that no attempt is being made to read anything out of the lecture notes; rather, the notes simply bring back to mind the lengthy discussion given when the material was originally taught.

Adonai—The Lord

We have already noted that this designation evokes the Lord of love, kindness, and compassion. The fact that God loves us confers a concomitant obligation upon us. When in the *Shema* we proclaim that God is our Lord and identify Him as the One Lord, the next verse proclaims: "And you shall love the Lord, your God." The sequential logic is obvious. If He loves us, we are required to love Him in return. For if we do not reciprocate, He may well withdraw. If love is rejected, it may not last. When God spoke to Adam and identified Himself, His very Name would proclaim the second of the universal laws: the injunction against blasphemy. Cursing the Almighty is a serious crime denying the very basis of the most significant human relationship.

Elohim

This name of the Almighty has, in its Hebrew form, a plural ending (*im*). For our Sages that explains a seemingly erroneous sequence for the opening words of Genesis. The Hebrew words are *bereshit bara Elohim*. God's name, Elohim, is the third word following the verb *bara,* "created." One would have expected the phrase to follow the more logical sequence where the subject precedes the verb, i.e., *bereshit Elohim bara.* When the Sages were first forced to translate the Bible for King Ptolemy in the famous translation known as the Septuagint ("the seventy," named after the number of translators), they reversed the order of the words so that the pagan king would not assume that a god by the name of "Bereshit" created another god called "Elohim." Yet the text needs explanation. Why is the verb before the subject? The commentators explain that this formulation prevents a horrible heresy from gaining acceptance. Since Elohim is a plural word, some might have assumed that the Bible is suggesting a plurality of gods. How does the Torah make clear that this is not so? Since in Hebrew a verb agrees with the subject both in gender and number, the fact that *bara,* "created," is singular indicates that the subject of the sentence is singular as well. So important is this clarification that the verb in this instance precedes the subject. Thus, there is not even a moment in which any reader could assume that what is being discussed is the handiwork of many gods rather than the creation by One.

The plural ending of Elohim is something that always had to be carefully guarded against misinterpretation. One might therefore logically ask, why use a name with such potential danger? If the most significant teaching of Judaism is monotheism, why would God adopt a name that suggests multiplicity?

The answer goes to the heart of the root of the word Elohim. Hebrew words derive from a basic three-letter source or sometimes from a shorter two-letter word. The three-letter root of אלהים (Elohim) is אלה (Eleh) which means "these." Looking around the world, the pagan mind was impressed with a multiplicity of objects—mountains, seas, trees, grass, flowers, clouds, stars, and planets. Each one must have power. For each there must be an Ultimate and Supreme force, a "god of the mountains, of the seas," etc. The shorter two-letter root of אלה (ELeH) is אל (EL), which in fact does mean "strength" or "power." "These powers" (ELeH EL) suggested the existence of many gods. Diversity created idolatry.

But where the pagan was misled by multiplicity, the Jew found

confirmation of monotheism in the very diversity of His handiwork. אל (EL, or God) with the power of אלה (ELeH), all these,
suggested a unity that explained the source of everything.

Perhaps the greatest intellectual contribution of the twentieth
century was Einstein's grasp of the unity between matter and
energy. Two seemingly totally different aspects of existence were in
reality one. Einstein, it is said, spent the last years of his life
attempting to find a single unifying force of the entire universe, a
fact of which he was certain. We Jews believe we have found that
Ultimate Unity: God is the Oneness of the world, the power (EL)
behind everything. His Name is plural to convey His existence
within all. The first words of the Torah explain what Einstein was
seeking to find. Elohim may appear via the manifold aspects of
His creation to represent many, but *bara* (created) is singular.
Unity within diversity. That is the secret of the universe.

To understand it is to reject idolatry. That is why the third
word was shorthand for the third principle addressed to humanity,
the rejection of idolatry.

'Al ha-Adam—To Adam

The wording *'al ha-adam* is strange. If the text means to convey
the idea that God spoke *to* Adam, the Hebrew preposition should
have been *el*. *'Al* in Hebrew means "on" or "with regard to." The
verse in fact teaches that God first commanded Adam a law with
regard to human life. Violation of this law would later warrant
punishment for Cain when he slew his brother Abel. *'Al ha-Adam*
is biblical shorthand for the injunction against murder, the fourth
universal law preceding and exclusive of the 613 mitzvot.

Leimor, Saying

Although *leimor* is usually translated as "saying," the translation is both incorrect and redundant. When the Torah states "And
God spoke to Moses, saying," are we to infer that, without the last
word, the text would imply that God spoke to Moses without saying? *Leimor* (with the infinitive lamed preceding the three consonants EMR) really means "to say," i.e., "to say over, to repeat,

to transmit to others." Used in connection with Moses, it represented his mission to teach the Jewish people. Spoken to an individual, as here to Adam, it refers to the mitzvah of transmitting the law to our children, as the Torah will subsequently teach us, *veshinantam le-vanekha,* "And you shall teach your children."

Each person is a link in the chain of eternity. Progeny require the past for direction; parents need children to ensure survival, both for themselves and their values.

This major mitzvah, crucial to continuity, entails one fundamental prerequisite. To teach one's children, one must know who they are. Sexual immorality is condemned not only for the harm it does to the present but for its effects on the future. It negates the soundness of family life. Unbridled sensuality leaves in its wake generations of children whose paternal lineage is unclear. For such people, the pedagogic duty toward one's children, inherent in the word *leimor,* is impossible to fulfill. This is why the injunction against sexual immorality was the fifth principle Adam was taught in anticipation of the Seven Noahide Laws.

Mi-Kol Eẓ Ha-gan—"Of Every Tree of the Garden"

"From the trees of the garden you may eat." God defines the property that is off limits to Adam, as well as the property he may have. Clearly what is inaccessible to Adam is forbidden, and to take that would be theft. The concept of property and ownership was established here. *Gezel,* robbery, became the sixth of the seven Noahide laws.

One question has not yet been raised. If these seven are, in fact, universal laws differing from the 613 because they relate not solely to the Jew but to all humanity, why are they attributed specifically to the children of Noah? True, after the flood, the only survivors were Noah and his family. We do, in a sense, descend from him. But the origin of the human species goes back further. Adam is the common ancestor for all. Laws rooted in Adam's creation in the image of God do go back to the first man. Why do we not refer to the universal laws as the Seven Laws of the children of Adam? The answer resides in the last of the seven laws, which could not have been given to Adam because the area of its concern only became relevant after the Deluge.

Adam was a vegetarian. To him God had said: "Behold I have given you every herb-yielding seed which is upon the face of all the earth and every tree in which is the fruit of the tree-yielding seed. To you it shall be for food" (Genesis 1:29). The next verse proclaimed, "And to every beast of the earth and to every fowl of the air and everything that creepeth upon the earth, wherein there is a living soul, I have given every green herb for food." Humans and animals were herbivorous, and humans were not permitted to destroy any living thing.

So it was until after the flood. Only after Noah and his family stepped forth from the Ark did God allow what had previously been forbidden: "And God blessed Noah and his sons and said onto them, 'Be fruitful and multiply and replenish the earth. And the fear of you and the dread of you shall be upon every beast of the earth and upon every fowl of the air and upon all wherewith the ground teemeth and upon all the fishes of the sea. Into your hand are they delivered. Every moving thing that liveth shall be for food for you as the green herb have I given you all'" (Genesis 9:1–3).

Our Sages disagree as to why this major change concerning food came about after the Deluge. Some suggest it represented an acknowledgment of Noah's greater eminence and spirituality. Noah was the survivor, the man the Torah described as "righteous and wholehearted . . . Noah walked with God" (Genesis 6:9). Our only conceivable right to the slaying of animals possessing "souls of life" (*nefesh ḥayah*) is to elevate animal existence by incorporating it into human life dedicated to serving God. Does not the Talmud teach us that "a man of the earth," i.e., a boor, is forbidden to eat flesh (*Pesaḥim* 49b)? Those who are no better than the animals, in terms of their spiritual life, have no right to eat meat. Their lives are not qualitatively better than the life they extinguish to satisfy a personal craving. Noah could now eat meat because he was holier than Adam.

Others take their cue from the messianic vision, which implies that in a perfect world everyone will again be vegetarian. Slaughtering any living thing, beast or fowl, will be considered cruel and barbaric. Adam's lifestyle as originally ordained by God is the one identified with the Garden of Eden. If Noah was permitted to eat what Adam could not, it was as a result of a special concession required for an educational purpose. In the time of the flood, people sinned because they considered themselves no holier than animals—"the end of all flesh is come before Me" (Genesis 6:13). God saw that generation as *basar,* the word for "animal meat," because that is how *they* perceived themselves. They lived like animals and even mated with animals. After the flood, God felt it necessary to set up clear distinctions between these two kinds of existence. Hence, Noah was taught "You may eat the meat of every moving thing that liveth," but "who so sheddeth man's blood, by man shall his blood be shed" (Genesis 9:6). God instructed Noah that he dare not slay a human being. Men are not animals. Noah's new food supply would serve as a constant reminder of this crucial distinction.

Both views are valid. The role of vegetarianism in Judaism today is not fully settled. The former Chief Rabbi of Israel, Rabbi Goren, did not eat meat, in accord with the view that taking the life of any living thing is at best a compromise, not a formal requirement. Others emphasize that whenever we require rejoicing, such as on Sabbath and holidays, there must be meat and wine present, so that we elevate and internalize animal flesh in the holy worship of God.

All views agree, though, that Adam was not permitted to eat any meat whatsoever. The seventh of the universal laws prohibits the removal and consumption of any part of an animal while it is still alive (*ever min ha-ḥai*). This had relevance only to Noah and his descendants. To them the Torah stated: Although you may eat the animal after it is dead, you can never condone the kind of cruelty practiced in many parts of the world, where a limb is chopped off an animal and consumed while the beast howls in pain and terror. Indeed at Sinai, the covenant with the Jewish people will extend this principle to require a special method of slaughter, *sheḥitah*. Ritual slaughter reflects special concern for the manner in which an animal may be put to death. For the sons of Noah, who for the first time were permitted to eat meat, the restriction against *ever min ha-ḥai* was considered sufficient.

The seven universal laws as we know them today, including the last, are given to the descendants of Noah, who are eaters of meat. Adam was not a carnivore but he too had seven laws. His "food law" differed from ours. It restricted not a limb of a living thing, but far more. Any and every animal was forbidden. That is why the verse alluding to the seven laws concludes: *Akhol tokheil*, in English, "You may surely eat." The word "surely" in translation is meant to suggest the repetition of the word *akhol*. More correctly, however, the phrase ought to be translated as "food you shall eat," i.e., what has already been proclaimed edible for you is what you shall eat and nothing else. There is much that is off limits, not only in location (i.e., *gezel*—that which is not yours) but in type. Adam could not take life; later Noah would be forbidden to tear away the limb of an animal while it is still alive.

Judaism does not maintain that God came to Adam long ago in Paradise and gave him, as a first restriction, a ban against the fruit of a tree. What transpired was a message that would, if observed, ensure that all people could create an ongoing Paradise throughout history. Perhaps, had Adam and Eve not sinned with the Tree of Knowledge, these seven laws would have been sufficient. People would not have needed more safeguards. The self-discipline demanded from them might have kept human beings holy. Once they were banished from Eden, God knew that true spirituality requires 613 mitzvot. That is the requirement for the highest level of sanctity. For those not yet ready to commit themselves to this Sinaitic level, the basic essentials remain incumbent upon all. Jews must obey the Torah; Gentiles are judged by their fulfillment of the seven universal laws.

22

The Two New Years

he existence of universal laws is constantly recon-firmed for the Jew by a seeming peculiarity in the calendar.

When does the year begin? Rosh Hashanah is observed on the first day of the Hebrew month of Tishrei. It is identified by most with the moment of Creation. Some have even suggested that the Hebrew word for "genesis" (*BeREShiYT*) with a slight rearrangement of letters, indicates the exact day when Creation took place: בראשית—*be-Alef TiShREiY,* on the first of Tishrei. Rosh Hashanah is also the Day of Judgment. The link between Creation and annual judgment is obvious. On the very day when God created the world, He chooses to review it and see whether it is worthy of His ongoing assistance, without which the world would cease to be.

The world was not created and then left to run on its own. As our prayers indicate, "Blessed be the One Who continues to make the act of Creation." Were the world not to be willed to exist on an ongoing basis, it would simply cease. God makes His decision concerning every human being as well as the universe on the day that commemorates the initial Creation.

Yet, the Jews leaving Egypt were taught to observe another

new year. This was the very first commandment given to the Jewish people as a nation. "And the Lord spoke unto Aaron and Moses in the land of Egypt, saying, 'This month shall be unto you the beginning of months. It will the first month of the year to you'" (Chapter 12:1–2). The month was that of Nisan; the commandment was that it be considered "first."

What purpose was served by giving Nisan this distinction? The Sages explain that it would calendrically serve as a reminder of the exodus from Egypt. It would constantly make us recall not the Creation of the world, but the creation of the Jewish people, the birth of a nation.

Counting from Tishrei, Nisan is the seventh month. Just as there are six weekdays followed by a holy day, the Sabbath, so, too, do the months now gain their Sabbath—a seventh one of holiness welcoming the Jewish people after six months of "winter," identified by the existence of a world not yet acknowledging its Creator. Metaphorically, Tishrei is the world, Nisan is the Jew. Tishrei is Adam, Nisan the totality of Israel.

Small wonder that the very first mitzvah given to the Jewish people makes us aware of our uniqueness and commemorates our beginnings. Nevertheless we must ask, once Nisan was deemed the first month, why did Tishrei remain with its holiday? We are now God's people. Should we not be judged on the first day of Nisan? Should not the holy day begin with the moment of birth of the holy people?

It is extremely important to note that Rosh Hashanah, the Day of Judgment, still remains the first day of Tishrei, because even with the birth of the Jew, the rest of the world was not rejected. The New Year prayer states: "Today is the day of judgment when all peoples of the world stand before God." The most important prayers of the High Holy Days proclaim God as King over the entire universe.

Much as God loves us, He still is the ruler of the whole world. He still judges everybody. Perhaps the Jew by a higher standard, but the non-Jew still with love, care, and concern. There is not a blessing in our faith that does not convey this truth. When we bless God we say, *Eloheinu,* our God, but immediately afterward we say the words *melekh ha-olam,* King of the Universe. He is the

God of Nisan, but also and always the God of Tishrei. We are important to Him. But the Creator of the entire universe cannot simply renounce or reject all of His other children. That is why the Jewish role is to be a kingdom of priests and why we are called "my son, my firstborn." Thus, the festival of Shavuot is the holiday of the first fruits. But we, together with God, still look forward to the final harvest of Sukkot, the time of complete rejoicing.

The seven universal laws serve as an ongoing reminder that God is the father of all people. Long ago, a woman added 606 more laws to her original seven, and her name became Ruth. The day will come when her descendant, of the House of David, will see to it that all humankind will join in acknowledging God and the reality of His Torah. His name will be the Messiah. His task will be to bring to completion what began a long time ago in the month of Nisan. There will come a day when all will worship the Creator of the heavens and the earth.

Part VIII

Is Study the
Greatest Mitzvah
of All?

23

Study or Deed?

ne mitzvah of the 613 is *Talmud Torah,* the study of Torah itself.

Is this mitzvah perhaps qualitatively different from any other? We may not distinguish between mitzvot. Yet we found some that were patently unique and in a category by themselves. We noted the separate sets of seven and three, the Seven Universal Laws and the Three Laws of Martyrdom. Is the study of Torah different by definition because of its role in fulfilling Jewish law? Does it perhaps occupy a central place in all of Judaism because it permits a human being to become linked intellectually with God Himself?

The Talmud in *Kidushin* discusses the relationship between study and deed, scholarship and saintliness of action.

R. Tarfon and the Elders were once reclining in the upper storey of Nitza's house, in Lod, when this question was raised before them: Is study greater, or practice? R. Tarfon answered, saying: Practice is greater. R. Akiva answered, saying: Study is greater, for it leads to practice. Then they all answered and said: Study is greater, for it leads to action. [*Kidushin* 40b]

Once again we encounter the attic of the house in the city of Lod!

We noted this location earlier in the discussion about martyrdom. Here one may identify the question as the opposite side of the coin: for what should a man live? What ought to be the greatest ideal? And if the question was raised in the attic, the text reminds us that the problem came to the fore at a time when persecution threatened Jewish survival. It was then that the rabbis wanted to resolve an issue raised by philosophers as well as theologians of all faiths.

Which is greater, study or deed? Who is the man more to be admired, the Sage who knows all, or the unlearned who nonetheless is committed to religious practice?

The Talmud seems superficially to present us with two disparate views, an unresolved controversy between the Sages. Rabbi Tarfon had selected deed; Rabbi Akiva was the proponent of study. Note the conclusion. They all responded and said, "Study is greater, for it leads to action."

Whose view did they consider to be the halakhically acceptable one? At first glance, it seems as if they were siding with Rabbi Akiva. But anyone familiar with talmudic terminology must surely note the remarkable omission of Rabbi Akiva's name in the response of "all of them." The text should simply have read: "They responded, 'The law is like Rabbi Akiva.'" We were already familiar with both opinions. The conclusion should have sided with one over the other. Clearly, in this fundamental issue, the rabbis chose to conclude neither like Rabbi Tarfon nor like Rabbi Akiva, but to present us with a third view that is an amalgam of both. *Talmud Torah,* study, is not the greatest mitzvah as an isolated act. The philosopher in an ivory tower, who attains total familiarity with the text and will of God, cannot be the greatest hero if his knowledge simply remains ensconced in the mind, if intellect produces no tangible results in life lived on this earth.

No, the rabbis concluded, study is greater because it leads to action. It is only when the sequence "to learn and to teach, to observe and to do" is completed that mastering God's will has meaning.

The Mishnah teaches: "not study is of main import, but the deed" (*Ethics of the Fathers* 1:17). If that is the case, how could the Talmud in *Kidushin* have placed primacy on study itself? The two do not contradict each other. One speaks of means, the other of ends.

Torah study is given its lofty significance because without it one would not know how to carry out the mitzvot properly. Visiting the sick is all well and good. But what if one visits late in the evening when the patient would prefer to sleep? What if one visits a person embarrassed by his or her incontinence? Halakhah takes into account all possibilities and rules for them.

That is the real meaning of the famous phrase from the Talmud (*Shabbat* 127a) that we recite daily in our prayers: "*Talmud Torah keneged kulam*—the study of Torah stands opposite all of them." The text had just taught: "These are the precepts whose fruits a person enjoys in this world but whose principal remains intact for him in the world to come. They are: the honor due to father and mother, acts of kindness, early attendance at the house of study morning and evening, hospitality to guests, visiting the sick, providing for a bride, escorting the dead, absorption in prayer, bringing peace between man and his fellow."

The conclusion concerning study does not imply that Torah learning exceeds all other items previously mentioned in terms of religious value. It simply suggests that study is "*keneged kulam*." *Keneged* means "opposite" like a mirror so that all the aforementioned mitzvot must be viewed in the context of study. Deeds become holy only if performed in accordance with the parameters clarified by the Torah. Neither study nor deed alone is sufficient; they are both necessary and interdependent. Study is not a goal or ultimate end in Judaism. It is merely the means to the good life, the way in which we learn what God asks us *to do*.

Study and deed are as inseparable as the phylacteries of the head and hand. The phylacteries are in fact symbols. They indicate subservience of the two poles of our existence. We subjugate the mind and acknowledge that He knows more than we do, that our intellect is inferior to His, that we must study to know what He desires, rather than rationalize our own motivations into a creed of ethical behavior. With the subjugation of the mind, however, must come the subjugation of the hand. When a Jew puts on the phylacteries of the head and hand, he may not talk between the placement of one and the other, for they must be inextricably linked. Both together remind us of the two words that defined our greatness at Sinai: *na'aseh ve-nishma,* "we will do and we will hearken." The Talmud relates that angels themselves were amazed at the profundity of the Jewish people. Who, they asked, revealed to the Jews the secret that the deed must take precedence even over study (*Shabbat* 88a)?

If Torah study assumes such priority in Jewish life, it must only be viewed as a stepping-stone to a greater good. Torah study is the greatest priority, but only because it leads to proper action and allows us to properly perform the will of the Almighty.

24

The Three Crowns

tudy is in a class by itself. True, it is not greater than all other mitzvot in the sense that one might set aside performance in preference for study, but as Maimonides succinctly states

> There is no mitzvah amongst all the mitzvot which is the equivalent of the study of Torah, but rather the study of Torah is opposite all mitzvot for study leads to action; therefore study precedes action in every place. [*Hilkhot Talmud Torah* 3:3]

This is why the scholar is so admired in Jewish life. Torah study is also the ultimate measure of aristocracy amongst our people. That aristocracy is democratic, since it is open to any Jew who wishes to join it.

A crown may be real or symbolic. It expresses a concept of royalty, an aspect of preeminence. Maimonides, analyzing a passage in *Ethics of the Fathers,* elaborates upon the crowns that exist among our people:

> With three crowns were the Jewish people crowned: The crown of Torah, the crown of Priesthood, and the crown of Kingship. The

crown of Priesthood was merited by Aaron, as it says, "And it shall
be to him and his descendants after him a covenant of Priesthood
forever." A crown of Kingship is merited by David, as it says, "His
seed forever will be in his throne as the sun in my presence." The
crown of Torah, behold, is placed and stands and is prepared for all
of Israel, as it is said, "The Torah commanded to us by Moses as an
inheritance for the congregation of Jacob." Whoever so desires it
may come and take it. Lest you perhaps say those crowns [Priest-
hood and Kingship] are greater than the crown of Torah, behold, it
says "By Me kings reign, and princes decree justice. By Me princes
rule." Thus you may learn that the crown of Torah is greater than
both of them. [*Hilkhot Talmud Torah* 3:1]

Priesthood is a crown of service. It was given to Aaron and belongs
to his descendants thereafter. It is a hereditary honor transmitted
from one generation to another. A non-Priest may never join
those who serve in the sanctuary. The same is true of kingship. The
descendants of David are so honored. Others dare not aspire to
that position.

Heredity ensures the performance of certain tasks. Even as it
honors, it places demands. The word *kavod* in Hebrew means both
respect and "heavy," i.e., a difficult burden to be carried.

Judaism does not content itself with the two crowns that are
inaccessible to the majority of Jews. There *must* be a crown open to
all. It is the crown of Torah, and our Sages have taught us that it
deserves the highest praise. "The crown of Torah is greater than
the two others."

In no culture can a commoner aspire to be king. Among Jews,
any youngster can hope to become someone greater.

Upon whom is honor bestowed? Hereditary positions do carry
certain privileges. Nevertheless: "Our Sages have said a bastard
who is a scholar takes precedence over a High Priest who is an
ignoramus, as it says יקרה היא מפנינים'—it [Torah] is dearer than
precious stones, [dearer] than a High Priest who enters לפני ולפנים,
into the innermost sanctuary'" (*Hilkhot Talmud Torah* 3:2).

A *mamzer* may be born with seemingly unrectifiable deficiencies. There is no way in which he can ever undo the tragedy associated with his sinful birth. Yet if he drinks from the waters of
Torah and absorbs the words of God, then the poorest boy from

the smallest village with the meanest background must be revered among our people more than the King or High Priest! Can there be a greater democratic ideal than this? The High Priest who seeks glory simply because of his heritage is mistaken. The pedigreed ignoramus is far inferior to the bastard who compensates for his poor beginnings through a commitment to study and personal growth.

Maimonides and Jewish law, however, are extremely careful to qualify this emphasis on Torah study. An ideal perverted may turn into idolatry.

Thus, we are taught: "If one had before him the performance of a mitzvah as well as the study of Torah, if it is possible for the mitzvah to be done through others, let him not cease his study. But if this is not the case, then let him perform the mitzvah and [only] subsequently return to his studies" (*Hilkhot Talmud Torah* 3:4).

Study takes precedence only if the righteous deed will be done. If not, no matter how great the Sage, the biblical or talmudic tome must be set aside and the righteous act performed.

Jewish history knows all too well the inherent dangers of a community in which intellectualism is admired to an extreme, in which piety is misunderstood as mental mastery of material rather than righteous practice. That was the key to the rift between hasidim and their opponents, the mitnagdim.

The hasidic movement took root because there were too many incidents such as the one recorded by Ya'aqov Yosef of Polnoy. This renowned rebbe had met the Ba'al Shem Tov and asked: "They say that you are an expert at story telling. Perhaps you will favor me with one of your tales."

"I am prepared," replied the founder of Hasidism, the BESHT, "to fulfill your wish and will relate to you an incident that truly happened. In a certain house there lived two Jewish men and their families. One was a scholar, the other a poor laborer. Every day the scholar would rise from his sleep at the break of dawn and go to the synagogue where first he would study a page of Talmud and then, as the pious men of old were wont to do, wait a short time, direct his heart to heaven, and say the morning prayers quietly and slowly, drawing out his worship until almost midday. His neighbor, a poor laborer, also rose early and went to work, back-breaking work that strained the body and soul at once, until noon—there being no time to go to the synagogue to pray with the congregation at the proper hour. It was precisely at midday that the scholar left the synagogue to return home filled with a sense of self-satisfaction. He had busied himself with Torah and prayer and had scrupulously performed the will of his Creator. On his way from the synagogue he would invariably meet his neighbor, the poor laborer, hurrying to the House of Worship where he would recite the morning prayers in great haste, with anguish and regret for his tardiness. When the poor laborer passed his neighbor on the street, he would utter a mournful groan. It was a groan born from the recognition that the other had already finished his study and prayer in leisure and he himself had not yet begun. It was then that the lips of the scholar would curl mockingly, and in his heart he would think: Master of the world, see the difference between this creature and me. We both rise early in the morning. I rise for Torah and prayer—but he?

"So the days, weeks, months, and years passed. Each of the two men's lives was spent in a different fashion. One lived in the freedom of Torah and prayer, the other in the slavery of earning a livelihood. And when from time to time their paths would cross, the scholar would smirk and the laborer would groan.

"As it must to all men, death came, at last, to the scholar and, shortly afterward, to his neighbor, the laborer. The scholar was called before the Heavenly Tribunal to give an accounting of his deeds. 'What have you done with the days of your years?' a voice from on high called out. 'I am thankful,' replied the scholar with a firm voice in which could be detected more than a little pride, 'that all my days I served my Creator, studying much Torah and praying with a pure heart.' 'But,' commented the heavenly Accuser, 'he always mocked his neighbor, the poor worker, when they would meet near the synagogue.' The voice from on high was heard: 'Bring the scales!' On one side they put all the Torah that he had learned and all the prayers that he had prayed, while on the other side they put that faint smirk which hovered over his lips each day when he met his neighbor. Lo and behold the weight of the smirk turned the scale to—Guilty!

"After the case of the scholar had been complete, they brought before the Heavenly Tribunal the poor laborer. 'What have you done with your life?' asked the voice from on high. 'All my life I have had to work hard in order to provide for my wife and children. I did not have the time to pray with the congregation at the proper time. Nor did I have the leisure to study much Torah, for there are hungry mouths at home to feed,' answered the laborer in shame and grief. 'But,' commented the heavenly Advocate, 'each day when he met his neighbor the scholar, there issued from the depths of his soul a groan. He felt that he had not fulfilled his duties to the Lord.' Again the scales were brought and the weight of the groan of the poor worker turned the scale to—Innocent!''

Study alone may not be sufficient to open the doors of the Kingdom of Heaven. It may only be idealized as a means to a greater end.

Who Must Study?

Who is required to fulfill the mitzvah of *Talmud Torah*? Here, too, Jewish law is clear.

> The beginning of judgment for every person is for nothing other than study and afterward for all one's deeds. Therefore our Sages have said one should always occupy oneself with Torah either for its own sake or not for its own sake. For even if one studies not for its own sake, one will eventually come to studying for its own sake.
> [*Hilkhot Talmud Torah* 3:5]

Every person must face a final accounting. Jews know what will be asked of them. One of the first questions will revolve around our fulfillment of the mitzvah of study.

The exact phrase of the question, we are taught in the Talmud, is *Qavata itim la-Torah?* "Did you set aside time for the study of Torah?" Within the precise wording of that question rests a fascinating response to a problem some have posed concerning the "fairness" of this mitzvah.

All of us are born with different abilities. "All men are created equal" may refer to legal rights, but not to talents. That "inequality of genetics" is acknowledged in the famous passage in the Talmud where we are told that an angel "takes the drop of semen and places it before the Almighty to be judged whether to be wise or foolish . . ." (*Nidah* 16b). Our intellectual capacities are foregone conclusions from the very moment of conception.

In that case, how is it possible for a person to be judged on intellectual attainments?

Indeed, the answer is simply that we are not. To the student who once cried that no matter how much he studied he could not seem to remember, and his efforts were therefore pointless, the renowned teacher Reb Yisroel Salanter (1810–1883) responded: "Where did you ever hear of a mitzvah which demanded that you become a great scholar? The mitzvah is only that you study Torah." So, too, at the end of our days, we are not asked how much of the Torah we memorized, or how many novel interpretations we were able to create. The question is simply "Did you set aside time for the study of Torah?" What you remember is not as important as how much time you put into the effort. Here is an instance where we are not judged by whether we reached our goal, but rather by the effort put forth in our journey.

The Mishnah in *Ethics of the Fathers* (5:26) teaches us: "In accord with the pain is the gain" (*Lefum ẕa'ara agra*). Modern report cards, which now place greater emphasis on effort than on academic growth, have much in common with this perspective.

That orientation also struck a responsive chord in the hasidic movement. An excessive emphasis on intellectual achievement had clouded the vision of many with regard to the sanctity of those whose personal limitations restricted how much they knew, but whose personal greatness was all the more enhanced by the extent to which they struggled.

Who has not heard the hasidic story of the poor shepherd who wept bitter tears because he did not know how to pray? He could not read the words in the prayer book and felt incapable of properly approaching the Almighty. In his grief, all he found himself capable of doing was to read the letters individually. Plaintively, he cried out, "*Alef, Beit,*" and the other Hebrew letters that he remembered. Then, with the total sincerity of his soul, he said to God: "I cannot read the words. Instead I offer You the letters. You know how to put them together properly. I beg of You to please make of them words pleasing unto You." And when the holy

Rebbe himself soared to the heavens to learn what would be the fate of his people, he heard the decree from Above: "God will answer the petitions of His people because of the beauty and sincerity expressed by the prayer of the shepherd." Judged merely by content, the shepherd's prayer was surely not the most powerful one, yet the strength of its conviction and the sincerity of its enthusiasm outweighed by far all the other verbal offerings of the Jewish people.

The hasidic movement righted the imbalance of a world that failed to remember the dictum "in accord with the pain is the gain." Of course the great scholar was to be respected, admired, and emulated. But one ought never to forget the profound insight of the tale taught by Rabbi Ya'aqov Yosef of Polnoy. The scales of heaven weigh the smirk and the groan more than they do the number of texts committed to memory or the novel insights produced by God-given genius.

When Shall One Study?

The conduct of our lives follows from the direction of Torah perspective. That is why Torah must come first. Maimonides teaches us:

> Perhaps you will say until I will gather sufficient money will I turn and study, until I acquire what I need I will remove myself then from my occupation and engage in learning; if this thought enters your heart, you will never merit the crown of Torah forever. But make your Torah study fixed and your work incidental, and do not say when I shall have leisure I shall study, lest you never have leisure. It is written in the Torah "For it is not in the heavens nor is it across the seas." It is not in the heavens—not in the arrogant is it to be found nor amongst those who travel across the seas. Therefore our Sages have said, one who engages overmuch in business transactions will not become wise. And our Sages have commanded, diminish preoccupation with business and be preoccupied instead with Torah. [*Hilkhot Talmud Torah* 3:7–8]

We all say, "someday," when we have time, we will sit and study. Someday when we retire, we will have the opportunity to

relax and then we will give our minds an opportunity to grow and
to develop.

The most obvious response to that is simply: "It will never
happen."

There is a famous story told by Tolstoy. It captures powerfully
the tragedy of "Everyman." In various forms, it has parallels in
midrashic tales. It is, in fact, the idea expressed in the *Ethics of the
Fathers* (2:5): "Do not say when I shall have the opportunity, I
shall study, lest you never have the opportunity."

A nobleman, goes the story, wished to reward one of his feudal
serfs. He told him that he would bestow great blessing upon him.
He would give him the gift of a large piece of land, the exact size of
which would be determined by the serf himself.

Next morning he would grant him the opportunity to arise
early. From sunrise to sunset he might walk and encircle a parcel of
land. Whatever he would succeed in walking round would be his.
There would be only one condition: the serf must return exactly to
the starting point or he would forfeit everything.

How grateful the serf was for this once-in-a-lifetime opportunity! His plan, to fulfill the requirements, was simple. He would walk
in one direction until the sun would be directly overhead. Then,
knowing it was noon and obviously half his time had elapsed, he
would begin his return journey. In that way he could be certain to
be back at the starting point by sunset. That would give him a great
parcel of land. That would allow him and his family to be rich
beyond his wildest dreams.

And so he set off on his journey, his road to personal fulfillment
and riches. He quickened his pace as the sun continued its ascent.
Every additional step meant additional land, all his rushing would
be rewarded with more riches. When noon arrived, he could not
bear the thought that this would mark the end of his opportunity
for acquiring land. If he were to go a little further and hasten his
steps on the return journey . . . if he would extend the first part,
mapping out more, and then run the entire way to return to the
starting point in order to meet the condition, why then he might not
be just a wealthy man, but a very, very, rich man. He might have
enough not only for his children and grandchildren, but even for
countless generations to come.

And so he walked to acquire new land for half an hour, an hour,
two hours beyond noon. Panic overtook him as he realized how far

he had gone and how great the distance in order to make it to the point from which he started his journey. Jogging, running, racing—he *must* make it back or else all of his efforts would prove futile. It was on the return journey that people stopped him to ask him for different things. One needed a favor desperately, it was a matter of life and death. "Tomorrow," he shouted out, "tomorrow I will help you. Today I do not have the time." Another was his own child who was hurt and begged, "Father, father, please heal my wound, comfort me with words. I need you, Daddy." "Tomorrow, my child, tomorrow. Tomorrow I'll have time to spend with you. Tomorrow I will have time to play with you. Tomorrow, not today. Don't you see how busy I am? And I'm doing it all just for you."

His wife, too, rushed forward to speak to him in the midst of his busy race. "Just one word, my husband. Just one word. I cannot solve this problem myself. I need to speak with you or I will go mad. I need you to talk to me the way you did when we were courting, when you were my pillar of strength, when you were my everything, when I could turn to you no matter what I needed." "Tomorrow," said the husband to his wife, "tomorrow, tomorrow I will have all the time you need." And he rushed right by her.

The race now was between the sun on the horizon and his frantic footsteps to the starting point. So far had he misjudged his ability to retraverse the ground he had covered that it now seemed almost impossible for him to complete his journey. Faster, faster, and faster still. Now he had to race with all the effort superhumanly possible. His heart beat faster, his legs felt as if they would cave in beneath him.

The sun had almost disappeared. The master was in the distance waiting at the prearranged spot. With one final lunge, the serf leaped to the required spot at almost the very last second, legally fulfilling the condition set upon him. He smiled the smile of the victor. The smile froze on his face in a death mask as his soul departed from him.

"Take this peasant and bury him in a plot six feet long, two feet wide," commanded the master. "Let him lie there. Let the land be his. That is all the ground he really ever needed."

We race through life and we ignore those who are truly important to us. For each of them we have an answer: Tomorrow. Tomorrow and we shall help you. Tomorrow and we shall be with you. Tomorrow and we shall have time for everything. Today I must make my fortune. Today I must still hurry. Yet tomorrow never comes as we live out our days, rushing to possess those things that will allow us a comfortable future—a future we forfeit in the present as we constantly occupy ourselves with foolish pursuits that prevent us from ever engaging in the truly meaningful tasks of life.

These were the words of Hillel the Elder: "And do not say, when I shall have the opportunity I shall study, lest you never have the opportunity" (*Ethics of the Fathers* 2:5).

It is in this vein that Rabbi Yoshiah in the Talmud explains the symbolism of matzah. In Hebrew, מַצּוֹת (matzot) is identical to the word מְצִוֹת (mitzvot). The two are identical because matzot contain a message crucial to the performance of mitzvot. Matzah is unleavened bread. Its opposite is *hamez,* the forbidden food on Passover. Yet the ingredients of both are exactly the same. *Hamez,* which is so strictly forbidden that anyone who eats it on Passover is punished with excision (*Karet*) is nothing other than matzah, *just a little bit later.* The villain is time; the difference between what is mitzvah and sin is having allowed eighteen minutes to go by (18, perhaps because in gematria it represents the word *hai,* the Hebrew word for life), disregarding the matzah and letting it turn to leaven.

From matzot we learn the concept to be applied to all mitzvot: *mizvah ha-ba'ah le-yadkha al tahmizenah,* "A mitzvah which comes into your hands, do not allow it to become sour." Mitzvot, like matzot, are to be taken care of immediately—lest the passage of time turn the best of intentions sour.

Torah cannot be studied last. It must be a priority. If it comes first, then Torah study will lead to action; one's entire life is transformed, for fulfillment of the first priority has rearranged all others as well.

But Do Not Forsake the World

Torah study, as means to an end, is not to be viewed as an escape from responsibility.

Maimonides adds one last major stricture:

Anyone who presumes in his heart that he will occupy himself in

Torah and do no work, supporting himself from charity, behold, this person has desecrated the Divine Name and shamed the Torah as well as extinguished the light of religion, and caused evil to himself, and has removed his life from the World to Come; for it is forbidden to derive benefit from the words of Torah in This World. Our Sages have said, anyone who derives benefit from the words of Torah removes his life from the world; and they have further commanded and said do not make them [the words of Torah] a crown with which to be glorified nor a spade with which to dig; and further they have commanded and said, love work and hate rulership. And all Torah which does not have with it work, its end will to be negated and it will lead to sin; and the end of that person will be that he will come to rob his fellow man. [*Hilkhot Talmud Torah* 3:10]

Maimonides could not have described his personal philosophy of life better. Tradition has it that "From Moses [son of Amram] to Moses [Maimonides, son of Maimon] there arose none like Moses." Nevertheless, Maimonides made his living from the practice of medicine. He used Torah study not as an excuse to run away from life, but rather as a way to ennoble everything else that he did.

This orientation, according to most commentators, is the meaning of the passage in *Ethics of the Fathers*: "Great is the study of Torah together with the way of the world" (2:2). Man is to make a living, be a wage earner, perfect and improve the world. True, perhaps a very select few may spend all of their time in study so that the rest of the community can benefit from their perfection. But study in isolation surely cannot be justified. Study with no identifiable good for the greater community was not God's will when He compared Torah to water, whose purpose is to fructify, irrigate, and improve the entire world.

Maimonides did not include in his condemnation those who gave of their Torah scholarship to others, be it by way of teaching or preaching. If they dedicated their entire existence to transmitting Torah and had no other means of livelihood, the greater community should recompense them. They deserve support for their work, which benefits the multitude. But Maimonides strongly condemned study that produced no good outside the ivory tower of scholarship.

Judaism believes in study and in work. Adam lived in Paradise, but even in Paradise he had a task to perform: "to work it [the Garden of Eden] and to maintain it." The Sabbath law, which teaches us the concept of a day of rest, is prefaced with the words, "Six days shall you labor and do all your work" (Exodus 20:9). But work, labor, and the "way of the world" can only be Godly activities if they are joined to Torah study. *Talmud Torah* must come first and be the guide for all of life's activities. It may not be set aside as something we hope eventually at the end of our days to fulfill.

Three crowns were created for the Jewish people. Priests and kings were given their marks of royalty at birth. Every Jew can and must strive for the greatest crown. The democracy of our faith demands we all struggle to become aristocrats of Torah.

Part IX

Summing Up

25

The Deeds
That Define Us:
In Retrospect

e began by declaring that Judaism is primarily a religion of deed and not creed. That is why we chose first to analyze the deed-system of our "faith," a faith far more concerned with practical consequences than with conceptual theories. Its vocabulary is primarily that of Halakhah, the law, rather than the catechism of belief.

Are there essentials of deed? Are certain laws to be considered "more important?" A fundamental principle we established was that "All mitzvot are created equal." The easy mitzvah and the hard mitzvah, the sending away of the mother bird and the honoring of parents, both have identical rewards. The Ten Commandments are in fact not commandments; they are the principles summarizing all of Jewish law. They were originally spoken together in one instant to convey the unity of law and its indivisibility.

Yet several possibilities exist for dividing Jewish law. These divisions suggest the existence of certain priorities. If the two tablets of the Decalogue teach us that religion entails dual responsibilities to God and to humanity, the Torah—by both story and law—stresses the preference we should give to the interpersonal

219

laws. Other human beings so often require our assistance, in contrast to God, Who can truly manage for Himself.

Negative commandments, unlike positive laws, which contain no reference to different rewards, express by their severity of punishment the degrees of divine displeasure. Although Judaism does not actually desire capital punishment to be carried out, the "threats" of the Bible are meant to teach us the various levels of evil implicit in various sins.

Among the 613 mitzvot, there are also several that stand out either by themselves or by representing unique theological principles.

For three things we must be prepared to die. Life is meaningless without them. They are the "ultimates" of the three categories into which all of Jewish law may be divided. Conversely, for the other 610 mitzvot, the principle remains "life above all." For Judaism is indeed concerned with life here on this earth. God's kingdom *is* of this world, and our role is to perfect it. Holiness consists not in rejecting what God created, but in refining and sanctifying it.

Seven laws are meant not only for the Jew but for all peoples. God has not given up on the rest of the world. They are simply slower to recognize what the Jews accepted at Sinai. They, too, will join in the universal symphony of praise to God some day, and that day is envisioned by the Messianic Era.

To hasten that day and to live by Torah means that we must study Torah. *Talmud Torah* may be the one mitzvah in a class by itself. It is the cardinal tenet of Judaism. Provided that it is recognized as a means to an end, Torah study is the greatest, for it leads to deed.

With that we have concluded our overview of the "deed" dimension in Judaism. But we have not come to the end of our journey. For although deed is more significant than creed, the latter cannot be ignored. Without any belief, the halakhic structure topples. Without a belief in "I am the Lord, your God," the nine other principles have no rationale for being. So we continue our journey of self-discovery by turning from the world of mitzvah to the world of *emunah* (faith), from the arena of "This I shall do and this I shall not do" to the realm of "This I believe, this is my faith."

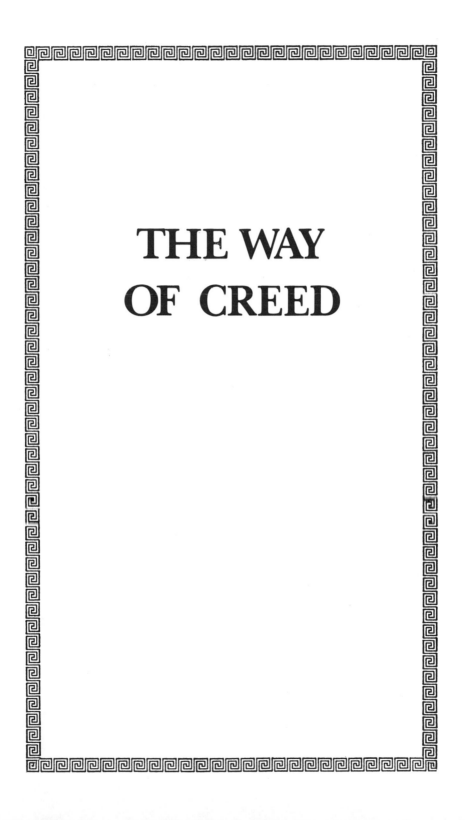

THE WAY
OF CREED

Part X

Must a Jew Believe?

26

The Thirteen
Fundamentals
of Belief

he Covenant of Sinai is primarily a commitment to
deed. God is concerned with "This thou shalt do"
and "This thou shalt not do" (*aseh* and *lo ta'aseh*).
Earlier we noted the comment of the Jerusalem Talmud on the
passage in Jeremiah where the prophet, speaking for God, bewails
the fact that "Me they have forsaken and My Torah they have not
kept: Would that they would have forsaken Me as long as they
would have kept My Torah."

The law of the Rebellious Elder (*zaqen mamre*) emphasizes the
primary area of biblical concern. The Mishnah in *Sanhedrin* (86b)
teaches us:

An Elder rebelling against the ruling of a Beth Din [is strangled],
for it is written (Deuteronomy 17:8), if there arise a matter too hard
for thee for judgment. [This proves that the verdict for the legal
issue involved is not explicitly mentioned in the Torah, since the
question is deemed "too hard" for judgment.] Three courts of law
were there [in Jerusalem], one situated at the entrance to the
Temple Mount, another at the door of the [Temple] Court, and the
third in the Hall of the Hewn Stones. They [the Elder and the
members of the court who contest his ruling] [first] went to the Beth
Din, which is at the entrance to the Temple Mount, and he [the

Rebellious Elder] stated, thus have I expounded and thus have my colleagues expounded; thus have I taught, and thus have my colleagues taught. If [this first Beth Din] had heard [a ruling on the matter], they state it. If not, they go to the [second Beth Din] which is at the entrance of the Temple Court, and he declares, this have I expounded and thus have my colleagues expounded; thus have I taught and thus have my colleagues taught. If [this second Beth Din] had heard [a ruling on the matter], they state it; if not, they all proceed to the great Beth Din of the Hall of Hewn Stones whence instruction issued to all Israel, for it is written, [which they] of that place which the Lord shall choose [shall shew this] (Deuteronomy 17:10). If he returned to his town and [merely] taught again as heretofore, he is not liable. But if he gave a practical decision, he is guilty, for it is written, and the man that will do presumptuously, [shewing] that he is liable only for a practical ruling.

The Rebellious Elder is not condemned for rebellious thought. Improper theology is a sin rooted in stupidity and does not become true heresy until it is affiliated with action and consequences.

How different from the witch trials of Salem, which were concerned simply with the charge of mistaken creed. Sufficient for them was the possibility of false belief. In Judaism what truly matters is how a person lives, what a person does, the way of Halakhah, which literally means "the path one chooses to take."

There have been some, such as Moses Mendelssohn (1729–1786), a philosopher of the German Enlightenment and spiritual leader of German Jewry, who have taken this to mean that Judaism renounces any interest whatsoever in theological categories. Judaism is not a "faith"; it is rather a guide for living, a manual for proper behavior. One may, according to Mendelssohn, believe anything as long as one lives by the law. Belief is irrelevant; what matters is simply observing the commandments. Piety is a function of practice, not of faith.

All classical Jewish commentators disagree with this view. Just as the Ten "Commandments" are impossible without the first, which proclaims the existence of God, so does acceptance of the 613 become not only impossible but perhaps irrelevant if not prefaced by a minimal commitment to a Creator and lawgiver. What if a Jew were to observe out of habit or peer pressure? What if a Jew observes the Sabbath and holidays merely out of enjoyment or out of deference to custom and tradition? What if a Jew simply chose to dance to the tunes of that magic fiddler on the roof who promises the joy of being part of "Jewish tradition"? Is such a person truly Jewish, is such observance the meaning of true religion?

Our daily prayer book has, it would appear, accepted the view of Maimonides. At the conclusion of the morning service we find an abridgement of the classic Thirteen Principles of Faith, which Maimonides posits as the basic theological prerequisites of a Jew. Although it is not an obligation of prayer, there are many who recite it on a voluntary basis.

The Thirteen Principles each begin with the phrase *Ani ma'amin be-emunah shelemah* ("I believe with perfect faith"):

I believe with perfect faith . . .

1.   . . . that the Creator, blessed be His Name, is the Author and Guide of everything that has been created and that He alone has made, does make, and will make all things.

2.   . . . that the Creator, blessed be His Name, is a Unity, and that there is no Unity in any manner like unto His, and that He alone is our God who was, is, and will be.

3.   . . . that the Creator, blessed be His Name, is not a body and that He is free from all the properties of matter, and that He has not any form whatsoever.

4.   . . . that the Creator, blessed be His Name, is the First and the Last.

5.   . . . that unto Him alone, it is right to pray, and that it is not right to pray to any being besides Him.

6.   . . . that all the words of the Prophets are true.

7.   . . . that the prophecy of Moses, our teacher, peace be unto him, was true, and that he was the chief of the Prophets, both those who preceded him and those who followed him.

8. . . . that the whole Torah now in our possession is the same that was given to Moses, our teacher, peace be unto him.

9. . . . that this Torah will not be exchanged, and that there will never be any other law from the Creator, blessed be His Name.

10. . . . that the Creator, blessed be His Name, knows every deed of the children of men, and all their thoughts, as it is said, "It is He that fashioneth the hearts of them all, that give heed to all their works."

11. . . . that the Creator, blessed be His Name, rewards those that keep His commandments, and punishes those that transgress them.

12. . . . in the coming of the Messiah, and though he tarry, I will wait daily for his coming.

13. . . . that there will be a revival of the dead at the time when it shall please the Creator, blessed be His Name and exalted be His Name forever and ever.

Several centuries later, the Thirteen Principles were reworded in poetic form and became far better known as the prayer *Yigdal.* The latter is included in the morning service and is today recited by every observant Jew.

One should not conclude from this, however, that Maimonides' listing enjoys universal acceptance. There are in fact three major disagreements with this approach, each one of which commands respect.

RaDbAZ (**R**abbi **D**avid **b**en Shelomoh Ibn **A**bi **Z**imrah, 1479–1573), when asked whether he accepted the formulation of Maimonides, wrote:

I do not agree that it is right to make any part of the perfect Torah into a principle, since the whole Torah is a principle from the Mouth of the Almighty. Our Sages say that whoever states that the whole of Torah is from Heaven with the exception of one verse is a heretic. Consequently, each precept is a principle and a fundamental idea. Even a light precept has a secret reason which is beyond our understanding. How then dare we suggest that this is inessential and that fundamental? ... My opinion is that every detail and inference of the Torah is a "principle," a foundation and a fundamental belief and whoever denies it is an unbeliever and has no share in the World to Come.

In short, Radbaz does not accept Maimonides because he does not believe that the Thirteen Principles go far enough. An objection of a totally different sort came from the Spanish philosopher and preacher Yosef Albo (c. 1380–1445), author of the *Sefer ha-'Iqarim* (Book of Principles):

A person is only called an "unbeliever" [*kofer*] who knows that the Torah lays down a certain principle, but willfully denies its truth. It is the element of rebellion against the clear teaching of the Torah which constitutes unbelief. But a person who upholds the law of Moses and believes in its principles, but when he undertakes to investigate these matters with his reason and scrutinizes the texts, is misled by his speculation and interprets a given principle otherwise than it is taken to mean at first sight; or denies the principle because he thinks that it does not represent the sound theory which the Torah obliges us to believe; or erroneously denies that a given belief is a fundamental principle, which, however, he believes as he believes the other dogmas of the Torah which are not fundamental principles; or entertains a certain notion in relation to one of the miracles of the Torah because he thinks that he is not thereby denying any of the doctrines which is obligatory upon us to believe by the authority of the Torah—a person of this sort is not an "unbeliever." He is classed with the Sages and pious men of Israel though he holds erroneous theories. His sin is due to error and requires atonement. [p. 496]

For Albo, Maimonides has gone too far. What if a pious, observant Jew believes—on the basis of his erroneous understanding of the Torah—that God does, in fact, have a body, that the phrase "Hand of God" is not a metaphor but is to be taken literally? Is such a man to be classed "heretic" simply because his mind was incapable of grasping the meaning of a metaphor? What if a Jew seriously wished to accept the Torah but misunderstood it in other ways, so that in all sincerity he believed he was accepting the Covenant of Sinai but did not understand its implications fully?

Such a Jew could not be an outcast or condemned to eternal damnation. Albo could not in good conscience consign someone who mentally erred to the same fate as a person who willfully chose to rebel. Perhaps Maimonides, the great rationalist, always assumed intellectual errors to be willful, but Albo was far more understanding. Even one who sides with Maimonides in accepting his list of thirteen tenets might not necessarily be required to accept the full force of Maimonides' ruling, according to which negation of any of the thirteen automatically consigns the skeptic to the punishments of the heretic.

A third criticism of the list offered by Maimonides is made by Naḥmanides (1194–1270), Crescas (d. 1412?), and others. They do not question the fact that there are basic principles. What they cannot accept is the specific list of thirteen as given. Nevertheless, Maimonides' summary seems to have gained the widest acceptance. Other lists have not been incorporated into the prayer book. The complaint of Radbaz that thirteen is far too minimal a list did not prevail. The profound distinction drawn by Albo, between error and rebellion, may be incorporated by us into an acceptance of the Thirteen Principles and serve as a qualification of them.

What we must analyze is why Maimonides codified precisely these thirteen principles of creed. To do so we must turn to the passage in the Talmud on which Maimonides based his list. The Thirteen Principles come from a passage in his master work, the *Perush ha-Mishnayot,* his commentary on the Mishnah. It is to the final chapter of the tractate *Sanhedrin* that we must now turn.

27

All of Israel
Have a Share in
the World to Come,
Except . . .

ll of Israel have a share in the World to Come" is the opening phrase of the final chapter in the tractate of *Sanhedrin*. Previous to it, the subject matter discussed the four different death penalties and the various situations that would warrant them. What connection could there possibly be between death penalties and the theological statement of hope and promise that all Israel is promised a portion of eternal bliss? Rabbi Shemuel Eliezer Edels (the MaHaRShA, 1555–1631) suggests a novel interpretation: "We have been talking about criminals who committed capital crimes. They are put to death by the courts, and one of the purposes of execution, we are told, is expiation. Even as one who has been given lashes is subsequently to be treated as 'your brother,' so, too, are those put to death by the courts then to be considered cleansed of their sins. 'All of Israel have a share in the World to Come'—even the ones we had just previously studied who committed capital crimes. The death penalty serves not only as punishment; it also secures atonement and forgiveness sufficient to allow a place in eternity."

Kol Yisrael ("all of Israel") means everyone. Some commentators even offer a remarkable allusion to the divisions within the

231

Jewish people. KoL is an acronym for *Kohen, Levi. Yisrael* includes all others. Thus, everyone has a share in the World to Come. Yet the Mishnah immediately thereafter seems to contradict its original premise when it adds, "And these are the ones who have no share in the World to Come." This share is denied to (1) one who rejects the principle that resurrection of the dead is a Torah-derived belief; (2) one who denies the divine source of Torah; and (3) the heretic. What seems incomprehensible is the apparent contradiction between the second phrase and the first: All of Israel have a share—and these are the ones who are excluded. How can we list a number of exceptions if the Mishnah had just told us unqualifiedly that *all* Jews have a share in the World to Come? If we did not mean "all," then at the very outset the Mishnah should have said, "All with the exception of three have a share in the World to Come." The text is clearly contradictory.

How should one explain this passage? Indeed both phrases are correct. All of Israel have a share in the World to Come at birth. All Jews are equally granted a portion of eternity. We cannot accept that some may be given grace at birth and others not. "O Lord," we recite as one of our first prayers every single day, "the soul that Thou hast given me is pure." We start our lives with purity of soul and therefore with an unqualified claim to a Heavenly portion. All have this justifiable claim. "And these are the ones who do not have a share in the World to Come"—because they forfeit their claim during their lifetime.

How can one forfeit the blessing of eternal bliss? Only one Mishnah in the entire Talmud deals with the requirement for proper belief. We are taught that three specific crimes, not of deed but of creed, are in fact so crucial that they result in a person losing the right to eternal life (*olam ha-ba*).

What Is *Olam Ha-Ba?*

Before proceeding, it is imperative for us to know the meaning of the term that describes the punishment as well as the blessing.

"A share in the World to Come" relates to three basic beliefs concerning afterlife:

1. The World of Souls (*olam ha-neshamot*). Death is the separation of the soul from the body. The soul comes from God and must return to Him. Like God, it is immortal. This soul has consciousness and awareness. Death does not dim its powers nor diminish its ability to be aware both of self and of others. The Talmud describes souls "speaking to each other" after death. At the time of death, the soul hovers near the body that served it well. It "hears" the eulogy; it "sees" the friends who come to pay final respects. The soul goes through a purification process after death to cleanse it of the sins that adhered to it during its lifetime. This purification process is universal, since "There is no one so righteous upon this earth who does only good and sinneth not," Ecclesiastes teaches us. All sin must be "washed away." Every soul must go through some period of purification and punishment after death. For the most pious it may last but a moment. For the most wicked it can last a maximum of twelve months. There is a reason why Kaddish is recited for eleven months. It allows mourners to pray on behalf of the deceased for a period sufficient to cover even an extremely terrible sinner. At the same time, the deceased is spared embarrassment because the mourner stops reciting Kaddish in the twelfth month. This implies that the deceased was not a terrible sinner and his or her degree of punishment after death was not long. Once the purification process is completed, the soul survives in the "presence of God," drawing ever closer to the Almighty on the anniversary of the day of death, a fact commemorated through celebration by survivors as they commemorate the *Yahrzeit*. In this world of souls, there is peace and contentment, there is no pain or suffering.

2. *Messiah*. God created the world as a Garden of Eden. Paradise was the way Creation was meant to be. Sin

forced Adam and Eve to be cast out, but the Garden was not destroyed. "So He drove out the man and He placed at the east of the Garden of Eden the Cherubim and the flaming sword which turned every way to keep the way to the Tree of Life" (Genesis 3:24). God never destroyed the Garden. That is because He intends for us someday to return to it. The Messianic Era is nothing other than history coming full circle. What was, is what will be; the way God intended the world to be must someday come to fruition. We cannot know all the details of the "World to Come." We do know, however, that it was described as Paradise by God Himself and that is sufficient for us to long for its return.

Although *olam ha-ba* is used to describe both of these future ideals, in English we might well call the world of souls the "World to Come" and the Messianic Era the "Coming World."

3.   Resurrection of the Dead. Perhaps fairness to most of recorded history demands belief in this third concept as a fitting bridge between the first and the second belief. Billions of people have died in the course of time. True, after death their souls have the bliss of continued existence in Heaven. But the Messianic Era is life as it was meant to be lived here on this earth. What of all those who are not destined to be alive at the time when the Messiah will finally be revealed? Will all those never know the glory, the joy, the indescribable bliss of human life here on earth in the reign of the Messianic Kingdom? Resurrection of the Dead means that sometime after Messiah appears, those who passed on will rejoin the living, those from the "World to Come" will taste the delights of the "Coming World."

Our Sabbath prayers refer to all three as aftermaths to our existence here on this terrestrial sphere:

There is no comparison to You, Hashem, our God, in this world, and there will be nothing except for You, our King, in the life of the

World to Come; there will be nothing without You, our Redeemer, in Messianic days; and there will be none like You, our Savior; at the Resuscitation of the Dead.

When the Sages use the term *olam ha-ba,* depending on context they may be referring to part or all of the afterlife categories. The prooftext adduced by the Mishnah for their statement "All of Israel have a share in the World to Come" is "As it is written, 'Thy people are all righteous; they shall inherit the land forever, the branch of My planting, the work of My Hands, that I may be glorified'" (Isaiah 60:22). That verse alludes to the Resurrection of the Dead. "Forever" they shall inherit the land. Eternity is connected here, with earth. We are obviously speaking not of souls but of people. Earth inherited forever obviously alludes to Resurrection of the Dead. Similarly, the second of the categories considered unworthy of receiving this gift is one who denies the future Resurrection. Denying the validity of a gift negates one's right to receive it.

The Backward Sequence

Maimonides clearly sees these three—rejection of Resurrection, rejection of Divinity of Torah, and Heresy—as headings for three much broader categories. It is these three that become thirteen, because every one of them must be understood logically in terms of its fullest implications.

Resurrection is not simply the belief in souls returning once more to be joined with bodies. Included in it is the concept that God knows the deeds of all humanity (Principle 10); that He rewards and punishes (Principle 11); that He will bring the Messiah (Principle 12); and finally that He will bring about revival of the dead (Principle 13). What in the Mishnah is but one phrase branches into four separate and important statements in the *Ani Ma'amin.*

Similarly, to believe in the Divinity of Torah, one must acknowledge four things: that the words of the Prophets are true (Principle 6); that the prophecy of Moses was true and that he was the chief of the Prophets (Principle 7); that the whole Torah is the same as given to Moses (Principle 8); and that this Torah will not be exchanged (Principle 9).

Finally, a heretic does not accept God as we know Him. There are those who may claim to believe in God and yet really reject Him by misdefining Him. That is why five principles are necessary to clarify what acceptance of God entails, in order for it to be considered monotheism and proper belief: God is the Author and God of everything (Principle 1); He is a Unity (Principle 2); He is not a body (Principle 3); He is the First and the Last (Principle 4); and to Him alone it is right to pray (Principle 5).

Maimonides has extended the categories of the Mishnah to include thirteen clear implications of the three statements. What seems strange is his apparent reversal of the sequence.

When the Mishnah lists those who have no share in the World to Come, the order reads: Rejection of Resurrection, Divinity of Torah, and Heresy. Maimonides, however, begins with the five principles that are the antithesis of heresy; he proceeds to the next four dealing with proper acceptance of Torah; and he concludes with the last four, dealing with the fuller implications of Resurrection.

The reason for his reversal is obvious when one reflects upon his purpose, which is distinct from that of the Mishnah. Maimonides is speaking in positive terms: he is itemizing a list of affirmations required of every Jew. To affirm one's belief system, one must properly begin with God. God is clearly the first step. Hence, we must clarify the five aspects of proper faith in God as we understand Him. Once we know God, Jewish theology demands acknowledgment of communication between Him and us. God's message to us would be codified in the Torah. A Jew must affirm that link as the second major step of his or her theological *Weltanschauung*. And Torah only becomes meaningful if its acceptance has consequences. God knows, He rewards and punishes, and there is an eschatological dream for our people. That dream is Resurrection and all that goes with it.

The sequence of affirmation is exactly as Maimonides posits it. The Mishnah, however, had a different message. Its intent was to discuss the subject from a totally different perspective. "And these are the ones who lose their share in the World to Come." How does one lose what one had? The assumption is that we are dealing with someone who was a member of the Jewish people. Such an individual, having been in the faith community, would not remove himself by immediately rejecting an essential principle. Rather, history has shown that heretics begin by attacking something that they deem inessential, a belief they consider not crucial. Rejection may well start with the denial of Resurrection. That is too "mystical" a concept. Does one really need reward and punishment in order to be good? Was that not simply a candy thrown out at theologically immature ancients in the hope that they might come to understand the beauty of religion, whose essence does not require an afterlife? From there it is but a short step to rejection of the Divinity of Torah. After all, could we not respect the Bible even if we reject God as its author, proclaiming its esthetic kinship with Shakespeare rather that its authenticity as a divine document? Those who did away with the mystical elements of *olam ha-ba* were soon ready to reject divine authorship. From there, no great leap was necessary to unseat the Almighty Himself from His throne. The road to total denial progresses from Resurrection to Revelation and then to Reality of God. That was the theme of the Mishnah. To create the Jew rather than to describe how he is undone is what Maimonides sought. The Thirteen Principles follow the correct order, in which we are to teach Judaism and become stronger people of faith ourselves. Maimonides and the Mishnah are in harmony.

Let us now understand the remarkable insight Maimonides added to what he maintained was the third in the series. Resurrection of the Dead became for him the most crucial theological belief, because he understood it not simply as an article of faith, but rather the key to the proper solution of the most fundamental problem faced by a believer.

28

Why Do Bad Things Happen to Good People?

very pious person must at some point confront this problem.

People who follow God's ways are supposed to be blessed. The Torah teaches: "I call Heaven and earth to witness against you this day, that I have set before thee life and death, the blessing and the curse, therefore choose life, that thou mayest live, thou and thy seed" (Deuteronomy 30:19). It is the major theme of the Bible. Obedience spells blessing; disobedience, death.

And yet reality teaches us otherwise. Righteous people often suffer, and wicked people prosper. Daily our faith is tested by the contradiction between biblical promise and the testimony of our own experience.

Job long ago sought to find a proper response. Every human being since then has either been able to resolve the matter to some personal satisfaction or renounce religion. Our Sages acknowledge it as the most significant difficulty of faith: There is a righteous person and it is evil for him; there is a wicked person and it goes well with him (*zadiq ve-ra lo, rasha ve-tov lo*). How can that possibly be if we accept two initial premises: (1) An all-powerful God rules the world; (2) He promises us His blessings as recompense for observance of His commandments? Either God or Torah cannot be true if our eyes bear witness that the wicked prosper, the righteous suffer.

That problem must be addressed. According to the Talmud, it was once asked by Moses of God Himself. The answer given then represents the most important insight of Judaism concerning this difficulty.

It was immediately after the story of the Golden Calf. Moses had prayed for a long time and finally God had forgiven the Jewish people their sin. It was during this special time of conciliation that Moses found the strength and the nerve to express his most profound quandary of life.

"And he said: 'Show me, I pray Thee, Thy glory," (Exodus 33:18). Superficially it would appear that Moses was asking to see God. We know that that is impossible. Surely Moses knew it as well. God has no body; that is one of the thirteen principles of our faith. To view Him in corporeal terms is to misunderstand His essence. Moses had already been on the very top of Mount Sinai and spent considerable time with the Almighty. What then is the meaning of "Show me, I pray Thee, Thy glory"?

How is one to understand God's response: "And He said: 'I will make all my goodness pass before thee, and will proclaim the Name of the Lord before thee; And I will be gracious to whom I will be gracious, and I will show mercy on whom I will show mercy.' And He said: 'Thou canst not see My Face, for man shall not see Me and live.' And the Lord said, 'Behold there is a place by Me, and thou shalt stand upon the rock and it shall come to pass, while My glory passeth by, that I will put thee in a cleft of the rock and will cover thee with My Hand until I have passed by. And I will take away My Hand, and thou shalt see My Back, but My Face shall not be seen'" (Exodus 33:19–23).

The final part of the response seems to grant Moses' request: "You will see My Back, but My Face shall not be seen." How can anyone see the Back of God? Does that not refute all we believe about the incorporeity of the Creator? And does not the final verse fly in the face of the initial portion of the response: "For man shall not see Me and live?" If man cannot see God and live, how could Moses be told that he would be enabled to see His Back?

The passage only makes sense if we understand it through the eyes of our Sages. God's response becomes clear when we grasp the intent of Moses' question.

"Show me, I pray Thee, Thy *glory*." Moses did not ask to see God Himself. Vision of the eyes was not at issue. It was rather insight he desired. The God who had just declared Himself as concerned with justice was confronted by Moses with a request for clarification. Perhaps Moses intimated to God that there were countless times when His ways seem inglorious and His dealings with man inexplicable. A young boy is stricken with paralysis; a young girl is riddled with cancer; a woman is widowed in the prime of life though her husband served God with all his soul and might; a learned Sage does not die easily but lies for months on his final deathbed in excruciating pain and affliction. Moses believed with all his soul that God was a God of love and compassion. Yet his experiences seemed to tell him otherwise. He asked God to help him reconcile the two; to be instructed and guided so that he might grasp the dimensions of His glory.

The Talmud (*Berakhot* 7a) teaches us that when Moses asked to see God's glory, he asked for nothing less than an answer for the ultimate religious dilemma "a righteous person and it is evil for him; a wicked person and it goes well with him."

What does God say in response? The first part of His answer places into perspective the limits of human comprehension.

"Man cannot see Me and live." Human intellect on this earth is too limited. We cannot possibly grasp the will of the infinite mind while we are restricted to finite existence here on earth. God's reply to Moses implies what He would later say in much longer form to Job, who was presented with the same difficulty:

> Where wast thou when I laid the foundations of the earth?
> Declare, if thou hast the understanding.
> Who determined the measures thereof, if thou knowest?
> Or who stretched the line upon it?
> Whereupon were the foundations thereof fastened?
> Or who laid the corner-stone thereof,
> When the morning stars sang together,
> And all the sons of God shouted for joy?

Or who shut up the sea with doors,
When it broke forth, and issued out of the womb;
When I made the cloud the garment thereof,
And thick darkness a swaddling-band for it,
And prescribed for it My decree,
And set bars and doors,
And said: 'Thus far shalt thou come, but no further;
And here shall thy proud waves be stayed'?
Hast thou commanded the morning since the days began,
And caused the dayspring to know its place;
That it might take hold of the ends of the earth,
And the wicked be shaken out of it?

[Job 38:4–13]

In simpler terms, how can you, Job, hope to understand? You are man—and I am God. "Man cannot see Me and live"—your mortality clouds the vision necessary for the perspective of eternity.

But even if we cannot fully comprehend, Moses is told where the answer lies: "You shall see My Back." If God's physical appearance is not meant, what does "Back" denote? The Sages explain that while the event is taking place it will seem to you cruel and incomprehensible; with the benefit of hindsight, in retrospect, you *will* know why, and all your questions will be answered. "My Face shall not be seen"—the face to face encounter of the immediate present does not allow you yet to understand.

God's four-letter name derives from the combination of three Hebrew words. They are the three tenses connoting existence: *Hayah, Hoveh, Yiheyeh,* "was, is, and will be." Only when all three tenses are combined can one understand the goodness of the Almighty and does His essence become understandable.

There are times when the hindsight required is but a few hours. A person who curses a flat tire on the way to the airport and is forced to miss an important flight, and who subsequently learns that the plane crashed, killing all aboard, is then in a position to acknowledge that the curse was in fact a blessing.

Life does not, however, always explain itself in such rapid sequence. True, there are scattered incidents where the next morning clarifies the perils of the preceding night. The story of Rabbi Akiva is a perfect illustration.

> . . . and so it was taught in the name of R. Akiva: A man should always accustom himself to say, "Whatever the All-Merciful does is for good," [as exemplified in] the following incident. R. Akiva was once going along the road and he came to a certain town and looked for lodgings but was everywhere refused. He said: "Whatever the All-Merciful does is for good," and he went and spent the night in the open field. He had with him a cock, an ass, and a lamp. A gust of wind came and blew out the lamp, a weasel came and ate the cock, a lion came and ate the ass. He said: "Whatever the All-Merciful does is for good." The same night some brigands came and carried off the inhabitants of the town. He said to them: "Did I not say to you, 'Whatever the All-Merciful does is all for good?'" [Because the lamp or the cock or the ass might have disclosed his whereabouts to the brigands]. [*Berakhot* 60b–61a]

But what if years pass and the tragedy still is not explicable, the pain and the suffering still have no rational explanation? How long will it take for the wisdom of retrospection to manifest itself? It may be years before a person can recognize that losing a job becomes the key to making one's own fortune. It may be decades before an injury suffered in youth is understood as being responsible for turning one's life around and choosing a totally different and rewarding career. But that moment of recognition may never come. And what does one say then? What if pain and suffering and tragedy endured by a righteous person remain until death itself and can never be understood in retrospect as misinterpreted blessings?

"For man shall not see Me and live." Even within the span of our lifetime, we have not seen all there is to see. A judgment cannot be rendered when one perceives only a small portion of a story. Imagine, the Lubavitcher Rebbe (Menachem Mendel Schneerson) once illustrated, if uncivilized barbarians were suddenly to step into the operating room of a modern hospital. Imagine their eyes gazing upon a man strapped to a table and white-garbed figures standing over him with cutting instruments. As they make their incisions and draw blood, those unfamiliar with the procedure would be certain that these doctors are cruel and bloodthirsty.

Their limited perspective of the entire scene leads them to totally erroneous conclusions. They do not know that what seems to them a prelude to cannibalism is the means to beneficent healing.

"For I am the Lord your Doctor" (Exodus 15:26). God, too, heals and sometimes must amputate. God heals and sometimes must make us swallow bitter medicine. God heals and at times appears to be cutting and drawing blood.

The Mishnah teaches us: "Just as we make a blessing for good things, so, too, must we make a blessing for 'evil'" (*Berakhot* 54a). The commentators clarify: The Mishnah does not teach us that we must be prepared to accept even the bad for the sake of the good, almost by way of compensation. The Mishnah demands rather that we bless God for the evil, because evil is nothing other than an as yet uncomprehended good.

If in a particular instance it appears that something cannot possibly be good because it is the source of someone's death, and we wonder what good can possibly exist after that, the verse assures us, "For man shall not see Me and live." It is solely within the context of this lifetime that you are unable to make a judgment as to what is good and what is evil. The same Rabbi Akiva whose habit it was to constantly bless God and say, "This, too, is for the good"; the Rabbi Akiva who found out on the morning after he was refused lodging that it was meant for his own good and part of God's blessing—that same Rabbi Akiva went to his death as one of the Ten Martyrs at the hands of Rome, blessing God and acknowledging His Unity and universality with his last breath, expiring immediately after completing the *Shema.* He acknowledged that although God may appear at times as the God of harsh and strict justice, He is actually the unity of *Hashem Eḥad,* the compassionate Lord whose goodness will eventually be comprehended, if not on this earth then with the retrospective view afforded by the next. Because death is not the end, it does not close the book on human existence nor does it deny the possibility for future understanding.

One word expresses this concept best. It is the key to God's opening verse in His response to Moses: "And He said I will make, all [*kol*] My goodness pass before you." When you see a portion alone, it will be incomprehensible. If you perceive *kol,* everything,

it is then and then alone that you will be able to proclaim the
Name of Hashem, the Lord of compassion, before you.

This idea finds powerful expression in the strange wording of a
prayer recited daily. Just before we acknowledge God's kingship
through the recitation of the *Shema,* we recite the following blessing: "Blessed are You, Hashem, our God, King of the Universe,
Who forms light and creates darkness, makes peace and creates
all."

The Talmud is intrigued by the text of this blessing. It contains
a quote from Isaiah (45:7), yet seems to make an error at the conclusion. The original reads: "and He creates evil." How dare we
tamper with the text? What justifies our changing a thought
expressed by a prophet? How can we say "creates all' when the
Bible itself employed a different phrase?

We are not changing the idea, but rather explaining it. How
can God be considered the source of evil if He is "all good"? It is
too shocking to read the words "the Creator of Evil" without clarification. How is it indeed that Evil is permitted to exist on this
earth if nothing could have been created without permission of the
Creator? Substitute the word *ha-kol* (all) for *ra* (evil) and you will
understand. For in the awareness of *kol,* the entirety of life and of
human existence, *ra* becomes comprehensible, even as light and
darkness are complementary.

Zoroastrianism attempted to solve the problem of good and
evil on earth by allowing for the existence of two powers, just as we
daily confront day and night, light and darkness. Temporal reality
reflects these metaphysical dimensions. Day and night are but
metaphors for the powers of light and darkness, of good and evil.
If these two give way one to another on a regular basis, it must be
because the two powers governing the universe have made an
arrangement between themselves to allow "equal time" one to
another. Zoroastrianism accepts dualism. Ormuzd is the god of
day and the force of goodness; Ahriman is the god of night, the evil
force behind all that is sinister, black, and wicked.

The Jew has a different way to deal with the apparent di-
chotomy between day and night. If darkness suggests evil, then the
very beginning of the Bible has already taught us the way in which
we are to reckon not only time, but its meaning: "It was evening

[*erev*] and it was morning [*boqer*], day one [*yom ehad*]" (Genesis 1:5). Night precedes day. Darkness is the prelude to dawn. When the sun rises, it is not only the daylight hours that are called *yom* (day) but also the preceding night. In the clarity of day, the darkness will be understood to have been a necessary prelude.

In the evening service (*ma'ariv*) we recite: "He forms light and creates darkness." The Talmud teaches that we are obligated "to include a reference of day in the prayer offered at night, and a reference to night in the prayer recited by day" (*Berakhot* 11b). The two are to be considered inseparable, different sides of the same coin, joining together to form the unity of Oneness of *yom ehad,* a single day.

Dualists will ascribe night to one god, day to a totally different deity. Judaism will acknowledge night as partaking of the dimension of *Elohim;* day offers the aspect of *Adonai.* Just as the verse "And there was evening and there was morning" refers to "one day," so, too, do the attributes of *Adonai Eloheinu* refer to one God, *Adonai Ehad.*

Every moment of darkness in life has a purpose. From the perspective of (*kol*) even death, the extinguisher of life, is not be viewed as tragedy. Rather, as the Indian poet Tagore wrote, "Death is putting out the lamp because the dawn has come." So, too, do our Sages speak of the afterlife as the time when "night will be turned into day."

"And you shall see My Back"—And you shall comprehend Me in retrospect. That is the only way in which people of faith can survive. If we are not clear about God's ways in the darkness of this night of our lifetime, we will someday become enlightened by the perspective of the morrow. That day of clarity must surely come. Even if it fails to become apparent here on earth because "Man cannot see Me and live," it will nevertheless be a part of our soul's insight in the world of eternity after our death.

Belief in the afterlife is the only thing that enables us to hope for a rectification of injustices we perceive here on this earth. Only a belief in some continued existence after the seventy biblically allotted years permits us to accept the answer that there is more, there is a "*kol*," a perspective of "all" that will clarify everything.

This is what Maimonides recognized as the deeper meaning of

the third category required for a believing Jew. Why is Resurrection of the Dead so significant that it is one of the major three categories of creed in Judaism? Because the belief in something after our existence here on earth is the only possible way to maintain our acceptance of a God who "knows all our deeds" (Principle 10), rewards those that keep His Commandments, and punishes those that transgress them (Principle 11). What reality contradicts, the future will reconfirm. If on a national level the Jewish people are downtrodden, and those who worship God seem to be the most accursed people on earth, then we express our faith in the coming of the Messiah (Principle 12), at which time the injustices of the world will be rectified. If on an individual level we have seen the righteous suffer and the wicked prosper, we believe with perfect faith that there will be a revival of the dead—and how can one compare the apparent injustices in the limited span of a single lifetime to the blessings set aside for the days when God will resurrect the righteous and demonstrate how darkness was a prelude to light?

29

"Amen"

he three categories of the Mishnah—denial of Resurrection, denial of Revelation, and heresy—became thirteen affirmative principles for Maimonides. The three were extended because he recognized that each one contained more than one idea.

Yet even as the three may ramify into more principles, they may also contract into one word of three letters, a word basic to our very definition of belief and acceptance of faith: **AMeN**, an acronym for the words El (pronounced Ail) **M**elekh Ne'eman (God, trustworthy King).

Let us first convey the main insight of every one of the three concepts with one simple word:

1. The first five principles: We must reject the world view of the heretical pleasure-seeker who denies monotheism. The first five principles both refine and define the refutation of heresy and our declaration of belief in God. One word does justice to a summary of all five and the entire grouping אֵל, *El*—the power and might of God.

2. The middle four principles: The antithesis of one who

rejects the Divinity of Torah is one who acknowledges not only a God (Principles 1–5), but a God who maintains a relationship with the world He created. God is interested in us and communicates with us. He speaks to prophets. The greatest prophet was Moses. To him He entrusted a law that would never be altered, because He *continues* to rule over us as a King who is concerned with his subjects. Judaism acknowledges the God of Creation as Ruler, or King, of the universe. Revelation is the greatest proof of God's ongoing relationship. Acceptance of God's law is talmudically referred to as *qabalat ol malkhut shamayim,* acceptance of the yoke of the *kingdom* of Heaven. If the first five principles are summarized by the word *El,* the middle four, referring to Revelation, are most aptly described by the word מֶלֶךְ (MeLeKH), or King.

3.   The last four principles—Resurrection: The one who denies Resurrection of the Dead declares that what we see here on earth is all there is to judge the wisdom of God's ways. Belief in Resurrection allows us to expand our horizons. It is more than a life span that determines the moral legitimacy of God's dealings with humankind. What may seem initially unjust may, in retrospect, prove the ways of a compassionate Healer. The third category allows us to maintain our view of God as just. What we have not seen by way of recompense in the present will be carried out in the future because God is trustworthy—נאמן, *ne'eman*—trustworthy is the one-word summary of the final category.

A God who is powerful (*El*), who is King (*Melekh*), and who keeps His word (*Ne'eman*) forms the triad of Jewish belief. How apt that the Talmud teaches us that precisely these three words are the acronym—AMeN—for the way Jews invariably affirm their belief in the Jewish religion.

"Amen" implies acceptance. It means more than "I believe." It also defines *what* I believe. It alludes to the very three things that serve as the three requirements for acceptance into the World to Come. Whenever Jews recite the word, they verbalize their agreement with the three principles of the Mishnah in *Sanhedrin*. Since the three, according to Maimonides, of necessity imply the thirteen, every Amen is Jewish shorthand for the Thirteen Principles of Faith.

The Introduction to the *Shema*

It is not merely coincidental that these three words, *El Melekh Ne'eman* (God, Trustworthy King) serve as the introduction to the recitation of the *Shema* when praying privately. They introduce our twice-daily acceptance of God most fittingly, because the *Shema* itself may be understood on three levels of meaning.

An affirmation of God (El): The simplest purpose of the *Shema* is to acknowledge our recognition of God. That implies five fundamental assertions: (1) He exists; (2) He is One; (3) He is incorporeal; (4) He is beyond time; and (5) To Him alone it is fitting to pray. When we recite the *Shema,* we must first and foremost perceive Him as the God whose very existence betokens five crucial definitions.

An affirmation of His Kingship (Melekh): We have already indicated the commentary of the Jerusalem Talmud on the phrase *Shema Yisrael.* This is an allusion to the moment when we as a people actually heard from the Almighty two of the commandments: *Adonai Eloheinu*—reference to the first commandment "I am the Lord, your God"; *Adonai Eḥad*—reminder of the second, "You shall have no other gods before Me." Sinai was Revelation, and the purpose of Revelation was for God to proclaim eternally that He was our King and Ruler (*Melekh*), the lawgiver who gave us commandments and expected our obedience.

An affirmation of His Trustworthiness (Ne'eman): Rashi, we have learned, gave us a third insight into the *Shema.* He writes that Jews firmly believe that the Lord—who at present is only our God because we are the only people who at this moment comprehend Him and accept Him—will be the One God of the universe. "Hear, O Israel" is the eschatological hope of our people. It speaks of our dream and our destiny. It confirms our faith in the Messianic Era. It aspires to a day promised by the One Who will unfailingly keep His word, the trustworthy God.

Three words precede the *Shema* by way of preface and commentary. Which interpretation is correct? They all are. To recite the *Shema* is to assent to the three, which are in fact thirteen. God, Revelation, and Resurrection are the sine qua non of our faith. They are the three ideals to which at all times and in all places a Jew must be prepared to say "Amen."

Part XI

All about God

🁢🁢🁢🁢🁢🁢🁢🁢🁢🁢🁢🁢🁢🁢🁢🁢🁢🁢🁢🁢🁢🁢🁢🁢🁢🁢🁢🁢🁢

30

Can We "Prove" God's Existence?

he first principle of Maimonides states: "I firmly believe that the Creator, blessed be His name, is the Creator and Ruler of all created beings, and that He alone has made, does make, and ever will make all things." A Jew must believe in the existence of God. Is this a belief purely based on faith or can it be proven? Does acceptance of God require a suspension of reason or does reason itself force one to no other conclusion? Is scientific verification of God at all possible? And if it is not, why indeed *should* we believe?

Much has been made of various "proofs" for God. All of them leave open the possibility for disagreement. That is not because the human mind is deficient but because there can never be a proof of God that offers total certainty. Indeed, certainty would prevent the possibility for belief.

The old adage goes, "Seeing is believing." That is not true. Seeing is knowing. To see removes all doubt. Where there cannot be doubt, what remains is not conviction but simple recognition.

One might well wonder, if God wishes to be accepted by humankind, why does He not proclaim His being in an irrefutable manner? Let a Heavenly voice boom forth morning and night: "I am the God who made everything. I demand obedience and submission." If God wishes the Torah to become universal law, why aren't the consequences of disobedience immediate, just as drinking poison is quickly followed by death?

The answer is simple.

Were God to do so, there would not be a single "believer" on earth, nor would there be anyone who ought be rewarded for observing the mitzvot.

Had He wanted to, God could have created beings who know Him unquestioningly. God could have fashioned creatures who comply with every command of their Maker. In fact He already did. They are called angels. Angels know God and praise Him, but they cannot be rewarded. An IBM computer that functions perfectly is not "ethically good"; it is merely performing as programmed. Angels may be perfect, but their built-in perfection precludes praise, for it is predicated on an inability to be or do anything else.

When God created Adam, He gave him the gift of free will—a gift that raised humankind higher than the Angels. Our Sages teach us that Angels are only permitted to recite God's name after repeating the word *qadosh* (holy) three times: *Qadosh, qadosh, qadosh Adonai zevaot, melo khol ha-arez kevodo*—"Holy, holy, holy is the Lord of Hosts, the Earth is filled with His glory." We, however, are permitted to express kinship with God after only two words: *Shema Yisrael, Adonai Eloheinu Adonai Ehad.* We are holier than Angels precisely because our goodness is freely chosen and determined by a conscious decision to separate ourselves from the evil of which we are capable.

Free will requires choice. That is why any divine manifestation that too clearly conveys God's will or His presence cannot be permitted.

How Did God Remove Pharaoh's Free Will?

The aforementioned concept explains a seemingly difficult passage in the Torah. God tells Moses in advance that the ten plagues will not convince Pharaoh to free the Jews: "And I will harden his heart and he will not listen to you" (Exodus 7:3). Yet if free will is a human privilege, how could it be denied to Pharaoh, no matter how wicked he was? Why was Pharaoh not given the right to choose whether he would obey God in light of the wondrous signs that God visited upon his land?

Naḥmanides and others suggest a profound answer: God hardened Pharaoh's heart not in order to deprive him of free will, but rather so that it might be returned to him. The Nile turning into blood, frogs leaping forth from the river, all the miraculous distortions of natural processes, which reached a crescendo with the death of every firstborn at precisely the same moment, would not have allowed Pharaoh to freely choose belief in God. Rather, these wonders weighted the scale in such a manner that Pharaoh could no longer have made a dispassionate decision. Were God suddenly to strike every Jew who is about to consume a ham sandwich with a bolt of lightning, Jews would no longer earn the reward for "choosing" to eat kosher. Had Pharaoh agreed to the plea "Let my people go" after witnessing ten irrefutable signs from God Himself, he would not have "acted on his own." Hence, God hardened his heart. He permitted Pharaoh to find some way in which to rationalize the significance of the plagues, to render their persuasiveness null and void, to reject them as inconsequential.

Why Then Believe?

When scientists speak of proof, they seek to demonstrate with absolute certainty. When theologians use the term with regard to God, they mean simply this: In an area where demonstrable proof is both impossible and, from God's perspective, undesirable, how can one nevertheless "prove" that, where a choice must be made between two ultimately unverifiable options, one is far more logical than the other? "Proofs" in this context refer to the most legitimate alternatives. It is in this sense that Jewish philosophers do not hesitate to offer highly convincing demonstrations—in fact so convincing that to reject them requires a suspension of logic and a "belief" in the unbelievable. Neither the believer nor the atheist can provide scientific proof based on demonstration. Ultimately both attitudes are merely "beliefs." The doubter is as much a "believer" as the one who accepts religious truths.

How can we prove to our own satisfaction that there is a God? In all probability the most basic way to "find" the Creator is to emulate the approach of the very first Jew.

How did Abraham "discover" God? The Midrash tells us: "Abraham was like a man who saw a mansion all lit up and said at first that there is no owner to the mansion. The owner looked out and said to him, 'I am the owner of this mansion'" (*Bereshit Rabah* 39:1).

Abraham saw a house gloriously built, a veritable mansion of many rooms that reflected the ingenuity of a remarkable architect. Because he did not see the architect, his first inclination was to disclaim his existence. Momentary reflection, however, screamed the obvious out to him. The house could not be here if it did not have an owner and builder. Its majestic design clearly demonstrates the existence of both a mind and a hand that preceded its creation.

What Abraham perceived is what King David would later poeticize in the Psalms: "The Heavens declare the glory of God and the works of His hand are proclaimed by the firmament" (Psalms 19:2).

The world in all of its complexity and design must have a Creator and a Designer. That simple truth is so obvious, one need not be a prophet to perceive it.

Jeremy Taylor, an Anglican clergyman and writer (1613–1667), quoted in *A Treasury of the Art of Living* exclaimed:

What can be more foolish than to think that all this rare fabric of heaven and earth could come by chance, when all the skill of art is not able to make an oyster? To see rare effects, and no cause; a motion, without a mover; a circle, without a center; a time, without an eternity; a second, without a first. These are things so against philosophy and natural reason that he must be a beast in understanding who can believe in them. The thing formed says that nothing formed it; and that which is made, is, while that which made it is not! This folly is infinite. [Greenberg 1964, p. 325]

Meditate on the words of scientist Howard J. Shaughnessy:

> I once was satisfied that the origin of life, and of the universe, could be explained by blind force and chance. My views changed as I grew older and more mature. The more I saw of that invisible world, teeming with its myriad forms of microscopic life, the more I became convinced that my original concept was wrong. The complexity and beautiful order of the microbiological world is so wonderfully constructed that it appears to be part of a divinely ordained system for check and balance in the regulation and continuation of all life. [Greenberg 1964, p. 324]

Are you convinced by statistics? Hear what perhaps the most famous pollster and statistician of all times, Henry Gallup, asserted:

> I could prove God statistically. Take the human body alone—the chance that all the functions of the individual would just happen is a statistical monstrosity. [Greenberg 1964, p. 324]

The phrase Gallup uses is also the operative credo of the atheist: "a statistical monstrosity." Yet those who believe in God are often dismissed as "unrealistic," as willing to ignore logic and grasp at the straws of unconfirmed, improbable theological convictions.

The truth is what William L. Sullivan so powerfully suggested: "The best proof of God's existence is what follows when we deny it." Life without God is not only meaningless; it is inherently impossible. Even the age of science and the vast increase of human knowledge do not threaten religious sensibilities, but rather reinforce them all the more. The intricacies of the atom and the genius of creation implicit in DNA confirm what Louis Pasteur said long ago: "A little science estranges men from God; much science leads them back to Him."

Maimonides, the intellectual giant, once conveyed this very point to a nonbeliever in a remarkable incident. Perhaps the story is apocryphal. Yet it is no more than a fitting illustration of a concept that Maimonides phrased more succinctly in his *Guide of the Perplexed.*

A heretic met with Maimonides and sought from him some proof that might allow him to renounce his doubt. Yet no matter how profound his arguments, Maimonides was unable to convince the questioner. Excusing himself for a few moments, Maimonides asked the atheist to leave the room, saying that he had to take care of a few pressing matters. Upon the other's return, Maimonides produced a parchment on which was written a beautiful poem, perfect in rhyme and in meter. "How remarkable," said Maimonides to his guest. "While you were out, the ink spilled over on my desk and, as it blotted, it created, by accident, these words." The man laughed vigorously and could not imagine why Maimonides was asking him to believe such a foolish impossibility. "Why do you reject what I am telling you?" asked Maimonides. "Because," the man responded, "there are words here, words of sense and of meaning. This is a poem of profound wisdom. It could not have come about simply by accident." "Let your own ears hear what your mouth has said," replied Maimonides. "If you cannot believe that a simple poem could have come into being by a quirk of fate, how much more so the entire universe, whose wisdom encompasses so much more, and whose profundity surpasses all human understanding."

Science ought not to be viewed as being in conflict with religion. Quite the reverse: the more science proves the complexity of the universe, the more apparent it becomes that the highly complex orchestration of atoms and molecules, of DNA and of chromosomes, could never be the result of an unsupervised "Big Bang" or an unguided evolutionary development.

Again, from *A Treasury of the Art of Living* comes this quote from the philosopher and historian Lord Edward Herbert (1583–1648), who said: "Whoever considers the study of anatomy can never be an atheist" (Greenberg 1964, p. 326). Such was the thought of Kind David when he wrote that "The Heavens declare the glory of God and the works of His hand are proclaimed by the firmament" (Psalms 19:2). To view the Heavens in their glory and to remain unmoved is impossible. To be aware of their magnitude and magnificence, and not to acknowledge a Creator, is a suspension of reason.

It is the atheist who refuses to acknowledge reality. It has been said that an atheist cannot find God for the same reason that a thief cannot find a policeman. In the words of Plato: "Atheism is a disease of the soul before it becomes an error of the understanding."

No atheist can ever satisfactorily deal with the problem of first cause. Even if one suspends reason and accepts the possibility that this fully developed universe is a result of pure accident, denial of a Creator demands some logical alternative that posits a beginning, an initial cause. Pasteur proved that spontaneous generation is impossible; life cannot come from nonliving matter. The scientist's rejection of God is replaced by an acceptance of spontaneous generation not only for life, but for all existing things in the universe.

If "the Heavens declare the glory of God," then to disbelieve bespeaks a refusal to listen. If God affirms His existence in every blade of grass, in every tree of the field, in the wondrous workings of every human being, then philosophically it becomes possible to understand how Judaism can command a mitzvah of belief.

At first glance the mitzvah of belief is self-contradictory. I can only be commanded to believe if I already believe there is a Commander. Yet that makes the commandment itself unnecessary. If I do not already believe, what purpose is there in telling me that I am commanded to do so by someone in whom I do not believe?

That seemingly vicious cycle is addressed by Maimonides in *The Laws of the Foundations of the Torah* (*Hilkhot Yesodei ha-Torah*). "This revered and awesome God, there is a mitzvah to love and to fear Him, as it says 'And you shall love the Lord your God,' and it says 'The Lord your God you shall fear'; and what is the way to come to love and to fear Him? At the time when a person meditates upon His actions and wondrous creations, and sees from them His wisdom has no limit nor end, immediately he [man] loves and praises and glorifies and desires with great desire to know the Almighty" (2:1–2).

A person can come to believe. Nature, the world, the universe, all shout out God's presence. We are not commanded to believe. We are commanded to listen. In listening, we will hear the divine symphony. Of necessity, we will become believers. We will choose God because we will recognize that any other alternative is theologically and intellectually impossible.

The Second Way

The proofs of God from the world and Creation are known as teleological and cosmological. The world has *telos,* a purpose, as well as a fixed beginning. These proofs, however, leave us merely with a Creator who need not necessarily be involved in our history and our destiny. They lack a personal reference. They may allow us to agree with Einstein, who acknowledged that the profundities of the universe necessitate a Creating Mind, but that still does not give us our God, the God of our fathers, the God of Abraham, Isaac, and Jacob.

That is why we had to have a personal encounter with God at Mount Sinai. When the Creator mandated belief in His existence, He did not predicate it on personal philosophic speculation, but rather on the acknowledgment of a historic encounter: "I am the Lord your God Who took you out of the land of Egypt, the house of bondage" (Exodus 20:2).

From this time forward, the conclusion that a world without God is "a statistical monstrosity" would always be merged with an even greater reason to acknowledge the existence of the Creator: He is still involved in our affairs, He intervenes in our history, and at one moment in our past He even deigned to speak directly with us.

One may perhaps question the possibility of this encounter. Does not the fact that He showed Himself to us, that we actually heard His voice, remove freedom of choice from us? Was this not too great a manifestation of His presence, rendering all further lack of belief impossible?

Indeed Jewish philosophers are concerned with this problem. How could God reveal Himself so fully? Because, our Sages suggest, Revelation took place with a people of whom it had already been said: "And they believed in the Lord and in His servant Moses" (Exodus 14:31). Since they already believed with a total belief, God's revelation added no more to what they had already achieved on their own in terms of divine recognition. God was able to reveal Himself at Sinai because we had already made that discovery on our own.

Revelation meant that God gave us a portion of Himself. Torah, the mystics teach us, is a rearrangement of the names of God. On a deeper sense, this implies that all of Torah is His essence. To study Torah in future generations is therefore to be given the opportunity once more to know Him as did the Jews at Sinai. To immerse ourselves in the Five Books is to merge with Him. Belief is the automatic consequence of sincere Torah study. We thereby recapture the moment when God made Himself "visible," leaving no room for doubt. Study enables us to regain the certainty of His being, which we enjoyed when we stood at Sinai. Perhaps that too is why "the study of Torah is equal to *all* other mitzvot."

The Two Blessings Before *Shema*

The performance of every mitzvah is preceded by a blessing. So, too, a benediction precedes the recitation of the *Shema*.

The Talmud teaches us that not one, but two blessings are to be uttered before we recite *Shema* and acknowledge our belief in His existence. Why do we require two blessings in order to verbalize our acceptance of belief in God? The answer relates to the two ways in which one can find one's way to the Almighty.

The first blessing opens with the words "Blessed are You, Hashem, our God, King of the Universe, Who forms light and creates darkness, makes peace and creates all." It concludes with "Blessed are you, Hashem, Who fashions the luminaries."

Between the introduction and the conclusion of this first blessing are the magnificent passages that describe the genius of creation:

He Who illuminates the earth and those who dwell upon it, with compassion; and in His goodness renews daily, perpetually, the work of creation. How great are Your works, O Lord. You make them all with wisdom, the world is full of Your possessions. The King Who was exalted in solitude before creation, Who is praised, glorified, and upraised since days of old, Eternal God, with Your abundant compassion to us—O Master of our power, our rocklike stronghold. O shield of our salvation, be a stronghold for us. The blessed God, Who is great in knowledge, prepared and worked on the rays of the sun; the Beneficent One fashioned honor for His Name, emplaced luminaries all around His power; the leaders of His legions, holy ones, exalt the Almighty, constantly relate the honor of God and His sanctity. May You be blessed, Lord, our God, beyond the praises of Your handiwork and beyond the bright luminaries that You have made—may they glorify You—Selah!

So glorious are God's creations that even the Angels sing unto Him. The prayer continues: "Holy, holy, holy is the Lord of Hosts, the Earth is filled with Glory." What we have in short in this first blessing before the *Shema* is our awed response to the majesty of Creation. It precedes our claim that the Lord is our God and that He is One because it is the first "proof." This approach to God is that of Abraham and David, of scientists and statisticians. Here, a deductive process leads to the awareness of God and an acknowledgment of a Creator.

But that is not sufficient. A second blessing introduces the recitation of the *Shema*. This blessing is also recited before a man begins his daily study of the Torah:

With an abundant love have You loved us, Lord, our God; with exceedingly great pity have You pitied us. Our Father, our King, for the sake of our forefathers who trusted in You and whom You taught the decrees of life, may You be equally gracious to us and teach us. Our Father, the merciful Father, Who acts mercifully, have mercy upon us, instill in our hearts to understand and elucidate, to listen, learn, teach, safeguard, perform, and fulfill all the words of Your Torah's teaching with love. Enlighten our eyes in your Torah, attach our hearts to Your commandments, and unify our hearts to love and fear Your Name, and may we not feel inner shame for all eternity. Because we have trusted in Your great and awesome holy Name, may we exult and rejoice in Your salvation. Bring us in peacefulness from the four corners of the earth and lead us with upright pride to our land. For You effect salvations O God;

You have chosen us from among every people and tongue. And You have brought us close to Your great Name forever in truth, to offer praiseful thanks to You, and proclaim Your Oneness with love. Blessed are You, O Lord, Who chooses His people Israel with love.

The theme of the second blessing differs from the first. Its emphasis is no longer Creation but Revelation. It reminds us of the second way in which we come to believe in God. It emphasizes not the product of philosophic speculation, but rather the joy of personal encounter. It reminds us that God chose to reveal Himself to us. We met through the law and we may continue to meet in that manner. Together, nature and love of the law lead us to the *Shema*. It is the respective themes of these two blessings that allow us to firmly assert: We believe as a result of our own free will. We believe not as Angels who have no alternative, but as human beings who have utilized our God-given gift of free will and reach the correct conclusion because we were willing to listen—to the symphony of the universe, to the music of Sinai. One who listens attentively will be convinced that "I am the Lord, your God, who took you out of the land of Egypt, the house of bondage."

31

Who Is Satan?

he first commandment demands recognition that there is a God. The second is concerned with His exclusivity: "Thou shalt have no other gods before Me." The first without the second is meaningless; a God who does not stand alone is not all-powerful and therefore not worthy of being called a deity.

In the days of the Talmud, Jews lived in a culture that accepted the reality of two major powers. Babylonian dualism recognized a god of darkness and a god of light, a god of evil and a god of goodness. The theological problem of the suffering of the righteous and the success of the wicked was muted in the assumption that a Satanic force was as much ruler of the universe as the power that sought the reign of righteousness.

The Mishnah taught: "If one [in praying] says, 'We give thanks, we give thanks' [i.e., in the major prayer of the Eighteen Benedictions, where the proper phrase is to recite 'We give thanks' but once], he is silenced" (*Berakhot* 33b). The Talmud explains the reason for this concern. We silence a man who reiterates thanks to God because we suspect him of acknowledging "two powers." Perhaps he is attempting to placate two different deities. His very prayer to God would become an abomination. His very words would betray the cardinal creed of Judaism: "Hear, O Israel, the Lord our God, the Lord is One."

But isn't there at least a measure of truth in the reality of Satan, the powerful figure whom Milton describes in *Paradise Lost,* "Fierce as ten furies, terrible as hell, . . . what seemed his head the likeness of a kingly crown had on?" Did not Satan lead the Heavenly Courts to rebellion against God Himself? Is he not as Shakespeare wrote in *Hamlet,* "the devil who hath power to assume a pleasing shape," deceiving us throughout the generations in his evil desire to reign supreme on earth?

Satanic cults may to this day feel a need to appease the devil incarnate. But Judaism knows of a certainty: "Unto thee it was shown, that thou mightest know that the Lord, He is God; there is none else beside Him" (Deuteronomy 4:35). "Know this day and lay it to thy heart, that the Lord, He is God in Heaven above and upon the earth beneath; there is none else" (Deuteronomy 4:39).

Satan does indeed exist. In fact he has two other identities: Satan is the incarnation of the evil impulse as well as the Angel of Death (*Baba Batra* 16a). In each of these guises it is crucial to grasp that he is not an independent entity capable of conflict with God; he is rather a messenger from the Almighty sent to perform an unpleasant, albeit necessary, task.

The Satan of Job

Satan makes his first biblical appearance as the "prosecuting attorney" of Job in the Heavenly Courts. We are introduced at the outset of the first chapter to a man who seemed perfection itself; "There was a man in the land of Uz whose name was Job, and that man was wholehearted and upright and one that feared God and shunned evil." Indeed he was blessed by the Almighty with all things—sons and daughters, sheep, camels, oxen . . . "a very great household, so that this man was the greatest of all the children of the East." It was this man whom Satan questioned and sought to harm. It was his sincerity that Satan would not accept as true piety: "Doth Job fear God for naught? Hast not Thou made a hedge about him, and about his house, and upon all that he hath, on every side? Thou hast blessed the work of his hands, and his possessions are increased in the land. But put forth Thy hand now, and touch all that he hath, surely he will blaspheme Thee to Thy face" (Job 1:9–11).

Satan, it would seem, is the cause of all subsequent tragedies that befall Job and his family. Yet the most important verse in this section is the one that follows Satan's diatribe: "And the Lord said onto Satan: 'Behold all that he hath is in thy power. Only upon himself put not forth thy hand.' So Satan went forth from the presence of the Lord."

God gave Satan permission to proceed and he was able to accomplish what he sought. Satan went forth only because he went "from the presence of the Lord," that is to say, with divine permission.

The rationale for Satan's authorization is the theme of the Book of Job. Implicit in it are numerous concepts that classical commentators have chosen to emphasize. Perhaps Job had simply to learn the reproach of God's chastisement in Chapter 40: "And the Lord answered Job out of the whirlwind and said, 'Gird up thy loins now like a man. I will demand of thee and declare thou unto Me. Wilt thou even make void My judgment? Wilt thou condemn Me, that thou mayest be justified?'" (40:6–8). God's intellect is greater than Job's; questioning Him is not a right given to creatures fashioned by a far superior Creator. Perhaps, as others would have it, God allowed Satan to harass Job, just as even He, God Himself, had caused pain to Abraham when He commanded him to sacrifice his son, his only son, "whom thou lovest, even Isaac, and get thee into the land of Moriah and offer him there for a burnt offering upon one of the mountains which I will tell thee of" (Genesis 22:2). That was test; "God did prove [*nisah*] Abraham." In Hebrew the word *nisah,* related to *nes,* a banner, means both to test and to uplift. In being tested we become uplifted. We rise higher than where we previously stood. Adversity may purify, even as metal under fire. For the artist, suffering may be the key to creativity. For the saint, it can serve as a source of inner strength, the tapping of personal resources that might otherwise never have been uncovered.

To this day the Book of Job offers a myriad of possible explanations. One thing it teaches is a certainty. The evil Job endured came not from a power separate and distinct from God. Satan had to gain permission to do from the *one* God. Let us give the devil his due: Satan has no strength other than what God allows him.

Satan as Evil Inclination

This same Satan is also known to us in another guise. Freudian terminology has acquainted us with the id, ego, and superego. In talmudic and midrashic thought, the battle is waged in our personal lives between the inclination for good (*yezer tov*) and the inclination for evil (*yezer ha-ra*). Inside every one of us there is not an "id" but a "little devil" constantly imploring us to silence the voice of our conscience and quell our desire to do good, to shut out the influence of Torah and ignore the demands of our faith.

What is this evil impulse? Does its very presence not suggest the validity of dualism, the existence of a power in conflict with the God of goodness and righteousness?

Not at all. At the very end of the story of Creation, when the text states "And God saw all that He had made and behold it was very good" (Genesis 1:31), the Midrash explains that "all that He had made" refers to the evil inclination. Indeed, the very inclination for evil was created by God, and yet "It was very good." Without it, sexual desire would be nonexistent, people would neither marry nor have children, and the world would remain barren. Without it, people would not be tempted to do wrong and would therefore gain no credit for doing right. Without a predisposition to evil, there would be no *struggle* for righteousness and all of our efforts would simply be automatic responses, intuitive reflexes, preordained patterns of behavior devoid of conscious decision or noble character.

"And you shall love the Lord, your God, with all your heart." In Hebrew the word for "heart" is *lev.* "Your heart" in Hebrew, in the third person singular, should be written *libkha.* Yet, the Torah writes *levavekha,* the plural form, in its description of ideal divine service. The Midrash explains that *levavekha* implies "with both your hearts," with your inclination for good as well as your inclination for evil. We can achieve the noblest stature precisely because we can redirect, or in Freudian terms, sublimate, the bestial within us into the saintliness of divine service.

Only once, when Abraham welcomes the three strangers in Mamre, does the Bible refer to "heart" in the singular: *Ve-eqhah pat lehem ve-sa'adu libkhem,* "And I will fetch a morsel of bread and stay ye here your heart" (Genesis 18:5). The language is not in the plural, "and your heart*s* shall be satiated," but in the singular "heart." Why this one exception? Abraham offered his hospitality to what he assumed to be three Arab strangers, but who in fact were angels. And angels do not have "two hearts" since they lack the evil inclination. Their hearts are attuned only to the doing of good, which is why human beings are greater than angels. The adverb in the phrase "very good" can only be relevant on the sixth day of Creation, when the evil inclination comes into being. The evil impulse presents the challenge which, when successfully mastered, allows a human being to become almost the equal of God.

The evil inclination and Satan are one. They are "evil" only in the sense that their missions require them to perform highly unpleasant tasks. Yet the actions of both have a purpose made necessary by the wisdom of God. If they were not divinely acceptable, then clearly they would not come to pass.

Satan as the Angel of Death

There is one more role designated for the devil. From the human perspective, it presents Satan in his most awesome and fearful garb. It is the final meeting of every human being with this divine messenger: "The play is the tragedy, 'Man,' and its hero the Conqueror, Worm," wrote Edgar Allen Poe.

Here, too, the key word describing the one who causes what appears to be the ultimate evil, the end of life, is "angel." The *Malakh ha-Mavet,* the Angel of Death, performs a mission no less divine than birth itself. From our limited human perspective, that mission may seem cruel, but not from the divine perspective of eternity.

The Talmud records the story of a sage who almost rendered the Angel of Death powerless to continue his work. Rabbi Yehoshua ben Levi grabbed the sword from the hands of the *Malakh ha-Mavet* because he believed that in so doing he would bring great blessing to the world. It was then that God allowed the rabbi to hear a groan that issued from the four corners of the world. It was a groan of pain and of suffering, a groan filled with tears and sorrow. When the rabbi asked for the meaning of the hideous sound, God informed him that it was the cry of a world deprived of the relief of death. "You believe that the Angel of Death is only an angel of cruelty," said the Lord. "Know, my son, that the *Malakh ha-Mavet* is also a messenger of mercy." Death allows those who have done all they need to do on this earth to leave it for the celestial spheres. Death is the entranceway to Heaven. How beautiful were the words of the sage racked with pain, lying on his deathbed, who when asked how he felt, responded, "Almost well." The moment when he would be "well" would be the gift of God's angel—not one with autonomous power to wreak evil, but with authorization from the Holy One to allow the soul to move from the body to the precinct of the immortals.

That is why God said to Rabbi Yehoshua ben Levi: "Return the knife to him, for it is required by mortals" (*Ketubot* 77b). A world without death is a world encumbered forever by its material and physical limitations.

Indeed, Satan exists. He has three all-important functions. He is the voice of the adversary, pleading for trials and tests that allow humans to attain higher states of perfection. He is the evil inclination, whose smooth serpentine talk serves as the challenge to our conscience and accounts for our potential superiority over the angels. Satan is also the Angel of Death, whose "cruelty" on this earth is applauded by those in the other world as they welcome the newly freed "prisoners" from the confines of earth. In Shakespeare's eyes he may be "an enemy to mankind." The Jew, however, is certain that the Angel is not God's enemy but rather only His messenger. Dual powers are impossible. The Lord is our God, the Lord is One.

32

Are We
Really Created
in God's Image?

believe with perfect faith that the Creator, blessed be His Name, is not a body." If God had a body, He would suffer all of its limitations. A body is material; it is mortal and subject to decay. A body is restricted in space, confined to one location. To believe in a god of flesh and blood is to have distorted His essence so that He is no longer identical with the Creator.

Yet the Torah often speaks of "the hand of God," "the finger of God," "the mouth of God," "the Lord sitting on His throne." There is no doubt in the mind of Jewish commentators that these anthropomorphisms appear, in spite of their potential for misunderstanding, because "The Torah speaks the language of men" (*Berakhot* 31b). God simply has no alternative. Communication demands comprehension. If human beings "speak" by means of vocal chords, tongue, and mouth, then obviously the word is inappropriate for the incorporeal God. Yet, God does "speak" to us. He informs us of His will and He finds ways to create sound carrying His words. Hence we will say "And the Lord spoke" because we have no other way to describe it. As the philosopher Baḥya Ibn Paqudah wrote in *Duties of the Heart:*

The prophetic books express His nature in words drawn from the physical world, which are near to man's intellect and his power of understanding. Were they to describe God in a manner suitable for Him, namely, by using spiritual words and ideas, no one would understand either the words or the ideas. It would not be possible to worship the unknown, for how can one serve that which is uncomprehended? Consequently, it was necessary for the words and ideas used to be in accordance with their hearers' intellectual capacity so that, at first, the idea is comprehended in a corporeal sense through the use of words drawn from the physical universe. Afterwards, we can increase his wisdom by encouraging him to grasp that all this is purely figurative and symbolic and that the true idea is far more refined, advanced, elevated and remote than one can possibly understand, by virtue of its extremely subtle nature [p. 80]

"In the Image of God, He Created Him"

What then is the meaning of the classic verse indicating that human beings are fashioned resembling their Creator? We are, the Torah tells us, created in His image. What is it that we share with Him if not our physical appearance?

Maimonides felt this problem was so important that he chose to discuss it in the very first chapter of his major philosophic work, *The Guide of the Perplexed.* The key to its solution is the distinction between two Hebrew words, *zelem* and *to'ar.* The figure and shape of a thing is its *to'ar.* Thus we find, "And Joseph was beautiful in form [*to'ar*] and beautiful in appearance" (Genesis 39:6). "What form [*to'ar*] is he of?" (1 Samuel 28:14). Appearance is based on physical attributes. It is totally inappropriate to God. The term *zelem,* on the other hand, signifies the specific form that constitutes *the essence of a thing* whereby the thing is what it is: "the reality of a thing insofar as it is that particular being."

If I were to say that two people share the same *to'ar,* I would be indicating that they are alike in appearance. Nothing in my statement would presuppose a correspondence of personality or of character. If, however, I stressed a correspondence of *zelem,* I would suggest that the two people share in some crucial way an aspect of their very essence.

This is the intent of the Torah in teaching that Adam was created in the image of God, *beẓelem Eloqim*. For Maimonides, the superrationalist, this correspondence can only highlight the most important aspect that we share with the Creator: "and on account of this intellectual perception the term *ẓelem* is employed in the sentences."

Naḥmanides disagrees with Maimonides' identification of the attribute intended by the words *ẓelem Eloqim*. We do share with God what is most basic to our essence. But, from the perspective of the mystic rather than the rationalist, it is not mind but rather soul that receives major emphasis. We are in God's image, for although our soul is housed in a body, His essence is soul. "Real man" refers to the portion that "the Lord blew into his nostrils from His spirit." The spirit, being a part of the everlasting one, is immortal.

Many centuries later Jewish history would note the violent controversy between hasidim and their opponents, the mitnagdim. That controversy revolved around the question of priority in Judaism. For mitnagdim, most important of all was the mind and intellectual self-improvement and service of God through study. For hasidim, God desires the heart above all. It is devotion of the soul that ranks highest in the scale of pious observance.

These are precisely the two possible interpretations given to define our uniqueness in having been created in "God's image." According to tradition, many years ago the founder of the hasidic movement, the Ba'al Shem Tov, and his prime opponent, the Gaon of Vilna, were to have come together in a conciliatory meeting. For some reason the meeting never took place. Had they met, a popular folk saying goes, the Messiah surely would have come. For the greatest truth is that the hasidic movement and its leader, as well as the mitnagdim and their rabbinic head, each grasped part of the ultimate reality: Maimonides and Naḥmanides were equally correct in their definition of "the image of God," because we share with the Creator both aspects of His intellect as well as immortality.

Is God Man or Woman?

If God has no body, then why do we refer to the Almighty as "He"? Would not "She" be just as appropriate?

In this age of women's liberation, much has been made of the supposed chauvinism of religion. Sexism is concerned with the seeming male bias of language. "Turn to God; She will help you" is the credo of some feminist leaders.

Yet what is fascinating is that Judaism long ago acknowledged the validity of this feminine dimension of the Deity. The two names of God differ grammatically with regard to sexual connotation. The feminine ending in Hebrew is usually produced by appending the letter *Heh* and the vowel *qamaẓ*, e.g., *yeled*, boy, becomes *yaldah*, girl. The Tetragrammaton (YHVH), the holy four-letter name of God, similarly ends in that manner. The word for Lord is thus feminine; it refers to God as if "He" were in fact "She." Yet, as we have frequently noted, the Lord is also called *ELoHiYM*. That name ends with the *Yod* and *Mem* which, in Hebrew, form the masculine plural. Here, God is a "He" in *all* of His many manifestations of strength.

How can God be both "He" and "She" at one and the same time? And what do we mean when we apply characteristics of gender to God, whom we know has no limitations of body?

To answer that is to come to grips with a far more fundamental question: If human beings are created in God's image, and the single most important thing we know about God is that He is One—why did God create two kinds of people, male and female, after His likeness?

One might be tempted to suggest simply that God had to create man and woman in order to ensure propagation. Yet that clearly does not do justice to the question. We find many different forms of reproduction on this earth. Surely it would have been possible for asexual reproduction to be the manner in which we could have fulfilled "be fruitful and multiply." Fission rather than fusion would have worked just as well. But God chose to create two different kinds of people on this earth, not in spite of the fact that He is One, but precisely because God in the deepest sense of the word is really two.

Of course we do not suggest any kind of dualism implying separate identities. Rather, as the very names of God imply, there are two distinct aspects to the Deity. God is both masculine and feminine. This gender difference is not one of physical attributes but one of emotion and typology.

The masculine aspect of God is identified with *midat ha-din,*
the trait of strictness, discipline, and uncompromising judgment.
God created Adam *be-ẓelem Elohim,* for the world must have a
parallel to that divine trait here on earth. Yet, the text later states,
Va-yomer Adonai Elohim lo tov heyot ha-Adam levado, "And the
Lord God said, it is not good that the man should be alone"
(Genesis 2:18). *Elohim* may have been content with Adam, but
Adonai Elohim said it is not good for Adam to be alone. God is not
alone in the attribute of *Elohim,* but requires also the feminine
addition of compassion and mercy—the *midat ha-raḥamim,*
derived from the very same root of *reḥem,* womb—that is why
Adam requires Eve just as much as Elohim needs Adonai. *E'eseh
lo ezer kenegdo,* "I will make a helpmeet for him." A far better and
more correct translation for *ezer kenegdo* is not a "helpmeet for
him," but rather "a help opposite him," to represent the part of his
nature that is distinct and different. When father is strict, mother
must be compassionate. When mother is too giving, father must be
firm. What God can accomplish as One, in terms of the ideal
harmony between the feminine–masculine nature of Adonai
Elohim, requires two parents on earth, male and female who
through their union can create a child-recipient of the dual, ideal
characteristics inherent in the Creator.

We are indeed created in His and in Her image. It is not in our
looks or appearance that we resemble the Creator. It is in who we
are and what we must make of our lives. We have divine intellect.
We have an immortal soul. And we, descendants of Adam and
Eve, have the potential to be like our Mother and Father in
Heaven.

33

Do We Really Have
Free Will?

he fourth principle of Maimonides states: "I firmly believe that the Creator, blessed be His Name, was the first and will be the last."

Jews believe in two propositions that seem mutually contradictory. In *Ethics of the Fathers,* Rabbi Akiva simply states them side by side without any elaboration: *Ha-kol zafui ve-ha-reshut netunah,* "Everything is foreseen, yet the freedom of choice is given" (3:19).

God is omniscient. He is aware of everything, even before it occurs. Nothing humanity can do has not been foreseen centuries and even millennia before. Yet we are totally free to act in accord with our own desires. Our freedom is what places upon us responsibility for our actions. Before we are born, God knows who will be thief or saint, yet the choice is entirely ours. We can do entirely as we please.

In his major halakhic work, *Mishneh Torah,* Maimonides succinctly states the problem:

Perhaps you will say, but does God know all that is destined to be even before it will be. He knew that this one will be holy or

wicked—or perhaps He did not know. If He knew that one would
be holy, it is impossible that he will not be holy. And if you will say
that He knew that one would be holy, but it is still possible that he
might be wicked, then, in fact, He did not know the matter to its full
extent. [*Hilkhot Teshuvah* 5:5]

If God knows, then His very knowledge creates reality. In the
realm of human behavior, prescience must therefore preclude freedom of will. And freedom of will is what Maimonides himself
declared is the most basic of all rights given to every human being,
the crucial distinction between humans and the angels, and the
reason why we could be given the Torah.

Maimonides' answer seems in a sense to beg the question:

The mind of man can not perceive the nature of God's knowledge
even as it says, "For man can not see Me and live"—so, too, is there
not power within a human being to comprehend and to fully recognize the mind of the Creator. That is what the prophet said, "For
My thoughts are not your thoughts and your ways are not My
ways." But know without doubt that the deeds of man are in the
hands of man, and God does not draw him nor decree upon him to
do such and such. [*Hilkhot Teshuvah* 5:5]

"Man can not comprehend." How, then, does that solve the
problem? Is it not merely rephrasing the original question? The
Rabad, commentator and frequent critic of Maimonides, is
appalled not only by the response but by the temerity of the
question:

The author did not deal in the manner of wise men, for one does not
begin something and not know how to complete it, and yet he started by asking difficult questions and left the matter in difficulty,
returning it to faith. It would have been preferable for him to leave
the entire matter in the "wholeness of the whole" and not stir up
their hearts and lead their minds in doubt, and perhaps at a certain
time there will come difficulties in their hearts on this matter. [*Hilkhot Teshuvah* 5:5]

Why raise philosophic issues, is the argument, if you have no solid response to a problem? It is faith that must prevail; preferable to state so at the outset and not verbalize a difficulty or even attempt an answer.

Should we take the advice of the Rabad and drop this question from any further discussion? What seems almost incredible, in view of the Rabad's initial condemnation of Maimonides' effort to deal with the seeming contradiction between omniscience and free will, is that Rabad himself then proceeds to pursue the matter and to offer his own answer. Rabad seeks to strengthen the role of free will by diminishing the principle of omniscience. God does not know in full; His knowledge is incomplete, in the same way that astrological signs may give tendencies, but do not create certainty of the future. What troubles the reader is not so much the correctness of this response, but rather why it is written at all. Has not Rabad condemned Maimonides for dealing with the question and offering a response when the ideal approach ought to be simple faith? Should we not simply say we believe it even though we don't know how two contradictory truths can coexist?

Clearly Rabad was upset with Maimonides for bringing up a problem that should have remained unstated. However, once the question has already come to the fore, even Rabad will seek to give an answer, because having been raised, a religious problem must be dealt with.

One might have argued with Maimonides in the Middle Ages as to whether any discussion should have taken place on the subject, but all commentators agree that once the issue has been raised it warrants full analysis and attempts at resolution.

What did Maimonides mean? Was his answer no more than "you cannot hope to comprehend"? Would he have raised the issue only to brush it off in such superficial manner? He does allude to something far more profound, even as he indicates the limitations on our understanding of the concept. "Know that God does not know with the knowledge that is external to Him, as do people for whom they and their knowledge are two, but He, exalted be His Name, and His knowledge are One, and the mind of man can not grasp this thing."

Man knows events in terms of a second dimension. They occur

in time. For man one can speak of before, during, and after. As Maimonides explained in *The Guide of the Perplexed,* the fourth principle of faith imposes that time exists only for humans, but cannot refer in any manner to the Creator:

> In the beginning, God alone existed and nothing else; neither angels nor spheres, nor the things that are contained within the spheres existed. He then produced from nothing all existing things such as they are, but His will and desire. *Even time itself is among the things created* [emphasis added]; for time depends on motion, i.e., on an accident in things which move, and the things upon whose motion time depends are themselves created beings, which have passed from nonexistence into existence. We say that God existed before the creation of the universe, although the verb existed appears to imply the notion of time. We also believe that he existed in infinite space of time before the universe was created; but in these cases we do not mean time in its true sense. We only use the term to signify something analogous or similar to time. [*The Guide of the Perplexed,* pp. 171–172]

It is only when the Torah introduces creation that we find the word *bereshit,* "in the beginning." Before then, there was no beginning because there was no concept of time. The very first thing God had to create before Heaven and earth was, in fact, the "beginning of time." Only afterward did He make Heaven and Earth.

The four-letter name of God teaches us this remarkable principle. The Tetragrammaton unifies several states of being: was, is, and will be (see Ch. 10). Of course we believe that God is the God of past, present, and future. Yet, His Name does not combine the three tenses sequentially, but rather the three dimensions of time become one word, transcending the limits of temporality and proving that God is above time.

In the days of Maimonides, this concept may in fact have seemed so alien that he had to conclude that it was above the capacity of a human being to comprehend it. Yet in our days, in the aftermath of Einstein and the theory of relativity, modern scientists are aware of the idea that even as humans are limited in space, they are also limited in time. But time may be transcended; it is relative to the speed of light. It is conceivable for someone to be lifted beyond these limitations. That is precisely what we mean when we say that God knows all things even before they occur—not because He sees them "before," but because for Him there is no "before."

Though our minds reel at the concept, an interesting illustration may somewhat clarify it. Imagine a spool of film that contains a movie lasting all of two hours and portraying the life of a person from birth to death. If shown on the screen frame after frame, one can only follow the events as they unfold chronologically. Imagine holding the spool in your hand and looking at several frames of action at one time. If your vision is wide enough, you might be able to see a number of slides moving the action from one stage of life to another. Picture now someone who can unwind the entire reel of film and look at all of it at the identical moment, not being limited by the time necessary for showing the film in its normal two-hour duration. This viewer might have witnessed birth and death in one all-encompassing overview. So, too, do theologians understand God as the "eternal now."

The great hasidic sage, Rebbe Nachman of Bratslav, gave perhaps a more familiar illustration:

God is higher than time, as is known. This matter is truly marvelous and utterly incomprehensible. It is impossible for the human intellect to grasp such an idea. Know, however, that time is, in the main, a product of ignorance, that is to say, time appears to us as real because our intellect is so small. The greater the intellect, the smaller and more insignificant time becomes. Take, for instance, a dream. Here the intellect is dormant and the imaginative faculty alone functions. In the dream it is possible for seventy years to pass by in a quarter of an hour. In the dream it seems as if a great space of time has elapsed, but in reality only a very short time has passed. On awakening after a dream one sees that the whole seventy-year period of the dream occupied in reality but a minute fraction of time. This is because man's intellect has been restored to him by his waking life and, so far as his intellect is concerned, the whole seventy-year period of the dream is no more than a quarter of an hour. . . . There is a Mind so elevated the whole of time is counted as naught, for that Mind is so great that for It the whole of time is nothing whatsoever. Just as the seventy years which pass in the dream are, so far as we are concerned, no more than a quarter of an hour in reality, as we have seen, so it is with regard to that Mind, which is so far above mind that time has no existence for it whatsoever. [*Liqutei Maharan,* Part II, 61]

To believe in the fourth principle is to express our acceptance of the idea that "His existence has no beginning." The concept of beginning does not apply to Him. He does not know the things we do *before* we do them. He has all of history before Him. Einstein's thoughts, together with the fourth principle of Maimonides, allow us to grasp the theory of relativity—and to accept the notion of personal responsibility for our actions. Although He knows, He did not ordain whether we be righteous or wicked.

34

No Middleman

he fifth principle of Maimonides states: "I believe with perfect faith that to the Creator, Blessed be His Name, and to Him alone it is right to pray, and it is not right to pray to any being besides Him." In another of his works, Maimonides elaborates: "Let us adopt no mediators to enable ourselves to draw near unto God, but let the thoughts be directed to Him, and turned away from whatsoever is below Him" (*Commentary on the Mishnah*, Fifth Principle).

The Golden Calf

It was shortly after the Jews had received the Torah at Sinai. These were the very same people who had crossed the Red Sea in awe and wonder and proclaimed, "This is my God and I shall glorify Him, the God of my fathers and I will exalt Him" (Exodus 15:2). The Midrash teaches us that even a handmaiden at the sea perceived God far more clearly than any subsequent prophet. These people awaited the return of Moses from the top of the Mount on the fortieth day. And when, through miscalculation, he

did not appear at the appointed time, the Jews fashioned themselves a Golden Calf and proclaimed this idol as their god.

Is it conceivable that the Jews now totally rejected the God
they had so personally experienced, in favor of a man-made calf of
gold?

Yehudah HaLevi offers a fascinating insight that makes it
comprehensible. Of course the Jews believed in God. Of course the
Jews had no intention of rejecting the One who took them out of
Egypt, the One whose Voice they heard at Sinai, the One to whom
they swore allegiance when they made their covenant and accepted
His Torah as binding. But Moses did not return when they thought
he would. What would then be their link with God? Thus they
built the calf, which they knew was not divine, but which they
hoped would serve as a suitable god substitute. They would pray
to the idol and think of God. They would look at the calf and have
the Creator in mind. This type of substitution is precisely what
God strongly condemned as idolatry, and for which he instructed
the tribe of Levi to slay the sinners.

"Ye have sinned a great sin" (Exodus 32:30). Why was this
such a great sin? What harm if a symbol is used and worshiped,
but the object of homage is God Himself? It is simply because
Judaism understood the danger implicit in creating any kind of
intermediary to God, for that is precisely the ultimate source of all
idol worship.

In his halakhic code Maimonides dealt with the difficulty of
comprehending how paganism began. For those not working within the framework of the biblical story, the facts are quite simple.
People did not know God and therefore sought to explain creation
through the many powers visible to them. The progression from
polytheism to monotheism required countless years of thought as
well as spiritual and intellectual advancement. According to the
Torah, however, Adam and Eve obviously knew the truth. They
were monotheists who had communication with the one God.
How should we explain the manner in which this truth was forgotten? What is responsible for the progression from monotheism
to paganism? Maimonides replies in the first chapter of *Hilkhot
Avodah Zarah*:

In the days of Enosh, the descendants of Adam erred an exceedingly great error and the Council of Sages of that generation was exceedingly foolish. Enosh himself belonged to those who went astray. The following was the nature of their error. They argued thus: Since God created the spheres and stars to control their world, placing them on high and allotting glory to them, and since they are servants who minister in God's presence, it is only right to praise them and glorify them and accord them honor. It must be the will of God, those people argued, that men should aggrandize and pay homage to those He has honored, just as a king desires homage be paid to his ministers, so that to carry out this wish is to honor the king himself. No sooner had they reasoned in this way then they began to erect temples to the stars and to offer sacrifices to them, and they began to sing praises and hymns to them and bow down to them, in order to fulfill, according to their base reasoning, the will of the Creator. This was the chief idea behind idolatry and this is how the idolaters who knew this idea argued.

They began by wanting to worship the Father. But the Father was not visible. The sun could be seen and hence worshiped. In the course of time, worship of the sun replaced worship of the Father. This is indeed what developed in Christianity. First the son was worshiped as a means of coming to the Father, and in a relatively short time it was the son, Jesus, who became the focal point of attention and worship.

The great Spanish commentator Sforno (c. 1470–c. 1550) recognized this as the concern of the first words of the Ten Commandments. In the verse "I am the Lord, your God," "*Your* God" (*Eloqekha*) appears in Hebrew in the singular form. Yet God was speaking to all of the Jewish people! Why speak in a restrictive manner, as if to one individual? In order, says Sforno, to stress the idea that God is speaking to every single Jew directly and saying "I am the Lord, your God—I am speaking to you, one-to-one, not through any intermediary."

A Jew does not ask a priest for dispensation. He prays to God on his own. A Jew does not worship a calf, moon, stars, sun, or son, but has direct access to the Creator. A Jew knows that the Gates of Heaven are open equally to all. Gamliel, basing himself on the verse "You shall be holy because I, the Lord, your God, am holy" (Leviticus 19:2), wrote: "Holiness was not given to the Priests exclusively, but to all, Priests, Levites, and Israelites."

But Why Are *Kohanim* Different?

According to biblical law, a murderer must be punished. "And if the man come presumptuously upon his neighbor, to slay him with guile, thou shalt take him from My altar, that he may die" (Exodus 21:14). "Take him from My altar," that is to say, even if he is a priest engaged in an act of holy worship, he is to be forcibly removed for punishment. His position does not exempt him from responsibility. He is as liable as any other Jew.

What then does his status grant him? Not more lenient treatment, but rather greater responsibility.

A priest may not marry a divorcee. Is God opposed to divorce? Clearly not. "When a man taketh a wife, and marryeth her, and it cometh to pass if she find no favor in his eyes, because he hath found some unseemly thing in her, that he writeth her a Bill of Divorcement, and giveth it in her hand, and sendeth her out of his house" (Deuteronomy 24:1). It is not better for two people who hate each other to continue to live under the same roof. It is not better for children to grow up in a climate of hostility rather than to grow up in peacefulness, even if it is with one parent alone. Mistakes need not be divinely sanctioned or enforced onto eternity.

Yet, "even the Altar itself sheds tears when man and woman must separate" (*Gittin* 90b). Were there to be no consequences to divorce, society might well sanction "sequential monogamy," a perpetual series of marriages and divorces allowing for consecutive sexual partners almost at will. No, divorce even while permitted needs some divine statement indicating, if not disapproval, at the very least sadness. Those selected as priests serve to demonstrate this dimension. The *Kohen* is a member of a select group set apart to be spiritual guides and teachers, particularly via the conduct of their own lives. They do not marry divorcees so the Jews will recognize that divorce may at times be a required option, but it is still a necessary evil. The ideal is for husband and wife to find happiness with each other throughout all of their days.

A *Kohen* is different, but not because he is deemed holier. Rather, he is given a holy function. His is a greater responsibility. His personal life must serve to preach an important principle necessary for society.

It is in this vein that we are to understand yet another law distinguishing the *Kohen* from his fellow Jews. A *Kohen* may not come into contact with the dead. This law emphasizes that Judaism is a religion of life, not of death. How better to ensure it than by forbidding those entrusted with the spiritual destiny of the Jewish people to come into contact with dead bodies, for the domain of *Kohanim* is the living.

True, *Kohanim* bless the Jewish people. But when they do so, they remove their shoes, coming into contact with earth and reminding themselves of their own mortality. They are merely transmitting a blessing, not initiating it. "So shall they put My Name upon the children of Israel, and I will bless them" (Numbers 6:27). As the *Kohanim* stretch forth their hands in blessing, the Jewish people do not look at their faces, for we are not to confuse them with God, nor the words of the blessing with those who merely utter them.

Priests serve a function, but all Jews are holy. All Jews are commanded to speak directly to God without intermediary, because middlemen can very quickly become substitutes for the highest and holiest. God must be accessible to everyone without distinction.

We Don't Pray to the Dead

The *Shulḥan Arukh* (Code of Jewish Law) decrees that it is customary on the day before Rosh Hashanah, after morning prayers, to go to the cemetery and prostrate upon the graves of the pious. Supplications are then made "to stir up the holy pious to intercede for us on the Day of Judgment." We speak to the dead in prayer. Are we asking them to be middlemen for us? Is this not a violation of the fifth principle?

To understand the answer, it is extremely important to take note of a fine point of halakhic distinction. As stated by Ganzfried in *Code of Jewish Law,* we go there

> because it is the place where the pious are buried and hence holy and pure, and prayers more readily accepted being said on holy ground. The Holy One, blessed be He, will show mercy for the sake of the righteous. But one should not aim to implore the dead who rest there, for this would be almost included in "and he inquireth of the dead," but he should implore God directly, blessed be His Name, to have mercy on him for the sake of the pious who rest in the dust. [Ch. 128, para. 13]

We pray *through* the dead and not *to* the dead. The distinction is crucial. Here, too, Halakhah is deeply sensitive to the fact that middlemen may assume their own independent status. If golden calves can become God, how much more so spirits of the departed? "I am the Lord, *your* God," speaking directly to you, with no need for any middlemen.

Praying to the Righteous and Holy

Does the interdiction against intermediaries include even pious sages and holy men? Can we not turn to a rabbi, a pious and holy person, and ask that he intercede in our behalf for a loved one?

Custom makes clear that it is permissible, but we must understand on what basis. If the blessing of a Sage or saintly man is invested with efficacy, it is in light of a principle that must be grasped in general terms, as it relates to the validity for any prayers offered by one person for another.

Jewish philosophers long ago wondered how prayer by an individual might achieve any result in altering God's decree. If, for example, a person is ill, then logic demands we believe that God felt the patient deserved to be so. Prayer is tantamount to beseeching the Almighty to change His decision. On what basis should that be done? Should God be convinced that his initial verdict was unjust? Are we suggesting in our prayer that we think we would do things differently? Isn't prayer a daring and audacious attempt to have God alter His ways because of our pleadings?

The resolution to the difficulty implicit in prayer is contained in the Hebrew root itself. We do not "pray," a word derived from the Latin *precare,* to beg, suggesting that we beseech God to do something differently than He intended because we get down on our knees and implore Him to do so. *Lehitpalel,* the Hebrew transitive verb, is reflexive. The root, *p.l.l.,* means to judge, and *lehitpalel,* "to stand in self-judgment." It is we who judge ourselves and in judging, transform our identity. We become someone else. Rather than begging on our knees, the *Amidah* (Eighteen Benedictions) demands standing and asking God, "and make us righteous with justice"—because what You decreed for one person is no longer relevant for the new individual who now stands before You.

Prayer is therefore predicated on the transformation of the one who is praying.

That, however, can only make sense in terms of a prayer for one's self. The very effectiveness of the prayer results from the change that is happening within. For one person to pray for another would bring us back to the original difficulty. What good does my praying do for another person if he or she obviously deserves what God decreed?

The answer goes back to a story in Genesis. It is within the context of Abraham's prayers for the people of Sodom that we find a remarkable idea, allowing us to comprehend how the prayers of a stranger can affect God's dealings with another.

When God told Abraham of His decision to destroy the city of Sodom, Abraham pleaded with Him and said, "Wilt Thou indeed sweep away the righteous with the wicked? Per adventure there are fifty righteous within the city; wilt Thou indeed sweep away and not forgive the place for the fifty righteous that are therein? That be far from Thee to do after this manner, to slay the righteous with the wicked, that so the righteous should be as the wicked; that be far from Thee; shall not the Judge of all the earth do justly?" (Genesis 18:23–25).

Abraham speaks in the name of justice. But justice demands that the wicked shall perish! And why does Abraham suggest

"Wilt thou indeed sweep away the righteous with the wicked?"
God never spoke of destroying the righteous. It was only the
wicked concerning whom He said, "The cry of Sodom and
Gomorrah is great and verily their sins exceedingly grievous." For
whom was Abraham praying—for the righteous or for the wicked?
If for the righteous, God had never expressed any intent to harm
them. If for the wicked, justice does demand they be punished.
What can Abraham mean when he says, "That be far from thee to
do after this manner, to slay the righteous with the wicked"?

The confusion can only be clarified if one grasps the beautiful
commentary of Rabbi Yisrael Salanter on the verse "The Rock,
His work is perfect, for all His ways are justice" (Deuteronomy
32:4). What is the special intent of the words for "*all His ways* are
justice"? The answer is that they indicate a unique aspect of the
Deity, one that judges of flesh and blood cannot emulate. If a man
murders another, he is put to death. We call that justice because
the perpetrator is suitably punished. With his death, however,
comes the pain of a widow bereft of her husband, the cries of
orphans without a father, the wails of parents who have lost a
child. We cannot help that. We cannot take into account all the
ramifications of such a sentence. But God's work "is perfect, for
all His ways are justice." Someone who may deserve a specific
punishment might be spared—not on his account, but because it
would cause pain to another who does not deserve it. That in fact
is the very meaning of the concept of *zekhut avot,* the special mercy
shown to the Jews on account of our ancestors. There are times
when the Jewish people might have deserved total annihilation,
but that could never be done because Abraham, Isaac, and Jacob,
as well as all the other holy souls of our past generations, would be
pained beyond measure. And they do not deserve the punishment
even if we might.

For whom was Abraham praying? Not for the fifty righteous,
of course, because there was never a suspicion that the righteous
themselves would be afflicted. Yet Abraham was concerned that
the "righteous be swept away with the wicked" because, if the
righteous cared for the wicked, or were involved with them and
had befriended them, then the death of the wicked would in fact be
punishment for the righteous. They would suffer undeservedly.

"If there are fifty righteous men (*zadiqim*) in the city." Significantly, Abraham based his plea on the presence of fifty righteous people *in the midst of the city,* i.e., righteous people bound up in the lives of others, so concerned with the destiny of even the wicked that their demise would cause the righteous an almost "living death." Abraham had proper grounds on which to base a plea of defense for the wicked: spare the wicked—for the sake of the righteous.

God did not deny the legitimacy of the claim. It was simply that in Sodom one could not find fifty or even ten righteous and caring individuals who would suffer undeserved pain for another's death.

When we recite a prayer for a friend's recovery from sickness (*me she-berakh*), the theological aspect of the prayer is as follows: If he deserves what is happening to him, please God, take note that I also share his pain. His sickness makes me ill. And if I have any merit, then add that to the scale of his judgment. Let him be well, because I and so many others pray on his behalf. His judgment is our judgment. May our merits be his.

Turn to a holy man, a pious sage or rebbe, and tell him how your loved one needs God's help. The righteous man hears your pain and it becomes his. He prays to God, and God must then hear how the pain of a simple Jew has become the concern of a holy man, who certainly does not deserve this depressing intrusion on his well being. The holy man prays and God hears. Turning to another to pray not *to* him, but *through* him, is permissible as long as we keep in mind the main idea of the fifth principle. We do not accept intermediaries. We know that God spoke directly to every single Jew at Sinai. We affirm that "God is nigh onto all those that draw near to Him, to all those who call onto Him in truth" (Psalm 145:18).

Part XII

The Divinity
of Torah

35

Does God
Speak to Man?

"I firmly believe that all the words of the Prophets are true."

(Principle 6)

"I firmly believe that the prophecy of Moses our teacher, may he rest in peace, was true; and that he was the chief of the prophets, both of those who preceded and of those that followed him."

(Principle 7)

"I firmly believe that the whole Torah which we now possess is the same which was given to Moses our teacher, may he rest in peace."

(Principle 8)

"I firmly believe that this Torah will not be exchanged, and that there will be no other Torah given by the Creator, blessed be His name."

(Principle 9)

ong before Freud, Judaism recognized the significance of dreams. In the Talmud we are told: "A dream contains a sixtieth part of prophecy" (*Berakhot* 57a). Everyday experiences validated this seemingly mystical judgment. Sometimes in a dream people would be told of imminent death—their own or that of another's. Sometimes they would see events clearly months and even years before they occurred. At times, couched in symbolic language that psychiatry would learn to take seriously much later, there would be omens that, like the dreams of Pharaoh, needed to be interpreted for their prophetic content.

Yet the Bible readily accepted the reality of dreams as opportunities for God to send messages to human beings. Even more striking is the fact that those "blessed" with the prophetic insight of dreams were individuals not particularly worthy of special divine favor. Pharaoh was not a holy man, but he dreamed of the seven lean cows and the seven fat cows, the seven lean stalks and the seven full ones. The message had to be given, and so whoever could best serve as its receiver became the vehicle for transmission.

"A dream is one sixtieth of prophecy" implies that dreams are the lowest form in which God chooses to communicate. To this day there are still people who have dreams of startling clarity and vision, dreams with amazing insights into the future and clearly prophetic premonitions.

If common experience indicates the existence of a phenomenon in limited measure, then wisdom as well as tradition force us to acknowledge the validity of a far more powerful method for divine communication. If Pharaoh and countless others like him were allowed to dream with heavenly content, then people of greater stature must be found worthy of far closer intimacy with God. In his *Commentary on the Mishnah*, Maimonides summarizes four ways in which Moses reached the very highest level of prophecy:

1.   Whosoever the prophet, God spoke not with him, but by an intermediary. But Moses had no intermediary, as it is said (Numbers 12:8): "Mouth to mouth did I speak with him."

2.   Every other prophet received his inspiration only when in a state of sleep, as it is asserted in various parts of Scripture, "in a dream of the night" (Genesis 20:3), "in a dream of a vision of a night" (Job 33:15), and many other phrases with similar significance; or in the day when deep sleep is fallen upon the prophet and his condition is that in which there is a removal of his sense, perceptions, and his mind is a blank like asleep. This state is styled *maḥazeh* and *mar'eh* and is alluded to in the expressions

"in visions of God." But to Moses the word came in the daytime when "he was standing between the two Cherubim," as God had promised him in the words (Exodus 25:22): "And there I will meet with thee and I will consume with thee." And God further said (Numbers 12:6–8): "If there be a prophet among you, I, the Lord, will make Myself known to him in a vision and will speak onto him in a dream. My servant, Moses, is not so, who is faithful in all My house. With him I will speak mouth to mouth . . ."

3. When the inspiration comes to the prophet, although it is in a vision and by means of an angel, his strength becomes enfeebled, his physique becomes deranged. And very great terror falls upon him so that he is almost broken through it, as is illustrated in the case of Daniel. When [the Angel] Gabriel speaks to him in a vision, Daniel says (Daniel 10:8): "And there remained no strength in me; for my comeliness was turned in me into corruption and I retained no strength." And he further says (Daniel 10:9): "Then I was in a deep sleep on my face, and my face towards the ground." And further (Daniel 10:16): "By the vision my sorrows are turned upon me." But not so with Moses. The word came onto him and no confusion in any way overtook him, as we are told in the verse (Exodus 33:11): "And the Lord spoke onto Moses face onto face as a man speaketh onto his neighbor." This means that just as no man feels disquieted when his neighbor talks with him, so he (peace to him) had no fright at the discourse of God, although it was face to face; this being the case by reason of the strong bond uniting him with the intellect, as we have described.

4. To all the prophets the inspiration came not at their own choice, but by the will of God. The prophet at times waits a number of years without an inspiration reaching him. And it is sometimes asked of the prophet that he should communicate a message he has received, but the prophet waits some days or months before doing so or does not

make it known at all. We have seen cases where the
prophet prepares himself by enlivening his soul and puri-
fying his spirit, as did Elisha in the incident when he
declared (2 Kings 3:15): "But now bring me a minstrel,"
and then the inspiration came to him. He does not necessarily receive the inspiration at the time that he is ready
for it. But Moses, our teacher, was able to say at whatsoever time he wished, "Stand, and I shall hear what God
shall command concerning you" (Numbers 9:8). It is
again said (Leviticus 16:2): "Speak onto Aaron, thy
brother, that he come not at all times into the Sanctuary"; with reference to which verse the Talmud remarks
that the prohibition ("that he come not at all times")
applies only to Aaron. But Moses may enter the Sanctuary at all times.

Prophecy exists. But there are many different kinds of
prophets. Moses, however, remains in a class by himself.

Why Was Moses Special?

Was Moses born great or did he become great? Was he divine
from birth or was his greatness predicated on self-perfection?

Two traditions appear in Jewish thought. They are implicit in a
disagreement concerning the correct interpretation of the verse
describing the birth of the greatest man who ever lived. "And the
woman conceived and bore a son; and when she saw him that he
was good, she hid him three months" (Exodus 2:2). Yokheved,
Moses' mother, saw *ki tov hu*—that he was good. But what precisely did that mean?

Rashi, relying on a talmudic opinion, tells us she knew that this
was a very special child, perhaps destined to be the redeemer of the
Jewish people, because "the entire house became filled with light"
when he appeared. As farfetched as this interpretation may sound,
some commentators lend it credibility via a fascinating exegesis.
Words in the Bible often gain their full meaning from a comparison with their use in other contexts. In particular, the first usage of

a word in the Bible is significant and stamps a term with an idea that will be relevant for all future occasions in which it is used. The first time we find the word *or* in the Torah is in Genesis 1:4: "And God saw the light (*or*) that it was good (*ki tov*). Light was identified with goodness. Similarly, when the mother of Moses perceives something special about her son and it is biblically identified as *ki tov*, the implication is that there emanated from him some of the original *or* that pre-dated even the creation of the sun on day four—the light of the first day of creation, which is an aspect of God's immanence, the *Shekhinah*.

In the context of the story recounting Moses' birth, the miraculous accompaniment of light is neither obvious in the text nor necessary for understanding the story Jewish babies were hunted. A mere cry or whimper would give away a hiding place and prevent parents from hiding a child to avert the decree of extermination. In this case, "She saw that he was good." He made no unnecessary noise. She was, in fact, able to hide him for three months—three months, as our Sages suggest, because although the Egyptians (like the Germans) kept exact records as to when a child was due, Moses was born prematurely, after six months. Since he was quiet, his mother could keep his birth a secret from the authorities for the remaining three months.

The two different interpretations are crucial for proper understanding of the man Moses. His very relevance for the ages as a role model will depend greatly on whether we view him as a "normal" infant or as celestially distinguished from birth.

A famous legend repeated by the German rabbinic scholar Rabbi Israel Lipschutz (1782–1860) in his commentary to the *Mishnah* (*Tiferet Yisrael, Kidushin* 4:14, note 77) clearly supports the view that Moses was all too human. A king who had heard of the greatness of Moses commissioned a famous painter to visit the children of Israel and bring back a portrait of him. When he fulfilled his commission and returned with the portrait as requested, the king could not believe that this was indeed the man of whom he had heard so much. The painting clearly showed—if credence can be given to the king's belief in the theories of physiognomy—a wicked degenerate. His advisers confirmed his opinion. Upon hearing the artist's pleadings that he had, in fact, carried out his

298 THE DIVINITY OF TORAH

mission and brought back an accurate representation, the king himself journeyed to the camp of Moses to see whether the portrait was accurate. Much to his amazement, he had to admit that the painter had not lied. When he could not contain his surprise and admitted to Moses why he originally did not believe that this could have been the picture of a great man, Moses confirmed the king's original view. Indeed, the evil they saw in his face was there. Those were aspects of his character that were with him from birth. Precisely because he, Moses, was able to control and conquer those evil impulses, God had chosen him to lead the Jewish people.

This is a story so startling that a number of Sages could not believe its authenticity and sought to ban its further publication. Yet in his *Hilkhot Teshuvah* (*The Laws Concerning Repentance*), Maimonides himself obviously believes that at birth Moses was not divinely different. "Every person has the possibility to be either righteous as Moses, our teacher, or wicked as Jeroboam, or wise or foolish, or merciful or cruel, and so too all other traits" (*Hilkhot Teshuvah* 5:2).

Moses was not born without an evil inclination, totally "good" (*tov*) so that the rays of light emanated from him. Had he been an angel, he would have been not more but less than human. Without evil desires, there can be no reward for overcoming temptation. The crucial words explaining Moses' selection are not "and she saw that he was good," but rather: "And it came to pass in those days when Moses was growing up that he went out unto his brethren and looked on their burdens" (Exodus 2:11). Before God appears to Moses at the burning bush and invests him with his mission, we meet him in three separate incidents, each one of which repeats in a somewhat altered form the identical attribute. Moses sees an Egyptian smiting a Hebrew. He could choose the path of least resistance, the way of silence and passivity. Instead he intervenes, he does not mind his own business, he accepts wholeheartedly the notion of responsibility of one person for another. In this first case, the victim was a Jew, the assailant an outsider. One might perhaps be ready to strike out against a stranger who attacks one of our own. What if, however, both wrongdoer and injured party are Jews and there is no threat of anti-Semitism? The second story alters the situation in precisely this way, so that

Moses is recognized as someone who will not stand aloof and remain uninvolved even when he sees "two men of the Hebrews were striving together." In biblical law, a trait or action is confirmed as the norm when it is repeated three times (a *hazaqah*). Indeed, one more story appears in the text before we are told that God appears in the burning bush and commands Moses to assume leadership. Moses has fled to Midian. At a well he sees foreign women attempting to water their sheep: "And the shepherds came and drove them away" (Exodus 2:17). Strangers attacking strangers. Yet, Moses could not stand idly by. "But Moses stood up and helped them and watered their flock."

The Torah, so sparse in language elsewhere, details just these three incidents in the life of Moses because they emphasize what he became and why he deserved to be selected. Could anyone else have become a Moses? Theoretically the answer is yes. But did anyone reach those heights? Only Moses reached the level that allowed him subsequently to ascend Mount Sinai and bring the Torah down from the Heavens to humankind.

Why does the Torah preface Moses' birth with the verse "And there went a man of the House of Levi and took to wife a daughter of Levi and the woman conceived and bore a son" (Exodus 2:1–2) without naming his mother and father? Because in view of what Moses became, one might have been tempted to attribute divine parentage to him, to claim that he was not a son of mortals, but rather of God. Far more important, therefore, than the name of his father, Amram, and mother, Yokheved, is the need to indicate that there went a mere man and took a wife a mere daughter—human, mortal people of flesh and blood. "And the woman conceived and bore a son." Obviously if she bore a child, she must have first conceived. Why must this self-evident fact be stated? Again because there might be some who would conclude that a man rising to such greatness could not possibly have been the product of a normal act of intercourse. Perhaps in an attempt to deify him, some might go so far as to claim an immaculate conception for his mother or even a virgin birth.

Moses was human. He was born of flesh-and-blood parents and he died as all men do. His burial place would remain unknown for all time so that he would not become an idolatrous object of veneration. There must always remain a distance between the Creator and the created.

Moses was a man with defects. He had desires that had to be overcome—and that made him all the greater. He had physical defects as well—Moses was slow of speech and slow of tongue. Thus, one cannot say that owing to his great oratorical skills, he mesmerized an entire people to accept a message of his own making as the word of God.

But still Moses was different from anyone else who had ever lived. So different that the Bible itself records as his epitaph: "And there hath not risen a prophet since in Israel like onto Moses whom the Lord knew face to face; and all the signs and the wonders, which the Lord sent him to do in the land of Egypt, to Pharaoh, and to all the servants, and to all his land; and in all the mighty hand, and in all the great terror, which Moses wrought in the sight of all Israel" (Deuteronomy 34:10–12). These last words of The Five Books of Moses carry a judgment that is crucial for the proper understanding of the entire Torah and its claim upon the Jewish people.

Principles six and seven must serve as the preface to the eighth principle, which declares that the Torah is divine. Prophecy exists: "The rich gift of His prophecy He gave to the men of His choice, in whom he gloried" (*Yigdal,* Principle 6). "There arose not in Israel again another like onto Moses, a prophet who perceived His countenance" (*Yigdal,* Principle 7). If prophecy is not reality, then we create truth rather than accept it; prophets make God's will acceptable to us even as they prove His concern. Yet the possibility of error exists whenever a message is transmitted. Moses was far more than a prophet who can "preach in his own style," phrase matters in his own words, or give expression to divine truths in a language whose verbal limitations may modify or distort these truths. Moses was a scribe who reached the level whereby he could sit before the Lord and take accurate dictation.

Whenever we lift the Torah on high, the congregation gives utterance to the way in which we believe the Torah should be accepted: "And this is the Torah which Moses placed before the children of Israel through the mouth of the Lord by the hand of Moses." God spoke and Moses wrote. No other prophet could come close enough to the Almighty to fulfill a task of this magnitude. But if we believe in both prophecy and the uniqueness of Moses, we may proceed to the next level: acknowledging a Torah of truth (*emet*), a word whose Hebrew consonants comprise the first letter of the Hebrew alphabet (*Alef*), the middle letter (*Mem*), and the very last (*Tav*), for the Torah is true "from A to Z," including everything in the center.

36

The Whole Truth

hat does the Sabbatical year have to do with Mount Sinai?" That expression is often used whenever we find two seemingly disparate subjects yoked together in the same discussion. This Hebrew idiom originated in a question raised by Rashi on a biblical text. In Leviticus (25:2–5), we are taught the commandment concerning the seventh year (*Shemitah*): "Speak unto the children of Israel and say unto them, 'When ye come into the land which I give you, then shall the land keep a Sabbath unto the Lord. Six years thou shalt sow thy field and six years thou shalt prune thy vineyard and gather in the produce thereof, but in the Sabbath year the Sabbath of solemn rest shall be for the land, a Sabbath onto the Lord; thy field thou shalt not sow and thy vineyard thou shalt not prune, that which groweth of itself of thy harvest thou shalt not reap and the grapes of the undressed vine thou shalt not gather; a year of solemn rest shall it be for the land.'"

There is a Sabbath of days for the Jewish people as well as a Sabbath of years. After six days of labor, every person is to rest. After six years of agricultural use, the land is to lie fallow.

Most intriguing and peculiar about this law is the manner in which it is introduced: "And the Lord spoke to Moses on Mount Sinai, saying" (Leviticus 25:1). Every law was given at Sinai. Why is this particular one introduced with the statement describing its source? More succinctly, what connection has the sabbatical year with Mount Sinai? Don't all the commandments have their source from Sinai?

The accepted answer of our Sages is that the information that this law was given at Sinai is important, because the Torah makes clear many rules, details, and minutiae concerning it. For that reason we are taught that this law was given at Mount Sinai. It is to be a paradigm for us concerning all other laws: "Just as regarding the Sabbatical year there were stated its generalizations and its details and its minutiae from Sinai, so were all laws given in similar manner, i.e., their generalizations, details and minutiae from Sinai" (*Torat Kohanim,* Leviticus 25:1).

Shemitah becomes a model law for every other Halakhah. The sabbatical year is selected by God for full explication and stamped with the seal of "Mount Sinai" so that all other laws are understood in similar manner.

What this equation seems to ignore is the most fundamental question: If one commandment out of 613 had to be used to indicate a principle—i.e., that every aspect of its legislation, no matter how small, was directly given by God on the mountain of law— why did *Shemitah* deserve this singular distinction? What is the connection between *Shemitah* and 612 other mitzvot?

The answer offers us an insight into a dimension of Jewish law that might otherwise go unnoticed. For *Shemitah* introduces us to the category of natural law. By clarifying its link to all other laws given on Mount Sinai, we have a fascinating insight into the real claim of the law on the actions of humankind.

Scientists today understand that land cannot be worked without surcease, chemicals and minerals must be replenished. What the Bible calls a "Sabbath of the land" is what modern farmers refer to as fallowing. When the Torah teaches us that we must let the land rest every seventh year, and then we will be blessed with a double portion, it is not simply mouthing theological promises but recording what turned out to be realistic rules based on realities of natural law.

All of us readily understand that the universe has built into it incontrovertible principles. If, for example, Newton announces to us the discovery of a law of gravity, no matter how much one might be displeased with that particular rule, one is subject to its consequences. If one were to decide, in a fit of pique against the Lawmaker on High to reject this ruling and to jump off the Empire State Building, freedom of choice would make the action possible, but physical reality would demand a severe price for this foolishness.

The law of gravity demands almost immediate payment for infractions against it. Other laws of the universe, although equally rigid and unbending, are more lenient at least in terms of the time necessary for punishment. To survive, the human being needs both food and drink. If one is dissatisfied with this "law," fasting is possible. For some time, the body deprived of its requirements will rebel only minimally. Weakness, headache, and an inability to stand may follow after indeterminate intervals. Continue to disobey, however, and the consequences are unavoidable, both final and fatal.

What invests these rules with such overwhelming power? The fact that they were legislated by God as the ways in which the universe must run. The manner of the legislation is the same method that brought everything into being: "And God said, let there be." The Mishnah in *Ethics of the Fathers* teaches us "The world was created with ten sayings." God needed simply to utter—"and He said," "and it was." God's will creates the reality. If God ordained day to follow night, then no matter how much we might curse the darkness of evening or seek to remove the sun by day, our desires are null and void in the face of divine decree.

The same God who determined the law of gravity simply by saying "Let it be" also legislated laws of morality by proclaiming the Ten Commandments. Not to obey either one is not simply to sin but to pay the consequence of going against what is built into the very operation of the world by its Creator.

Why did God give the world a comprehensive code of instruction, a Torah guide of proper living? For the same reason that General Motors feels it necessary to present every purchaser of its automobiles with a manual for proper care of its vehicles, built according to certain specifications. The one who built the cars informs us that we must change the oil and grease on a regular basis. Can one get away with disobeying these instructions? Yes, for a short time the car will function even if not cared for exactly according to specifications. In the long run it must malfunction because the car was built according to certain principles. It cannot withstand treatment that goes against the plans of designer and builder. When God created Adam, says the Midrash, He "looked into the Torah and created the world."

God commands us to work the land for six years and then allow it to rest on the seventh. He promises that reward will follow, not as a special providential gift, but as an axiomatic result of a natural law that came into being because God said, "When ye come into the land which I give you, then shall the land keep a Sabbath onto the Lord." The commandment created the reality. And so, too, when God said, "Six days shalt thou labor and do all thy work and the seventh day is a Sabbath onto thy Lord," the very statement created the reality of the Sabbath built into both the human body and psyche, so that its negation would be as futile as attempting to avoid the consequences of the law of gravity.

Can one live without keeping the Sabbath? Can we drive a car without changing the oil every 3,000 miles? The owner's manual teaches us what must be done, because that is the way in which the object was created. But people may violate the Sabbath for decades. They may never observe the weekly day of introspection, which demands an analysis of why we pursue all our goals of vanity and foolishness throughout the six secular days preceding the Sabbath. But something will be amiss. There will be a subliminal recognition that a law of gravity is being denied, a law of Sabbath ignored. The one who does not rest on the seventh day might wind up resting on a psychiatric couch, wondering where his life has gone, what he's done wrong, why he finds no meaning or happiness in his existence.

There is a price to be paid for every violation of law, be it natural or spiritual. There is an automatic consequence to every infraction created by God's word, from refusing to replenish the body with food to failing to nourish the soul with mitzvot.

The connection between *Shemitah* and the rest of Jewish law is as follows: God chose a patently natural law of agriculture to illustrate the relevance and rationale for all other mitzvot. God gave a Torah of truth. The sun rises and the sun sets. That is incontrovertible. Jews must recite the *Shema* morning and night. That, too, is incontrovertible and unalterable. If *Shemitah* is observed, reality decrees that fallowing brings blessing. If Sabbath and Torah are observed, God has equally ensured that "Behold I set before ye this day a blessing and a curse: the blessing, if ye shall hearken unto the commandments of the Lord, your God, which I command you this day; and the curse, if ye shall not hearken unto the commandments of the Lord, your God, but turn aside out of the way which I command ye this day, to go after other gods which ye have not known" (Deuteronomy 11:26–28).

The Torah is a Torah of truth. Every generalization and detail comes from Sinai. That is our eighth principle—the Torah is true even unto its smallest detail.

37

Now and Forever

"I firmly believe that this Torah will not be changed, and that there will be no other Torah given by the Creator, blessed be His Name."
(Principle 9)

young man in the Midwest grew up in a home where Jewish practice was almost nil, where knowledge of Torah was absent. He was a youth of great religious sensitivity. When he went to college, one of his professors recognized his spiritual thirst and induced him to become a member of "Jews for Jesus," to which the professor belonged.

The young man became God-intoxicated. The Bible became his passion. He accepted everything he was told and became a fervent disciple. It was then that his mother became distraught. How could my son forsake the faith of his ancestors? Although in retrospect she recognized it was her own fault for never having given her son any religious instruction prior to this, she knew she had to do something to stop what she felt was a betrayal of her people.

She had no one to turn to and so she began to read the Bible by herself. She knew no Hebrew, and so the English translation had to suffice. Without the benefit of teacher or commentaries, she looked to the biblical text for some way to rebut the beliefs her son was now espousing.

Then two words struck her. Had she seen them in the original
Hebrew, they would have been *ḥuqat olam*; in English they were
translated as "everlasting statute." Countless times in the text, she
saw that God said of the laws He gave to the Jews that they were to
be "everlasting statutes," meant not just for one age or for one
generation, but for all times, forever, throughout all of human
history.

How could her son be told that biblical law was no longer relevant? That with the coming of Jesus, there was no longer a need
for observance? That the Son had the power to countermand the
words of the Father, given in perpetuity?

She shared the problem with her son. He was intrigued and
said he would look into it by turning to his superiors. The ones
whom he asked said they were not sufficiently erudite to answer
the problem, but they would get back to him. Up the chain of command, the question went. But no matter how wise or important the
respondent, the answer was never satisfactory.

That young man today is studying for the rabbinate. Because
he was not given a response that could justify the alteration of the
original laws given at Sinai, he returned to his roots. He recognized the simple truth that, in Judaism, the law is synonymous
with eternity. It is what the Sages understood from the words that
Moses pronounced: "For this commandment is not in Heaven"
(Deuteronomy 30:11). In other words, to anyone who mistakenly
believes that "another Moses" could bring us another law from
Heaven, the Sages answer: the Law was given to us on this earth by
Moses—for all time. There are no other laws left in Heaven for
anyone else to impart. God had declared that this is the only Law
He will give to us; nothing will ever replace it. "Rabbi Ḥanina
taught: 'The law and all the implements by which it is carried out
have been given forever more'" (*Devarim Rabah, Niẓavim* 8:6).

Judaism rejects Jesus not simply because he comes as Son to
replace the Father; far more serious is his transgression in abrogat-
ing God's commandments.

It was Jesus who, when walking with his disciples on a Sabbath
through the wheat fields, allowed his companions to pick and eat
ears of wheat. When rabbis censured them for desecration of the

Sabbath law, Jesus replied, "The son of man is master of the Sabbath" (Matthew 12:1–8). This was not a case of mortal danger legitimizing the violation of the Sabbath. There was no emergency, and yet Jesus permitted the desecration of the Sabbath. The old law could be replaced with the new. The Old Testament would be dismissed as secondary and nonbinding in light of the New Testament, which stressed faith over law.

There is an unresolved discrepancy between Jesus' practice and his claim "Do not suppose that I have come to do away with the law or the prophets. I have not come to do away with them, but to enforce them. For I tell you, as long as Heaven and earth endure, not one dotting of an 'i' or crossing of a 't' will be dropped from the law until it is all observed. Anyone, therefore, who weakens one of the slightest of these commands, and teaches others to do so, will be ranked lowest in the kingdom of Heaven; but anyone who observes them and teaches others to do so will be ranked high in the kingdom of Heaven" (Matthew 5:17–19). When Jesus and his disciples failed to observe a fast, the justification was: "No one sews a new patch of unshrunken cloth on an old coat; for if he does, the patch tears away, the new from the old, and makes the hole worse than ever, and no one pours new wine into old wine skins; for if he does, the wine bursts the skins. New wine has to be put into fresh skins" (Mark 2:21–22). The law was the old, and had to be done away with. If it had any justification, it was only for sinners: "I agree that the law is excellent—provided it is legitimately used, with the understanding the law is not intended for upright men, but for the lawless and disorderly, the Godless and irreligious, the irreverent and profane, men who kill their fathers or mothers, murderers, immoral people, men sexually perverted, kidnappers, liars, perjurers, or whatever else is contrary to sound teaching, as set forth in the glorious good news of the blessed God with which I have been entrusted" (1 Timothy 1:8–11). The righteous of faith do not need law. The dietary laws could be disregarded: "All foods are clean" (Mark 7:19). Clearly stated biblical laws could be disregarded: "They [the Jews] were told, 'Anyone who divorces his wife must give her a Certificate of Divorce,' but I tell you that anyone who divorces his wife on any ground except unfaithfulness, makes her commit adultery, and anyone who marries her after she is divorced commits adultery" (Matthew 5:31f).

The list is long. The facts are incontrovertible. The one who claimed he came not to do away with the law or the prophets acted contrary to this assertion. By his deeds he taught that what God said long ago could be revised, amended, and improved.

That is exactly what God had said could not be done. Maimonides states: "It is a distinct and explicitly stated feature of the Law that it is an Ordinance to endure for all eternity, and it does not admit of any alteration, diminution, or addition. Hence we learn that no prophet has permission to introduce any innovation at any future time. Should, therefore, a man arise, either from among the nations or from among Israel, and perform any sign or miracle and declare that God has sent him to add any commandments or to abrogate any commandment or to explain any of the commandments otherwise than we have heard from Moses, or should he declare that the commandments which have been ordained for the Israelites are not for all time for all generations, but were only temporary enactments—behold this man is indeed a false prophet, for he indeed comes to refute the prophecy of Moses" (*Hilkhot Yesodei ha-Torah* 9:1).

If we accept the Law as divine, then by definition it is meant to be everlasting. Its wisdom transcends the vagaries of different times and cultures. Its truth is timeless, its relevance for all generations.

The Only Exceptions to Unchanging Law

Only one group of laws needs to be emphasized as an exception to the rule. They do indeed appear in the Bible and yet Judaism acknowledges that the possibility for change is built into their initial legislation. That is because even when originally given, it was made clear that they stand apart in a category of law that we might best call the "*ki* grouping"—laws that are prefaced by the Hebrew word *ki,* meaning "when" or "if."

Let us cite one very important illustration. Does the Bible

believe in polygamy? Clearly it appears the answer is yes. Two of the Patriarchs had more than one wife. Nowhere in the Pentateuch is marriage with more than one woman forbidden. It was not until the Middle Ages that Rabbenu Gershom issued his famous decree banning polygamy.

Yet, one might ask, by what authority did this rabbi, no matter how great, go against the clear dictates of the Torah? If the Bible said yes, how could he say no?

It is here the Hebrew word *ki*—translated as "if" or "when"— must be recognized as crucial when it introduces a specific law. Indeed, if polygamy were a mitzvah or a desirable state in God's eyes, there would have been some biblical verse alluding not only to its permissibility but also to its desirability. In fact, the only legal reference to a polygamus union reads as follows: "If [*ki*] a man hath two wives, the one beloved and the other hated, and they have borne him children, both the beloved and the hated, and if the firstborn son be hers that was hated; then it shall be in the day that he causeth his sons to inherit that which he hath, that he may not make the son of the beloved the firstborn before the son of the hated, who was the firstborn, but he shall acknowledge the first-born, the son of the hated, by giving him a double portion of all that he hath, for he is the first fruits of his strength, the right of the firstborn is his" (Deuteronomy 21:15–17). The Bible does not state that a man "ought" have two wives, but *ki*—"if" a man has two wives. Then the Torah describes the results of a polygamous situation in which one is beloved and one is hated. It is almost as if the Bible predicts the impossibility of a happy marital triangle. The problem will then manifest itself not only to the wives but to the children as well. Fighting will revolve around rights of the first-born. Judges will have to render decisions stemming from familial disputes. Two wives mean one is beloved and one is hated; two wives lead to arguments over inheritance between the children, who share the same father but have different mothers.

Still more remarkable is the section that immediately follows. Having described a polygamous union and the ensuing dispute concerning rights of a firstborn, the law shifts to the section dealing with the "stubborn and rebellious son that will not hearken to the voice of his father or the voice of his mother." Does the sequence not clearly suggest that a family bereft of peace because of a marital triangle will also see the rise of rebellious children who have grown up in a household filled with discord and enmity?

The fact that the Torah permits something does not necessarily mean it considers it an ideal. In a time where the taking of many wives was a norm, perhaps its prohibition at the very beginnings of Jewish history would have been too severe, too difficult to accept, comparable to what the rabbis might later refer to as a "decree that the majority of the community could not tolerate." That kind of law, the Sages taught, could not be legislated no matter how noble or lofty its purpose. So, too, would God Himself limit legislating even a Torah ideal if the world and the Jewish people at the time of Sinai could not realistically accept it in practice.

How did Rabbenu Gershom know that God did not consider polygamy a paradigm of the marital relationship? How did he know that a man and woman seeking to re-create the state of original Paradise would only be able to find it in a one-to-one relationship? Because God revealed in His plan for Creation that it is one Adam and one Eve who made up the inhabitants of the first Paradise on earth.

When Rabbenu Gershom felt that the Jewish world was ready to accept the biblically expressed ideal as universal practice, he codified the prohibition of polygamy. He was not deterred by the verse "If a man hath two wives"—for that verse did not mandate the practice; it merely predicted the terrible outcome of a practice that had not yet become outlawed.

So, too, must we understand what the slaveholders of the South did not, when they justified their actions at the time of the Civil War in light of the Bible. How could a God-fearing Abraham Lincoln be opposed to a practice that clearly found favor in the eyes of the Almighty? If the Bible made slavery legitimate, why should the North and its leaders be so outraged by its legitimacy?

Here, too, the response must take note of the word *ki* as it introduces a legal section. Nowhere does the Torah command the purchase of a slave or demand a system of servitude. Indeed, the very first section of Jewish law in the portion *Mishpatim* (Exodus 21) deals with slavery. Why should God's law, which ought to revolve around the most ethereal concepts and categories, initiate its discussion about human relationships and responsibilities with ordinances concerning a slave? Because, our commentators respond, the law shows its greatness by its concern for the weaker vessels of society. It is not the wealthy or the truly blessed who must be the objects of our initial concern.

Let us begin with the laws concerning the slave, because God cares most about those whom others forsake. Thus, if (*ki*) you buy a Hebrew servant (in a world that saw nothing wrong with slavery and assumed it to be a given of human behavior, in which the strong can rule over the weak), then the very first law states: "Six years he shall serve and in the seventh he shall go out free for nothing" (Exodus 21:2). It is not slavery that is condoned, but rather everlasting servitude that is forbidden. A remarkable first step was thus taken centuries before the Civil War brought that same ideal to fruition in the United States. The same God who said "Let my people go" and Who proclaimed "I am the Lord, your God, who took you out of the land of Egypt, the house of bondage" demands: if you purchase a slave, you must at least recognize a basic limitation imposed upon your ownership, for "Six years he shall labor, but in the seventh he shall go out to freedom." God took the Jews out of the bondage of Egypt; God frees the slave after six years of servitude and demands that he be given his "Sabbath"—the seventh year must provide him with rest and with freedom.

The very nature of servitude itself is legally altered. The Torah not only limits length of service but also redefines what is permissible during the years the master–slave relationship is condoned. Indeed, so many rights are granted to the slave that the greatest biblical fear is that the slave may be willing to forfeit his freedom: "The servant shall plainly say: 'I love my master, my wife, and my children. I will not go out free'" (Exodus 21:5). What shall then be done to a man so foolish as to prefer continued slavery to freedom? "Then his master shall bring him onto God and shall bring him to the door or onto the doorpost, and his master shall bore his ear through with an awl and he shall serve him forever" (Exodus 21:6). Why was his ear pierced? The rabbis answer: "The ear which heard on Mount Sinai, for to me shall the children of Israel be slaves, and yet went and acquired a master for himself, let that ear be

THE DIVINITY OF TORAH

pierced." He who voluntarily chooses slavery obviously did not understand the message of Sinai. We are given free will; we are the masters of our fate. That is why the Bible allows someone to continue to be a slave, even though the text condemns the decision. With pierced ear, that is to say, an ear literally indicating it did not truly hear God's will, the man who loves his indentured status remains as he is: "And he shall serve him forever." Yet, even that is not accepted literally by our Sages. The fiftieth year, the Jubilee, serves to "proclaim liberty throughout the land unto all the inhabitants thereof; it shall be a jubilee unto you; and ye shall return every man unto his possession and ye shall return every man unto his family" (Leviticus 25:10).

Did the Torah command slavery? No, it condoned the institution only partially, redefining and limiting it. The Torah also makes clear that this was a temporary compromise with reality. The Torah projected an ideal, illustrated by the Jews who were taken out of Egypt in order to abolish slavery. The Emancipation Proclamation did not contravene the words of the Bible, but rather acknowledged that the time had finally come when God's ideal will could at last become the accepted law of the land. Once society reaches a higher stage of civilization, slavery will no longer be relevant; in the interim, it is severely restricted.

The prophet Samuel clearly understood this when he heard the pleas of the people for a king. Yet the populace was merely asking to fulfill a biblical ideal, the selection of a king. Why did Samuel object and argue against the request?

And they said unto him: "Behold thou art old and thy sons walk not in thy ways; now make us a king to judge us like all the nations." But the thing displeased Samuel when they said, "Give us a king to judge us." And Samuel prayed unto the Lord . . . and Samuel told all the words of the Lord unto the people that asked of him a king, and he said, "This will be the manner of the king that shall reign over you. He will take your sons and appoint them unto him, for his chariots, and to be his horsemen; and they shall run before his chariots. And he will appoint them unto him for captains of thousands and captains of fifties; and to plow his ground and to reap his harvest, and to make his instruments of war, and the instruments of his chariots. And he will take your daughters to be perfumers and to be cooks and to be bakers. And he will take your fields and your vineyards and your olive yards, even the best of them and give them to his servants. And he will take the tenth of your seed and of your vineyards and give to his officers and to his servants. And he will take your menservants and your maidservants and your goodliest young men and your asses and put them to his work. He will take the tenth of your flocks and ye shall be his servants. And ye shall cry out in that day because of your king whom ye shall have chosen you. And the Lord will not answer you in that day. [1 Samuel 8:5–6, 10–18]

How do we explain the prophet's displeasure with the people? Is not monarchy recorded in the Torah as the ideal system of government for the Jewish people? Are there not, in fact, laws for the king, implying that this is the form of government most sanctioned by the Bible?

Samuel was not going against biblical law when he discouraged monarchy. True, the Torah discusses kings and records specific laws relevant to them. But the opening verse of that section as well as the first word are what must be considered most crucial: *Ki tavo el ha-arez*—"When [or if] thou are come onto the land which the Lord, thy God, giveth thee, and shall possess and shall dwell therein and shall say, 'I will set a king over me like all the nations that are round about me'"(Deuteronomy 17:14). The laws of monarchy are thus predicated upon a specific condition, one that is clearly not favorable in God's sight since it is based on an attempt to imitate other nations. Having expressed their desire to be "like all nations" that are about them, the Jews are told that if they wish to have a king, "Thou shalt in any wise set a king over thee whom the Lord, thy God, shall choose. One from among thy brethren shalt thou set king over thee. Thou mayest not put a foreigner over thee who is not thy brother" (Deuteronomy 17:15). If you are going to do it, then at least choose one from amongst your own. Also, it is worthwhile recalling the maxim of Lord Acton: "Power corrupts; absolute power corrupts absolutely." If you do ask for a king, at the very least limit his powers as well as his prerogatives. "Only he shall not multiply horses to himself nor cause the people to return to Egypt, to the end that he should multiply horses, for as much as the Lord hath said unto you, 'Ye shall henceforth return no more that way.' Neither shall he multiply wives to himself that his heart turn not away. Neither shall he greatly multiply to himself silver and gold" (Deuteronomy 17:16–17). Monarchy may be permitted, but not absolute monarchy. A king is preferable to anarchy, but a king who fears no one is a threat to the people: "And it shall be when he sitteth upon the throne of his kingdom that he shall write him a copy of this law in a book out of that which is before the Priests, the Levites; and it shall be with him and he shall read therein all the days of his life, that he may learn to fear the Lord, his God, to keep all the words of this law and these statutes to do them; that his heart be not lifted up above his brethren, and that he turn not aside from the Commandment to the right hand or to the left, to the end that he may prolong his days in his kingdom, he and his children in the midst of Israel" (Deuteronomy 17:18–20).

Samuel did not abrogate the law. The law as originally stated only posited a possibility. Its suggestion that the Jews' future request would reflect their desire to be like other nations proves that Samuel's fears were already implied in the biblical qualifications of monarchy.

Monarchy, slavery, and polygamy were not banned outright. Yet God made clear His divine displeasure. A desire to live in terms of the higher ideal would obviously not be sinful; rather, it would represent a step forward in society's march to compliance with the will of the Almighty.

Some laws, therefore, when prefaced with the Hebrew word *ki,* allows for emendation. When God spoke in unalterable terms and said *ḥuqat olam,* "everlasting statute," then no Sage or Prophet has a right to change the law. The ninth principle in *Yigdal* is crucial to the acceptance of Torah: "This law God will not alter, and will not change for any other through time's utmost range."

Part XIII

The End of Days

38

Are We Close to the Time of the Messianic Era?

"I firmly believe that the Creator, blessed be His name, knows all the actions and thoughts of human beings, as it is said: 'It is He who fashions the hearts of them all, He who notes all their deeds.'"

(Principle 10)

"I firmly believe that the Creator, blessed be His name, rewards those who keep His commands, and punishes those who transgress His commands."

(Principle 11)

"I firmly believe in the coming of Messiah, and although he may tarry, I daily wait for his coming."

(Principle 12)

"I firmly believe that there will be a revival of the dead at a time which will please the Creator, blessed and exalted be His name forever and ever."

(Principle 13)

wo premises basic to the Jewish religion lead to two irrefutable conclusions. The first premise is that God knows everything that happens on this earth: "Great in counsel and mighty in work; for thine eyes are upon all the ways of the sons of man" (Jeremiah 32:19). That is the tenth principle of faith.

The second premise is that God rewards the righteous and punishes the wicked, a concept rooted in the very first commandment from God to humanity and reiterated throughout the Torah. Obey and you will be blessed; disobey, and face the consequences. That is the eleventh principle.

What must we say when these premises are refuted by reality? How do we reconcile God's awareness of our deeds and promise of reward and punishment with a world that, to all appearances, allows the wicked to prosper and the righteous to suffer? The two premises remain valid only if they are joined with firm belief in the final two principles. The reality of reward must be removed from the domain of the immediate present to a more distant future; the blessings promised to the Jewish people in return for their walking in the ways of the Lord may be deferred to the time of the Messiah; and the promise of personal recompense for every individual need not be within the span of this lifetime, but may be realized after Resurrection. The tenth and eleventh principles necessitate the twelfth and the thirteenth: What the Jewish people lack for now is part of our national destiny. What righteous individuals fail to receive is reserved for them in a setting far more precious, in the World to Come.

The Messianic Dream

A Jew must have the ability to view life from a perspective that transcends the present. This approach is rooted in the philosophy of a founding father of our faith. Abraham had two sons. One was destined to transmit all that he learned from his father to the future and become the second Patriarch of our people. This was Isaac. His name, *Yizhaq,* means "he will laugh." Abraham had yet another son. He became an outcast, unworthy of bearing the mission of his father. This Ishmael (*Yishmael,* in Hebrew) was patriarch of the Arab nations. The Torah uses one word to express what caused Sarah to recognize Ishmael's unworthiness: "And Sarah saw the son of Hagar, the Egyptian, whom she had born onto Abraham, *mezaheq*—making sport." *Mezaheq* is from the very same root as the name *Yizhaq;* both mean "to laugh." *Yizhaq,* however, is in the future tense, *meẓaḥeq* in the present. That is why the Sages suggest that Ishmael's laughter refers to idolatry, immorality, and bloodshed. He identified joy only with immediate reward; *meẓaḥeq* refers to the ideology known as instant gratification.

A Jew is called a *Yid.* The word that identifies us also represents a letter in Hebrew, the *Yod,* which grammatically turns a root into the future tense. A *Yid* is someone who knows that gratification of the moment is not as significant as the promise of the morrow.

How have Jews been able to survive throughout history while being forced to endure suffering more than any other nation? It is because Messiah and immortality meant more to them than curses and Crusaders. The horrors of the present could be ignored by clinging to hope for the future. Not now, said the Jew, but someday. To those who trust in the Lord, the words of King David spoke forcefully: "God will deliver you in the aftermath of a day of suffering" (Psalm 20:2). Long before the creation of the modern state of Israel, the unsung song of our national consciousness was always *HaTikvah*—"The Hope." Someday. And if not now, "I believe in the coming of the Messiah even though he tarries, nevertheless I await firmly his coming."

Messiah and the Jewish View of History

Messiah must come someday. The prophets who verbalized the promise were merely elaborating on the opening story of Genesis. The Messianic Era is nothing other than a return to the original plan, a fulfillment of the way in which God intended the world to exist when he placed Adam and Eve in the Garden of Eden and proclaimed the ideal world as Paradise.

Eden partook of precisely those dimensions that would later serve as our messianic vision: peace, wholeness, unity between humanity and nature, recognition of God, a life of purpose but not of pain. "Every tree pleasant to the sight and good for food"—the truth of beauty and the beauty of truth were one, giving physical satiation and enjoyment. Sin caused Adam and Eve to lose God's gift. It was sin that caused them to be cast out of the Garden and to live life as we know it today, gaining our food by the sweat of our brow and being wanderers over the face of the earth. Yet, for us, what is most important about the Garden of Eden story is how it ends. "So He drove out the man and He placed at the east of the Garden of Eden the Cherubim, and the flaming sword which turned every way, to keep the way to the Tree of Life" (Genesis 3:24). God chased Adam and Eve out, but He did not destroy the Garden. God forbade us from eating of the Tree of Life, but He did not uproot it. Had God desired that Paradise never more be the province of human existence, why guard the entranceway instead of burning it to the ground? Why place an angel at the gate as a guard? Why not simply make it disappear?

The Garden waits for us. The Tree of Life offering immortality is still an option. The Messianic Era must someday come to pass, because God's will cannot be denied forever. What He planned initially for humankind will some day materialize. The Garden will be available to those who live in the time of the Messiah as well as for those who will be resurrected. Resurrection is not a mystical concept, but rather a necessary reality for some future date, so that those who did not live to experience Paradise in the course of their lives would, at least at some point in the future, know the meaning of existence according to God's original plan.

Three views of history emerge clearly in human thought. The Western view pictures human development on a graph, with a steadily ascending line, indicating steady progress. The line, beginning with Creation, ascends as it moves forward, implying greater wisdom and achievement, the marks of scientific discovery and civilization. The Chinese would reverse the graph. Only with the Ancients was there true wisdom; only in the past was there real knowledge. The passage of time brought only steady diminution. Would that we could be like the Ancients. The third view is that of our people. History may be pictured as a circle, with its beginning at the apex, the highest point of perfection. The downfall of Adam and Eve is the decline from that Eden. The purpose of history is to return to the starting point. What once was, can be again. True, those who do not learn from history are condemned to repeat it, but those who do learn from history can be blessed even more by returning to what once was, by recapturing what God desired for the human race. "Renew our days as of old" is the prayer of our people.

How will the Messiah come? The answer to that question is simple—by reversing the way in which we caused our banishment from the first "Messianic Era," the time of the Garden of Eden. We sinned and we were expelled. Repentance will bring the Redeemer. When the Jewish people return to God, He will return to us. That, too, is an aspect of measure for measure, a derivative of the principle of reward and punishment.

There is another way in which the question may be asked: not *how* will Messiah come, but *when* will he make his appearance. The two are not necessarily identical. God has made a promise through the prophets that the Messianic Age must someday dawn. Jews may hasten his coming through repentance. The Talmud teaches us that if the Jewish people were but to observe two consecutive Sabbaths correctly, God would have no choice but to send the Messiah. Yet if the Jewish people persist in not giving up their wicked ways, God still has an obligation to live up to His commitment. That is how our Sages reconcile the seeming contradiction between two words in a biblical text. In Isaiah (60:22), God proclaims *be-'itah aḥishenah,* "In its time, I will hasten it." The Talmud asks: "Rabbi Yehoshua Ben Levi pointed out a contradiction. It is written 'In its time' [will Messiah come] whilst it is also written, 'I, the Lord, will hasten it'—hasten it implies before its proper time?" The Talmud responds: "If they are worthy, I will hasten it. If not, he will come at the due time" (*Sanhedrin* 88a). There are thus two options for the messianic dream to be fulfilled. Any time throughout all the ages, we, the Jews, could have made it happen by being worthy. The other alternative: God must live up to His commitment in the course of time even if we do not do our part. God cannot wait forever, because a remarkable tradition concerns the maximum length of time this earth was programmed to exist.

"Six thousand years shall the world exist" (*Sanhedrin* 97a, *Rosh ha-Shanah* 31a, *Avodah Zarah* 9a). Our count, as Maimonides has cogently pointed out, does not include the first "week of Creation." That "week" may in fact have lasted for millions of years. Obviously the phrase "It was morning and it was evening, day one" need not refer to a twenty-four-hour period, inasmuch as there was no sun until the fourth "day." All the "days" of the first "week" may represent indeterminate periods of time that include the evolutionary transformations from one stage of development to another, which were programmed by God. It is only when we reach the creation of Adam that time is measured in human terms and that days, weeks, and months must refer to time spans as we know them. For this reason, when geologists tell us that the earth itself seems to suggest an age of millions, if not perhaps billions of years, we are not troubled. Our count starts with Adam.

Within the context of that numbering system we have been taught that all of world history will be completed by the year 6000. Within that time span, and not beyond, must come the fulfillment of the messianic promise.

It is true that our Sages were profoundly disturbed with those who sought to deduce the actual year set aside for Messiah's coming. "A plague upon all those who calculate the times for the end" (Sanhedrin 97b) was the rabbinic attitude. If prophetic works suggest some clues for the timing of the Messianic Era, these interpretations ought to be discouraged and certainly not disseminated among the people. After all, Jews might have brought the Messiah much earlier through the method of personal worth, by way of ahishenah, "I will hasten him." The pessimistic prediction of the Messiah's arrival, positing a time that has not yet arrived, is not an unalterable decree, but rather a worst-case scenario.

Today, as we find ourselves in the last quarter of the predicted final millennium, the knowledge that a major aspect of our faith has but so short a possible time for fulfillment dare not be easily dismissed. Six thousand years is the life span projected for the world because we are taught "A day of the Holy One, blessed be He, is a thousand years" (Bereshit Rabah 19:14). If the original story of Creation spoke of six "days" and then a Sabbath, a period of rest and holiness, so too would all the days following the "week of Creation" be six thousand, to be followed by a Sabbath of history that can neither be imagined nor described.

The Talmud went even further in its parallel between the "week" of Creation and all subsequent human history: "The Tana D'bey Eliyahu teaches: 'The world is to exist six thousand years.

In the first two thousand, there was desolation; the next two thousand years the Torah flourished; in the next two thousand years is the Messianic Era'" (*Sanhedrin* 97a). Each of the two thousand years is marked by a major descriptive term. The first two thousand are called *tohu,* the biblical word for "unformed," because in them there was no Torah. Abraham was exactly fifty-two years old when he began to convert men to the worship of the true God. From Adam until Abraham's fifty-second year, two thousand years of world time elapsed. The next two thousand years, i.e., from Abraham's fifty-second year until 172 years after the destruction of the Second Temple, we witnessed the flowering of Torah, from Sinai to the Talmud. It is the last two thousand years, those in which we presently find ourselves, that represent the closing chapters of the earth. It is at the sunset of the sixth "day" that contemporary Jewry has witnessed both the horror of the Holocaust and the rebirth of the State of Israel.

I do not believe it is too daring to view both of these major moments in history as having a special bearing on the promised era that will materialize in the not-too-distant future. The rabbis in talmudic times prayed for the Messiah. Yet some of them were bold enough to say "Let him come, but let me not see him" (*Sanhedrin* 98b). They did not want to live in the time immediately before the advent of the Messiah because they knew that that era would be filled with "the birth pangs of his coming." When a student asked his master, "Give me a sign so I may know when the Messiah is near," the rabbi responded with a story: "When a father and son were walking through a vast desert and the son queries, 'How will I know when we are approaching civilization and that we are close to the end of our journey?' The father replied: 'You will know that a city is near when you see a cemetery at the outskirts.'" "So, too," the rabbi continued, "will you know that the end of our long journey of exile draws near to a close when you will see a cemetery, symbol of death on a grand scale, striking our people. That will be the sign for us as well that the end of our long journey draws near. Then, divine deliverance will follow, even as the verse teaches us 'God will respond to you in the aftermath of a day of tragedy'" (Psalms 20:2) (*Midrash Tehillim* 82:4).

What greater cemetery than the one formed in the mid twentieth century, marking the destruction of six million of our people?

If we have suffered many times in the past, surely the scope and the horror of the Holocaust has no equal. Is it merely coincidence that in 1945 we said Kaddish for six million, and in 1948 we proclaimed *mazel tov* over the return of our homeland after almost two thousand years of exile and dispersion? Had we been given the choice, perhaps we might also have said with Ulah and Rabah, "Let the glorious day of return to the Holy Land and the dawn of Redemption come, but may we not live to see it"—so that we not be forced to endure the sight of what precedes it. As Elie Wiesel so masterfully expressed: "We are the most cursed of all generations and the most blessed of all generations. We are the generation of Job, but we are also the generation of Jerusalem."

It is at the conclusion of the Seder on Passover night that we Jews sing a song that, at first glance, seems to have no meaning and is certainly irrelevant to the glorious message discussed throughout the Passover Seder. *Ḥad Gadya* seems to tell the nursery-rhyme tale of "one kid, one kid that father bought for two *zuzim*." What meaning can that possibly have? Why reserve for the very last a tale that has no significance? Obviously our first impression is wrong. In accord with the principle that the most important part of any blessing appears at the very end, the *Ḥad Gadya* is perhaps the most powerful conclusion to the night commemorating our commitment to our religious and national destiny. Seder means "order," because from the time that God took us out of Egypt we recognized that history is not merely coincidence, that events of our past are not simply the product of blind fate or foolish happenstance. "I am the Lord who took you out of the land of Egypt." God is in charge. He is not only the Creator, but also the ongoing Guide of all that transpires throughout the ages. God is in control of everything, and history itself follows a seder, a divine order. The beginning of that order involves one kid that a father acquired for two *zuzim*. The number two is obviously meant to suggest something. "Who knows two?" we sing at the Seder. The Haggadah had already answered the question. Two is a symbol of the two tablets. Now the message of the parable becomes clear. The "father" is obviously God. It is He who acquired the "kid" for two *zuzim,* the two tablets of the law. It is we, the Jewish people, who were acquired by the Almighty at Sinai through the covenant of the tablets. The *Ḥad Gadya* is therefore *our* story, the story of the Jews throughout history from the time we were chosen by the Almighty.

The evening dedicated to a retelling of the story of humankind encapsulates major events via the reference to a kid and its travails, representing the various empires that have played a role on the world scene. Each one of them, Egypt, Babylonia, Persia, Greece, and Rome has an emblem, a readily identifiable insignia alluded to in the song. The cat, the dog, the stick, the fire teach us of the decline and fall of every one of them, until we reach the ultimate conclusion preordained by the Almighty: "And the Lord appeared." God makes Himself manifest. He will be universally recognized.

Especially fascinating in the above prayer is the penultimate paragraph, which obviously refers to the time immediately preceding the Messianic Age, when "the earth shall be full of the knowledge of God" (Isaiah 11:9). God appears after the Angel of Death has played his important part. It is in the aftermath of death on a grand scale that final salvation will dawn. The Talmud's suggestion that a cemetery is the greatest sign that the end of a long journey is near finds a parallel in this closing prayer of the Seder night. For us, the meaning of the events of our generation has long ago been foretold. The Angel of Death performed his odious role in the days of the Holocaust. The year 1945 marked the close of the days when we witnessed "the cemetery." The year 1948, with the establishment of the State of Israel, commenced the period of rebirth and redemption.

"God will answer you in the aftermath of a day of tragedy." The tragedy did occur in our own lifetime, in the allegedly civilized twentieth century. But we, of all generations, were also privileged to witness the fulfillment of another biblical verse: "And the Lord, thy God, will turn thy captivity and have compassion upon thee and will return and gather thee from all the peoples whither the Lord, thy God, hath scattered thee" (Deuteronomy 30:3). Contemporary Kabbalists point out a fascinating and almost frightening fact relating to this prediction. Numerically, beginning with the very opening verse of the Bible, the sentence telling us that God will return us to our homeland and gather us in from all the lands of our dispersion is sentence number 5,708. The year 1948 on the Hebrew calendar, which saw the dream come to pass and the prediction become reality, was none other than the year 5708. Coincidence or Seder? Make of it what you will.

What is imperative for Jews to recognize is how much of biblical prophecy concerning the Messianic Era has already been realized in our times.

What still remains as an obstacle to the end of the story? Why have we come so far and yet not welcomed Messiah himself? The text does not end with the prediction of verse 5,708 concerning the return of the Jews to their land. It continues: "If any of thine that are dispersed be in the uttermost parts of Heaven, from thence will the Lord, thy God, gather thee in, from thence will He fetch thee. And the Lord, thy God, will bring thee into the land which thy fathers possessed, and thou shalt possess it, and He will do thee good and multiply thee above thy fathers. And the Lord, thy God, will open thy heart and the heart of thy seed to love the Lord, thy God, with all thy heart and with all thy soul, that thou mayest live. And the Lord, thy God, will put all these curses upon thine enemies and upon them that hate thee and persecuted thee, and thou shalt return and hearken to the voice of the Lord and do all these commandments which I command thee this day" (Deuteronomy 30:4–8).

If the Jews will not repent fully in order to bring Messiah before his appointed time, then God will return us to the Holy Land and assist us in turning towards Him, so that the spirit of *teshuvah* will sweep the earth, and our return to Him with all our heart and soul will allow Him, measure for measure, to turn to us in total Revelation.

It is in this light that we ought to view the controversy between two mishnaic scholars recorded in the Talmud (*Rosh ha-Shanah* 10b). Although we have already indicated that our Sages were extremely upset with anyone who dared to try to "reckon the end" and determine the year of deliverance, nonetheless they did not hesitate to predict what might at first glance seem something far more specific. Rabbi Eliezer and Rabbi Yehoshua disputed not the year, but the month in which God's redemption would occur. Two possibilities suggested themselves: the rabbis agreed that Messiah was meant to come either in Nisan or Tishrei. Which of the two, however, is reserved for being worthy of this greatest blessing is the subject of dispute between them. Rabbi Eliezer acknowledged that in the month of Nisan our ancestors were originally redeemed from Egypt. However, the final drama will be unfolded when Messiah is sent by God in the month of Tishrei, the month of Creation and judgment. Rabbi Yehoshua says just as the Jews left Egypt in Nisan, the time of spring and the month of love, so, too, in Nisan will we be redeemed in the time to come.

How can each one of them be so sure of the month in which Messiah will come? Why predict months if we are forbidden to be concerned with the year? Their controversy only makes sense if we are aware that they are disputants in yet another issue concerning not the time, but rather the manner of Redemption. In *Sanhedrin* 97b we find: Rabbi Eliezer said, "If Israel repent they will be redeemed. As it is written, 'Return ye backsliding children and I will hear your backslidings.'" Rabbi Yehoshua said to him, "But it is not written, 'Ye have sold yourselves for nought and he shall be redeemed without money—without repentance and good deeds.'"

Rabbi Eliezer makes repentance a prerequisite for the Messiah; only a deserving Israel will be redeemed. Rabbi Yehoshua believes that God will be moved by love, even when unaccompanied by deed, to save His children. It is precisely these categories that serve as the focal point of different months in the Jewish calendar. Tishrei is the time of judgment. In the astrological system of *mazalot* (the stars), it is Libra—the time when scales govern the universe. Rosh Hashanah and Yom Kippur represent the days when men stand before God in judgment. The same Rabbi Eliezer who believes only repentance can bring the Messiah makes Tishrei the ideal moment for redemption. Rabbi Yehoshua does not believe that God will be so demanding. If He redeemed the Jewish people once in Nisan, the season of spring designating the relationship of a lover and his beloved, then the future days of greatest glory will also dawn as an outgrowth of this very love, even when not deserved. For Rabbi Eliezer, Nisan and Messiah are inextricably intertwined.

At first glance one is tempted to agree with Rabbi Yehoshua. Of course Rabbi Eliezer's view obtains for the Messiah who comes as a result of "I will hasten him." A Messiah before the fixed time, who is brought by the worth of the Jewish people, must be a Tishrei deliverer. But if God has a promise He must keep, and Messiah comes no matter what we do, because within 6,000 years there must be a Messianic Era, then surely Nisan and the message of love are paramount. It is Maimonides, however, who, in a seemingly contradictory ruling allows us to see the possibility for both views prevailing.

In *The Laws of Repentance* (Chapter 7:5), Maimonides writes: "All the prophets commanded concerning repentance and Israel would not be redeemed other than through repentance." Clearly this is the view of Rabbi Eliezer. How strange then to read in Maimonides' concluding section of his work, in the law of Kings, that it will be the task of Messiah to return the hearts of the people to God in complete repentance. What previously appeared as a condition preceding Messiah's coming is now recorded as a consequence of his presence on earth! And if repentance follows Messiah, does that not prove that his appearance will be based on Rabbi Yehoshua's concept of Nisan rather than on Rabbi Eliezer's time of Tishrei?

The paradox seems unanswerable if one fails to take note of an all-important distinction. Redemption, even as the Jerusalem Talmud makes clear, is not a one-time act of fulfillment, but rather a step-by-step process. How will Messiah come?—asks a Sage. The answer: Like the breaking forth of dawn, piecemeal, with rays of ever-increasing brightness and intensity.

For that very reason, tradition recognizes two distinct categories. There is *ge'ulah shelemah,* the Final Redemption, and there is *athalta de-geulah,* the glorious onset. Each of these times requires its own determination with regard to cause and calendar. The question of when shall it begin is, in fact, the question of how shall it come about. Maimonides in his seemingly two contradictory rulings is giving us an answer for both the beginning and consummation of the Redemption. The first step may, and perhaps must be, an act of love—a Nisan experience. God must begin the process for us if we do not make the first move. "Stir, arise, awake my beloved," sings the lover in *The Song of Songs.* If the Tishrei experience of complete repentance is not present, then God will hasten the process. He will allow us to return to the Holy Land. The Jewish people will witness a spiritual re-awakening unlike any other in all of our history. The ba'al teshuvah movement will become a phenomenon recorded and analyzed by theologians, sociologists, and historians. Israel's very rebirth will serve as spur to religious consciousness of Jews throughout the world.

But that will not be enough for the complete Redemption. Rabbi Yehoshua and Rabbi Eliezer are both correct. Because of love, Redemption will begin. And then it will be our holy mission to intensify our understanding of the process of Redemption, so that the last step may be realized when spiritual awareness covers the earth like the waters cover the seas.

Where do we stand today in terms of the order of history? We are the survivors of the Holocaust, which we may well recognize as the birth pangs of the Messiah. We are the witnesses to the ingathering of the exiles (*qibuẓ galuyot*) and of the return of our people to our ancient homeland in 5708, the year marking the fulfillment of the 5,708th verse in the Torah. We have come back to Jerusalem, the holy city. Jews from all backgrounds are searching for spiritual meaning. Their thirst for Torah knowledge is truly the most remarkable phenomenon of Jewish rebirth ever witnessed.

We are like no generation that went before us.

Jews have come back to their home. Jews have come back to their faith. Jews have come back to their roots. It is not too much to hope that soon, very soon, in a month of Tishrei—if not this year then perhaps next—Rabbi Eliezer's dictum will be fulfilled. A redemption already started by way of God's love for us will be brought to completion for a people that proudly proclaims its allegiance to His kingship, His rule, and His law. In that day the words of the prophet Zechariah will come to pass: "The Lord will be One and His Name will be One."

Glossary

Adonai Lord.

Alef first letter of the Hebrew alphabet.

Aseret ha-Dibrot Lit., ten sayings. The Ten Commandments.

Avodah the sacrificial system instituted in the Holy Temple.

bein Adam le-atmo relationship to the self.

Beit second letter of Hebrew alphabet.

Dalet fourth letter of Hebrew alphabet.

dinim courts of law.

Elohim God.

emet truth.

emunah faith.

erusin betrothal.

ever min ha-hai removal and eating of any part of an animal while it is alive.

gematria numerology in which each Hebrew letter represents a numerical value.

gezel robbery.

Gimel third letter of Hebrew alphabet.

haftarah a chapter from the Prophets, read after the portion from the Pentateuch.

Halakhah body of Jewish law.

Hashem lit., the name. A name for God.

Heh fifth letter of the Hebrew alphabet.

Heneq death by strangulation.

heqesh a comparison between two laws (*halakhot*).

hereq death by sword.

Het eighth letter of the Hebrew alphabet.

hora'at sha'ah emergency measures.

hupah divine canopy.

Khaf twentieth letter of the Hebrew alphabet.

ki when, if.

Kohen priest.

Kohen gadol high priest.

kol Yisrael all of Israel.

le-dorotam throughout their generations.

lev heart.

malqut lashes.

mamon monetary or financial penalties.

mamzer (m.), *mamzer t* (f.) a child of an adulterous or incestuous relationship.

mamzerut illegitimacy.

Medinat Yisrael the State of Israel.

melekh king.

Mem thirteenth letter of the Hebrew alphabet.

met mizvah a corpse that is not properly attended to.

milhemet mizvah obligatory war.

mishkan tabernacle.

mishpatim ordinances.

mita death.

mitzvah (pl., mitzvot) commandment.

mot yumat you shall surely die.

ne'eman trustworthy.

nisuin marriage.

olam ha-ba eternal life; the world to come.

onan a person whose relative has died but has not been buried yet.

pikuah nefesh the preservation of life.

qidushin engagement or consecration.

qorban sacrifice.

ra evil.

rasha a wicked one.

seqilah death by stoning.

sereifah death by burning.

shalom welcome, farewell, peace.

Shekhinah God's immanence.

Shema Yisrael, Adonai Eloheinu Adonai Ehad Hear, O Israel, the Lord Our God, the Lord is One.

Shemitah the seventh year, in which the land is to lie fallow.

sheqer untruth, lie.

Shulhan Arukh The code of Jewish law, compiled by Joseph Karo.

talit prayer shawl.

Talmud Torah Torah study.

Taryag Mizvot the 613 commandments found in the Torah.

Tav twenty-second (last) letter of the Hebrew alphabet.

tefilin phylacteries.

tekhelet a blue thread, one of eight used to make up the fringes (*ẓiẓit*).

teshuvah return.

tov good.

Yahrzeit anniversary of the day of death.

yeẓer ha-ra inclination for evil.

yeẓer tov inclination for good.

Yod tenth letter of the Hebrew alphabet.

ẓiẓit fringes on a *talit* (prayer shawl).

References

Ganzfried, S. (1963). *Code of Jewish Law*. Trans. E. Hyman. Brooklyn, NY: Hebrew Publishing Co.

Gary, R. (1987). *The Dance of Genghis Cohn*. Trans. C. Sykes. New York: Schocken Books.

Greenberg, S., ed. (1964). *A Treasury of the Art of Living*. New York: Hartmore House.

International Encyclopedia of Quotations (1978). Chicago, IL: J. G. Ferguson.

Syrkin, M., ed. (1973). *Golda Meir Speaks Out*. London: Weidenfeld and Nicholson.

Wiesel, E. (1975). Speech at Hofstra University. Hempstead, NY. December.

Index

About the Author

Benjamin Blech has been Rabbi of Young Israel of Oceanside, New York, for over three decades, and is Assistant Professor of Talmud at Yeshiva University in New York City. He has served as Scholar-in-Residence in numerous congregations throughout the United States, Canada, and the Orient, and he has lectured to Jewish communities in Israel, Australia, and many other countries. Rabbi Blech has written articles for *Tradition, Jewish Life, Reader's Digest, Jewish Week, Newsweek,* and *Newsday.* He is the author of *The Secrets of Hebrew Words.*